BACKWA[...]

"Danison presents an account of spiritual beliefs gleaned from her near-death experience. . . . In her third book concerning near-death experiences, the author sets out to compare the spiritual truths she learned during the experience with ideas from organized religion. . . . Readers interested in near-death experiences may find the book compelling for its depiction of reality, but those who don't accept Danison's experience at face value will struggle with the text."—**Kirkus Book Reviews**

"What a fascinating and disturbing book (in a good way)." **Editor, FATE Magazine**

BACKWARDS and *BACKWARDS Guidebook*

"*BACKWARDS* . . . is an examination of this phenomena [NDE] in which it's questioned thoroughly with an educational eye, with a focus on the case of a true story of a big time lawyer being on the brink . . . . *BACKWARDS* is deftly written and researched, and highly recommended."–**Midwest Book Review**

"Forward thinking is fine in all, but one can find many answers just by looking back. '*Backwards Guidebook*' is a second in a series called '*Backwards*.' Asking many of life's questions, ranging from God to the meaning of life, Danison and company keep it secular while waxing philosophical in ways that will tax the mind, but leave it better from the exercise. A strong choice for those looking for answers about life, the universe, and everything, '*Backwards Guidebook*' is a definite purchase for those who have read the first and enjoyed it."— **Midwest Book Review**

"Consistent with works such as Conversations with God and A Course in Miracles, *Backwards* clarifies and simplifies the complexities that we tend to manifest into our lives."—**TCM Reviews**

"[A]re we all going to have to wait until we pass across to discover what that experience really is? In Nanci L. Danison's book these questions subside: here is a writer who is trained in observing and listening and summarizing and convincing as only a fine trial lawyer can. . . . [T]he author is very much worth reading and heeding."—**Grady Harp, Amazon Top 10 Reviewer**

"'*Backwards: Returning to Our Source for Answers*' will be well received by students of metaphysics, self improvement, and readers in the genre of spirituality. However, because of the nature of the material, there will be controversy and opposition from traditional academics, physicians, scientists, and theologians."–**Reviewer's Bookwatch**

"This is a book that lets you know what a near death experience is like and it will amaze you. The book will startle you with revelations that you never thought of and this is easily one of the most controversial books I have ever read. I am not sure I agree with it but it certainly gives me a great deal to think about."—**Amos Lassen, Amazon Top 100 Reviewer**

"Nanci went farther than most NDErs. . . . She looked at life, and death, from multidimensional perspectives—the human, the soul, the Light Being, and Source. . . . If you read just one new book about NDEs this year, make it this one."—**Vital Signs Magazine**

"Danison's elaborate but very readable story is summarized in her first book, '*Backwards: Returning to Our Source for Answers*' (A.P. Lee, 2007), and discussed more formally in her new book, '*Backwards Guidebook*' (Lee, 248 pages, $15.95). She spent many months taking notes from memory, recording as much as she could recall from her experience. . . . It's a pretty tough observation, which to me lends credibility: Danison is just telling us what she learned—no sugarcoating."—**The Spokane Spokesman-Review**

ANSWERS FROM THE AFTERLIFE

Also by Nanci L. Danison

Books

BACKWARDS: Returning to Our Source for Answers
BACKWARDS Guidebook
BACKWARDS Beliefs: Revealing Eternal Truths Hidden in Religions

Audiobook

BACKWARDS: Returning to Our Source for Answers

DVDs

Be Your Own Psychic
Interview by Ted Henry (ABC News)
Manifesting: Creation, Not Attraction
Meaning of Life
Nanci Danison at the Edgar Cayce A.R.E.
Our 5 Spiritual Superpowers
What Happens When We Die?

CDs

God Loves, Man Judges
Heart of New Age Beliefs
How to Access Universal Knowledge
How to Manifest Physical Reality
Life Plan From the Afterlife
Manifest Consciously with Unconditional Love
Manifest Healing
Primer on Life and Death
Purpose of Life
Revelations
Root of All Evil
Self-Healing
Soulless Humans

ANSWERS FROM THE AFTERLIFE

Nanci L. Danison

A.P. Lee & Co., Ltd.
Columbus, OH

AP Lee & Co., Ltd.
PO Box 340292
Columbus, OH 43234
"Evolving mankind, one book at a time."

Library of Congress Control Number: 2016948871
ISBN-13: 978-1-934482-37-7

Printed in Canada

Contents

CONTENTS

Acknowledgments

SOME OF THE TALENTED PEOPLE WHO HELPED produce this, my fourth book, include: the best Editor ever, Erin Clermont; Visual Artist Shawn Reeder (www.shawnreeder.com) who took the incredible time-lapsed photograph of the night sky and stars framed by an ancient bristlecone pine tree on the front cover; Karen McDiarmid, the incomparable graphic designer who created the cover design; Karen Lynch, author photographer extraordinaire; and my friends and family. I especially want to thank all my readers and YouTube viewers who have written to me with questions. I hope each of you wonderful Light Beings knows how much your interest and support make my human life worth living.

ANSWERS FROM THE AFTERLIFE

I

Getting Answers In The Afterlife

TRADITIONALLY, WE CONSULT RELIGIONS FOR AN-
swers to our questions about life, death, and the afterlife. Those less
religious may turn to the words of philosophers, or even self-labeled
channels or psychic mediums. My spiritual answers came to me the
hard way. I died. Then I returned to human life, rendering my demise what physicians call a near-death experience (NDE).

On March 14, 1994, I died and crossed over into the most extensive excursion into the afterlife ever recorded. While there, my mind
was deluged with far-ranging knowledge in a form I call "Knowings."
Knowings differ from "knowledge," as we use the term in human life.
Humans gain knowledge by studying materials produced by others
educated in a given field, by serving an apprenticeship with a master
craftsman, by personal experience, or through a combination of these
methods. All of this learning is filtered through a person's mind and
level of understanding, then consolidated into a personal knowledge
base on a particular subject.

Receiving Knowings is like having everything that could ever be
known about a topic suddenly splashed into your mind, complete
with total understanding of every drop of it. This phenomenon feels
as if we learned the information through firsthand personal experience rather than from any outside source. The net effect of receiving Knowings is having your mind blown. I learned in the afterlife

that Knowings are contained in an immense database that I call (for lack of a better term) Universal Knowledge. Universal Knowledge is everything that God/Source knows. We all have unlimited access to Universal Knowledge in the afterlife. And I learned during my NDE that we can also access Universal Knowledge from time to time during human life.

Knowings do not come in words. They are not communicated verbally or telepathically by another being or entity, such as guides, angels, or spirits. Knowings are pure understanding unfiltered by anyone's translation or interpretation. They come directly from the mind of Source.

Before and since my NDE, I have enjoyed instances when I could sit down and write a term paper or legal brief without consciously structuring it or thinking about what to say. The paper or brief generated this way is complete with heading sentences, appropriately placed quotations from relevant sources I read while researching, and concluding sentences summarizing each topic. These documents are organized, persuasive, and nearly perfect first drafts. An outsider witnessing this process might assume the writings are coming *through* me, rather than *from* me. But the ability to write this way is a normal human skill. Some people can simply read or learn a large quantity of material and mentally organize it in their own words. The output from using this skill is not automatic writing, channeling, or receiving information from the afterlife. It is nothing like having Knowings.

When I recount the chronology of the events of my NDE, and when I did interviews years ago on local TV stations' noon news for my bar association, I could talk for minutes at a time and have no idea what I'd just said. I remembered not a word of it after I stopped speaking. Again, this is a normal human consequence of being totally immersed in a subject that takes your mind off yourself. It is not channeling, even though it feels at times as if someone else is speaking through me because I have no memory of what I just said. This is nothing like having Knowings.

Receiving Knowings generates an emotional sensation of assuredness and total certainty, and of being the recipient of great scholarship that cannot be put into exact words. Knowings are not a compendium of words in your mind. Rather, they are telepathically absorbed wisdom.

Here is a detailed description of an incident of receiving Knowings I had while writing *BACKWARDS Beliefs: Revealing Eternal Truths Hidden in Religions*:

A profusion of emotions surged through my body and mind. My laptop keystrokes engraved a hard drive with my memories of awakening as Source as indelibly as a diamond cutter etches glass. I wept as I wrote—partly from the sorrow of being separated again from Source's unconditional love. Partly in response to reliving the most dramatic and life-altering moments of my present life.

Without warning, I transported back into the same level of Source's loving Energy that I experienced during the deepest part of my merger into Source. I expected to relive the same memories my fingers were translating into words. But an entirely new event unfolded.

Universal Knowledge opened to me. I could read through the lens of my mind's eye every single word that had ever been written, or ever will be written, in the English language. Books of every description. Poetry. Songs. Plays. Even little personal notes and office telephone message slips. My mind simultaneously held every written word ever produced by English-speaking humans. In many of these writings I noted for the first time the common theme that there is only One of us in the universe. One consciousness. One beingness. This message lifted off the pages of various writings and telescoped toward me in a shimmering display of light, as though backlit by a thousand suns. Regardless of genre, theme, or surface topic of the document, the message of Oneness percolated to the forefront from many of man's works as they displayed across my mental screen.

I recognized some of the writings from this human lifetime. Books I had read. Songs I could sing nearly word-for-word, including a recent one by Nickelback. Even movies and TV shows I loved. And I marveled that I had never before noticed the theme of Oneness in them. I felt utterly witless to have missed what was now so obvious. But I was overjoyed that Source had given the world so many millions of messages of truth in every conceivable way. No communication medium was overlooked. Not a taste in literature ignored.

Returning to my body after this brief, unexpected visit to the afterlife was a much shorter passage than when I died in 1994. But, unlike in 1994, the aftereffects of this visit were disturbing. My first instinct was to jump up from my computer and pace in circles. Energy coursed through me like a live wire. My nerve endings tingled and itched. My thoughts skittered and tumbled back upon one another like ocean waves as I tried to remember all the words I had seen highlighted in the Knowings episode. I felt, quite simply, that I had been electrocuted. It was not a pleasant feeling at all, which surprised me. I would have thought that the predominant aftereffect would be feeling Source's unconditional love. But for about two weeks, my muscles twitched and I paced around the house as I tried to dissipate the huge quantity of Energy I brought back from the afterlife.

This dramatic peek into Universal Knowledge far surpassed any other I have had since I returned from my 1994 NDE. But my description gives you an idea of what it is like to have Knowings downloaded into your mind.

All of the answers to questions and other material in this book are Knowings I received while in the afterlife in 1994, unless otherwise indicated. These Knowings are not my own theories. They are not my own thoughts or beliefs. My only input in relating these Knowings is that I chose the words to describe them, to share with you as accurately as I can what I learned in the afterlife. Sometimes my readers think I digested everything I learned in the afterlife and later drew my own conclusions about how we should change human life to make ourselves happier. The fact is that the material in all of my books—about how to take charge of our lives; and how to change education, advertising, and churches to better serve our eternal needs—came to me as Knowings while I was in the afterlife. What I remember of these Knowings, however, is very fragmented. I am able to give reasonably full answers to some questions and none at all to other questions. I recall quite a bit about some topics and very little about others. That's why there are big holes in my explanations and answers. I offer only what I remember from the afterlife and do not fill in any gaps with logic or human speculation.

Unlike others who have visited the afterlife, I was allowed to return to Nanci's body with extensive memories of what I learned about life, death, heaven, hell, the afterlife, our true spiritual nature, Source, and much, much more. The Knowings I received encompassed an entire cosmology of Creation, and why we are here, that may surprise you as much as it did me. What I remember of this comprehensive explanation of, well, everything, is contained in my books: *BACKWARDS: Returning to Our Source for Answers* (*BACKWARDS* for short); *BACKWARDS Guidebook*; and *BACKWARDS Beliefs: Revealing Eternal Truths Hidden in Religions* (*BACKWARDS Beliefs* for short). I recommend these books to you for more extensive background on the answers given here, and for a full description of my 1994 afterlife experience. These books are not autobiographies. They include only the story of my NDE and what immediately preceded and followed it. I will sometimes refer to a chapter in one of these books in answer to a question to give you more resources for understanding my response.

Until people started asking me questions, I truly believed that my books documented every single one of my afterlife memories. The questions made me realize I had misjudged what would most interest readers, as well as the level of detail they wanted. I have designed this book to supplement my three previous ones and answer questions my readers and YouTube Channel viewers have posed to me over the years. Included in this material are my newsletter articles through 2014, some of my posted YouTube comments, and many of my e-mails to all of the wonderful people who have expressed an interest in my mission. All of you have kept me going through hellish cancer treatments, grieving the deaths of four family members and loved ones, managing the many little physical disabilities that result from temporarily dying and from surviving cancer treatments, living with life-threatening illnesses, dealing with stalkers, and just being human (so to speak). For that, I thank you with unconditional love from the very bottom of my part of Source's heart.

I recommend reading the chapters in order because I use short-hand terms and concepts in later chapters that are explained in earlier ones. Without these definitions, it might be difficult to understand certain answers, or you might get the wrong impression from my answer. You will see that this has happened in the past when you read some of the questions I have been asked. For those of you who prefer to read the chapters that interest you most first, I have repeated in a shorthand form in many answers some of the crucial background from the beginning chapters.

The most important terms to understand are:

God–I do not use this name for our Creator because it is loaded down with religious meanings and human misconceptions. The Creator I met, the Source, is nothing like the God of my former religious understanding.

Source–the being or entity that most people call God, the Creator, the Supreme Being, Yahweh, Allah, and other names. My personal experience with Source is that it is more of an entity than a being. I experienced Source as an immense Energy field radiating intelligence, emotions, consciousness, character traits, and personality. But Source has no body or gender, unlike what the word "being" implies. I will occasionally refer to Source as "it" and mean no disrespect. Knowings and my personal experience in the afterlife convinced me that Source is the only consciousness in existence. I discuss the nature of Source in chapter 3 of this book. More detail is provided in chapter 2, "What Is God?," of both *BACKWARDS* and *BACKWARDS Guidebook*.

Soul–what most people call the part of the human that goes to heaven or paradise after death of the body. Knowings persuaded me the soul is not actually part of the human being. It is a far more sophisticated concept, which I explore in detail in chapter 5, "Humans

Get Souls," of *BACKWARDS Beliefs*. I use "soul" to describe the part of a Light Being that has been incarnated into physical matter.

Light Beings–what I call you and me after we cross over into the afterlife, recombine with the part of our Energy that stayed behind in the Light, and make the full transition back into our natural spiritual state. We are Light Beings. Near-death experiencers (NDErs) coined the name "Being of Light" for the beautiful, glowing spiritual beings they encounter in the afterlife. Knowings informed me that what NDErs perceive to be luminous spiritual beings are actually fragments of Source's focused awareness. Light Beings are characters and personalities Source imagined—as an author imagines book characters—to incarnate into the physical universe that Source also manifested in its imagination. A Light Being invests some of its Energy, awareness, and perspective into physical matter by incarnating into it, such as incarnating into a human. The rest of the Light Being's Energy and awareness stays in the afterlife during incarnation. Thus, what we call *souls* are the incarnated parts of Light Beings who have split their awareness between the afterlife and a human life. These mental characters allow Source to directly experience all that both the Light Being soul and its host encounter in physical life. Light Beings all share the same consciousness, that of Source, but they have different character traits and personalities.

Light Being nature is explored in chapter 5 of this book. I relate Source's creation of Light Beings in chapter 3, "Our True Origin," of *BACKWARDS Beliefs*. Our transformation back into Light Being form is detailed in chapter 19, "Death as a Process," of *BACKWARDS* and chapter 13 of *BACKWARDS Guidebook*. My personal experience living as a Being of Light during my NDE is documented in chapter 21 of *BACKWARDS*.

Spirit–I do not usually use the term "spirit" because it already has too many different meanings.

Humans–are animals indigenous to planet Earth. Source manifested them in its imagined universe in the same way we imagine people in our dreams. I learned in the afterlife that we are not humans. We just incarnate into their bodies. I detail what humans are, and our relationship to them, in chapter 3 of both *BACKWARDS* and *BACKWARDS Guidebook*.

Some of the answers in this book will sound repetitive. This is because my readers and viewers have posed their questions in a frame of reference I call the "human perspective." Human perspective is the way we all think as a result of being inside humans, sharing this planet, and being indoctrinated by our respective cultures and religions. The Knowings I received paint a multi-level perspective on everything, including human viewpoints, Light Being level of awareness, and Source's ultimate perspective. The way we look at life once we resume our eternal spiritual existence as Light Beings is vastly different than human perspective. Source's perspective is different than that of Light Beings. Thus I often repeat key concepts of Universal Knowledge in an answer to help the reader adjust his or her thinking to the new perspective. This is necessary to fully understand the Knowings the way I did while in the afterlife.

By the way, I may use the singular pronoun *he* or *she* in examples. I do not mean to exclude any females when I use the male gender or any males when I use the female gender pronoun.

2

What Death Teaches Us

FROM A HUMAN PERSPECTIVE, IT IS POSSIBLE FOR bodies to die temporarily and then come back to life, usually due to resuscitation by medical personnel. Sometimes we return spontaneously, like I did. Sometimes a person will remember being alive and conscious after his or her body's death. Physician and author Dr. Raymond Moody coined the phrase "near-death experience" (NDE) for these instances of remembered life after death. In 1975, Dr. Moody compiled his medical research into a best-selling book titled *Life After Life*.[1] Many other writers, researchers, and near-death experiencers since then have added to the wealth of empirical and experiential knowledge we have about NDEs.

Dying and going into the Light, that is, the afterlife, is actually an awakening process from the spiritual perspective. We wake up from the amnesia that allows us to believe we are humans leading lives on earth. This awakening usually results from trauma that has resulted in human death. But mortal trauma can occur before we souls are ready to leave human life—before we have accomplished our purpose for coming here. When we return home to the Light before our time has come, and awaken before we are supposed to, we may return to our bodies with memories of what happened after death, *i.e.*, an NDE.

The Nature of Near-Death Experiences

What is the Light that NDErs say they enter at death?

For a while after we leave our host human bodies at death we mentally continue to observe things the way we were accustomed to in human life using human senses. Humans perceive the outer layers of Source's Energy field as Light. I know from having been in the afterlife for an extensive period that we stop noticing this Light after we fully transform back into our natural spiritual state.

NDErs feel Source's Energy, or Light, as bliss. In the afterlife, we luxuriate in true unconditional love, complete and total acceptance of who we are despite what we have done in human life, and release from all pain and hardship. Who would want to leave this blissful Light? No one. The problem is that when our bodies die before we souls are ready to return home to the afterlife, we usually leave the bliss and return to what is probably a damaged body.

Why must anyone leave the bliss of the afterlife and return to his or her body?

We return if the part of us that remained in the afterlife still wants to finish what it started, to complete its goals for this human life. We Light Beings are not quitters.

I learned in the afterlife that reentering physical life after death is entirely an act of free will. No one can force us, assign us, condemn us, or compel us to return. It must be voluntary. Obviously, the soul part of us needs a very good reason to shift its intentions from staying in heaven to returning to earth. Reentering a pain-filled, damaged body in what we may consider to be a ruined life takes a *lot* of persuasion. If someone has died before his or her time, those Light Beings whose job it is to meet new arrivals will work with the soul's personality and character traits to create just the right incentive to return. We need these colleagues to do this for us because we still have amnesia about why we entered human life and whether we have met our goals.

For some, seeing deceased loved ones who say, "It's not your time," is enough. For others, the weight of responsibility for, or love of, someone still on Earth will suffice. For example, mothers will return to care for their children. For a few NDErs, nothing less than the God of their understanding can get them back to Earth. An NDEr like this may see Jesus, Buddha, Lord Vishnu, or whomever he or she perceives to be the Creator or Supreme Being in whatever form he or she would find believable, and will either be told to return to human life or assured that accepting return as the natural course of events when one comes home too soon.[2]

In sum, usually an NDE is a taste of heaven before the soul's normal time to return home. What the NDEr sees, hears, and feels during this home visit is designed to temporarily relieve the soul of the trauma of human life, to refresh it with new purpose, and to bolster it for reentry into the wilds of humankind. Each of us is unique, so each of us requires a custom-tailored NDE experience to accomplish these goals.

Why doesn't everyone have an NDE when they almost die?

My understanding is that "almost dying" does not usually trigger the automatic waking up process that clinical death does.

Is it possible that people near death have an NDE but just don't remember it?

Yes, it is possible. Each case would have to be looked at individually, and each person interviewed by someone open to hearing what the patient has to say. NDE researcher Pim von Lommel, MD, made it a point in one of his lectures to mention that many NDErs don't tell anyone about their experience for fear the person they tell will be dismissive or closed-minded about the concept of NDEs.

Why do some people have an NDE or similar experience when they are not near death?

I have limited exposure to "NDE-like" experience accounts. Those I have read do not bear a resemblance to what happens after death. From what I gather, the similarity between NDE-like events and NDEs is mostly in the aftereffects. Also, I do know that once someone has been through the dying process it is easier for them to go back into the afterlife state of existence without dying, to in effect, have an NDE-like experience. I have done it. But my NDE-like experiences did not include the transition into Light Being state that I went through during my 1994 NDE.

What is the purpose of the near-death experience?

When something as dramatic as an NDE occurs, we want to know why. Was it something about that person's life or religious beliefs? Did they need this as a slap in the face to change their lives? Why did it happen to him or her and not to me, or my nana, or another person I love who died briefly? Humans always try to find cause and effect relationships between events they don't understand. In this instance, they do it so they might have a better idea of how to control having or not having an NDE. Or they do it to ferret out facts that set some people apart from others, to form categories of some type that can be used to predict who will have an NDE.

My understanding of NDEs from Knowings I received in the afterlife is that they happen spontaneously when we leave our bodies at a time of serious illness or injury and start the automatic process of waking up to who we really are. There is no purpose to it any more than there is a purpose to things falling to the ground. Dying from physical life and returning to the Light is just an automatic part of the reincarnation process Source created. When death happens too early, NDErs are guided back into their bodies. When I died, however, I was informed that it *was* my time to leave human life. I was never told to go back, so I completed the entire transformation/ waking-up process. I then *chose* to come back to tell people what I had experienced in the hopes that sharing the Knowings I received might relieve someone else's suffering.

Are children's NDE accounts "purer" and therefore more valid than those of adults?

Several notable researchers have postulated that children's NDE accounts are more credible than adults' are because children, in theory, do not have the religious or anti-religious biases of adulthood. I was surprised to learn otherwise in the afterlife. We souls inside humans remember every single moment of human lives from the time we enter them. We hear everything said around and to us, even while in the womb, and integrate it into our worldview. The soul inside the child already believes everything it has heard. Therefore, it is not true that young children have not adopted religious or other beliefs about the afterlife. A prime example is NDEr Colton Burpo, who is credited in his father's book about him, *Heaven Is For Real*, with regurgitating numerous Bible concepts at age three. Colton's minister parents read Bible stories to him every day from his birth. Naturally, Colton's NDE at age four was filled with biblical imagery. There is nothing "purer" about a child's NDE account than an adult's. Both reflect expectations formed by unawakened soul beliefs.

Do very young experiencers forget their NDEs as they age?

Near-death experiencers I am aware of uniformly claim they remember their NDEs no matter how many years have passed, and no matter their age at the time of experience. They obviously do not recall every moment of the afterlife because of the amnesia blanket that drapes over memory upon reentering the human host. Yet NDErs never forget those elements of their beyond death experiences that they are able to remember despite the amnesia. Given this, I am surprised that *Heaven Is For Real* (mentioned above) is a hearsay account told by the Reverend Burpo to a ghostwriter, rather than the firsthand account of his son, NDEr Colton Burpo. The book was published when Colton was ten years old, presumably old enough to describe his experience to the ghostwriter. Colton once told an interviewer that he remembers most of his NDE but some of it has faded.[3]

Do child NDErs continue to have spiritual experiences after returning to human life like those reported by adult NDErs?

Yes, they might. Young NDErs may continue their relationship with the afterlife until they experience the full effect of the amnesia of human life. Children can also be more adept at accessing Universal Knowledge than adults.

Some children do not need to have an NDE to be able to report what deceased relatives look like and how they are doing in the afterlife, or even memories of previous lifetimes. When he was three, my friends' son, Liam, once took a break from playing with Tonka trucks to come up to me and ask, "Your dad's dead, isn't he?" I had never discussed my father's death (during my senior year in high school) with Liam's parents, much less with him. When I affirmed his statement, Liam said, "He wants you to know he's okay, he's all right." Liam at other times informed his mother why he selected her as his mother, told both parents about an earlier lifetime as a racecar driver who died during a race (the details of which, according to newspaper reports, turned out to be exactly as Liam described), and told me lots of things about souls and their nature. Many of us have probably heard similar wisdom from our children and grandchildren.

Why Should We Believe Near-Death Experience Accounts?

Why should we believe anything a near-death experiencer says about death, heaven, hell, and the afterlife in general?

NDE accounts are an excellent source of information because NDErs are eyewitnesses to death and what comes after it, and to a lawyer like me, an eyewitness is the most credible source of testimony. I am aware some scientific studies conclude that eyewitness perceptions can be decidedly wrong due to human sensory perception errors during times of extreme stress. But I believe that being out-of-body cures these sensory perception errors because the experiencer is no longer subject to the body's physical limitations. That, to me, gives the NDE account more credibility than any human eyewitness account.

However, the NDEr may very well interpret the experience like a human, with religious or spiritual bias, if he/she has not gone through the transformational processes in the afterlife that wash away human ways of thinking and refresh our spiritual memories and personalities. An NDEr's perspective can change dramatically the deeper into the afterlife the soul goes. For example, someone who goes into the Light and no further may interpret the Light itself to be God, instead of just part of Source's Energy field. That NDEr soul may think it has merged with Source, whereas someone who actually does merge into the core entity of Source will be able to look back and see in hindsight that the Light is just the outer edges of Source's aura, nimbus, or corona.

As we raise our awareness by greater degrees in the afterlife, different truths will download as Knowings. I know from experience that an understanding of Knowings that feels right and true at an early stage in the afterlife might be revealed as slightly erroneous with more enlightenment at later stages of afterlife. That is why I believe it is extremely important to know how far into the afterlife transition an NDEr has processed when considering his or her story. We NDErs feel an absolute certainty about everything we experience in the Light because the afterlife feels far more real than anything we live through here in human life. The combination of certainty and heightened reality fully convinces an NDEr of the truth of whatever it is he/she learned, though the soul might well have completely changed its understanding of those same concepts had it reached higher degrees of awareness within the afterlife. For example, someone who enters the Light and sees beautiful gardens, but goes no further, will be certain that heaven consists of an earth-like paradise. If that same soul had gone deeper into the afterlife, it would have come to realize that the gardens are manifestations created to comfort the newly arrived soul, or that the soul itself manifested them to match human expectations. Physical matter environments simply do not exist in a spiritual state like the afterlife.

Our first reaction upon hearing an NDE account might be to apply the advice "accept what resonates with you and leave the rest" because the truth for each one of us is always inside us. My memories of what I learned in the afterlife about humans tell me that "accepting what resonates and rejecting the rest" is a human perspective. Humans make snap decisions and knee-jerk judgments because being judgmental is necessary for survival. An animal must be able to decide in a few seconds whether someone is friend or foe, or whether a situation is safe or life threatening. That instinct taints our spiritual thinking until we achieve a degree of awareness free of human influence. Only after we have awakened to a sufficient degree of enlightenment should we trust our gut on spiritual matters.

I learned that while we are in the afterlife we are open to all thoughts and opinions and do not reject any of them. Source accepts and loves all opinions and beliefs with no judgment or condemnation whatsoever because experimenting with erroneous opinions and beliefs is part of the physical matter universe experience. In later stages of the afterlife we are, however, able to discern which opinions and beliefs are of human origin and which are eternal truths contained within Universal Knowledge.

Finally, as with everything we read, we must consider the NDE author's educational, experiential, and religious background, all of which influence language choices. For example, someone with a PhD in physics will interpret seeing a tunnel, void, or Light Being completely differently than someone with an eighth-grade education. A world traveler will have experiences to draw from and see analogies that are unknown to someone who has never traveled out of his or her home state. Someone who speaks three languages might be able to find the perfect word to describe a spiritual concept that English does not provide. Because of this, I think it is more important to get the gist of an NDE account and not attach much significance to the literal meaning of the words used.

In an NDE experience, the soul leaves the body. If the human body is dead, it has no active sensor mechanisms. So what NDErs report hearing and seeing isn't real, right?

Yes and no. Based on my own experience, and NDE accounts I have read, the illusion of human-like vision and hearing continues for a while in the spiritual world even without the body. This is more habit carried over from human life than actual sensory input. We Light Beings have no physical sensor mechanisms. But we have greatly expanded and heightened mental senses that operate very much like physical ones.

The physical manifestations an NDEr reports seeing are real to the NDEr who manifests them, just as what we all experience as human life feels real to us while we manifest life in these bodies. Manifestations are designed by Source to seem completely real.

After we transition fully into our natural spiritual state, we live an entirely mental life. This is nothing like the mental life we have while insides humans. Spiritual life seems completely real, unlike the ephemeral impression we get about daydreaming and thinking in human life.

Why allow NDErs to remember anything? Why allow them to be messengers? Won't having a hint at what we truly are ruin the experience of human life?

As I watched the history of religious developments among humans that I was shown in the afterlife, I realized that Source has given us millions of messengers over the ages. And still does. NDErs are among them. Source has never tried to hide the truth from us, as some might believe.

As for having a hint of our true nature ruining the human experience, my only source of information is my own life. I know I am not human but I still experience this life as totally real. Knowing something intellectually does not change my emotional responses much. Maybe that is true for other NDErs as well. The amnesia we don at birth is pretty effective.

Everyone goes through something different, meets someone different, sees something different, is told something different even though, yes, there are certain similarities—for example, feelings of peace and love, or merging with the Light. If everyone comes back with a different experience, how can we be sure we can trust NDErs to be telling the truth?

This reader's frustration with NDE accounts is natural. It stems from comparing NDE accounts about the afterlife to human experience. Most of us have been taught that heaven is a *place*, like an earth environment, or an *event*, like attending school, or a *lifestyle*, like living in a vacation resort. In human life, a specific physical place will look much the same to all of us. This gives rise to the expectation that heaven should look the same to everyone who enters. Shared human events tend to generate similar stories about the events. And those who experience the same lifestyle describe similar elements of their human lives. So we expect all NDErs to describe heaven in terms of the same scenery, events, and lifestyle elements. When they don't, we scratch our heads and wonder if they are lying. NDErs are telling us the truth about their experiences. What is false is our preconceived ideas about heaven.

Heaven is *not* a place, event, or lifestyle. There can be no places, events, or lifestyles because there's no physical matter. The afterlife exists outside the physical universe. Heaven/paradise is simply the continuation of our eternal lives within Source without a human body.

After we enter the Light, we live spiritual lives of intellectual and emotional beingness. Spiritual life is as different for each of us as human life is. It is also a big adjustment from what we were used to while inhabiting humans.

Those already in the afterlife help us acclimate to life without physical sensations or human drives. Most important, they help us remember who we really are, recapture our eternal memories, and transition from the grinding judgmental human perspective to an unconditionally loving spiritual attitude. This transformation is different for each of us because our individual needs are unique. Our personalities are unique. Our lives are unique. NDE accounts are different because the experiencers' personalities, lives, needs, and reasons for being in the afterlife are different. Their NDEs reflect who they are at core: precious and distinctive parts of Source.

NDE accounts are secret glimpses into the most intimate parts of an experiencer's life—his or her crossing over into the afterlife. Courageous NDE authors share their stories with us to give us hope and comfort. Their motivation is to spread the truth about the afterlife and dispel the prevailing belief that heaven is a fixed, one-size-fits-all place, event, or lifestyle.

My way of reducing the dissonance created by reading conflicting NDE accounts is to keep several factors in mind: (1) How far into the afterlife did the NDEr go? Ninety-nine percent of the NDE accounts I have read are very brief, toe-in-the-door experiences, though the NDErs themselves or researchers may think these are deep NDEs because they don't know otherwise. Data collected entirely from NDErs who did not go through the transition process I did while in the afterlife will be skewed toward human interpretations. (2) What are the writer's religious background and expectations? Religious interpretations may be projected onto non-religious elements of the afterlife. (3) What are the writer's education level and range of worldly experiences? This can dramatically impact how the NDE is described. (4) Did the writer get pulled back into the body early, such that he or she ended up believing that what he/she experienced is all there is? For example, someone who gets out-of-body but makes it only into the darkness, or void, and no further because he/she is resuscitated, may believe there is no life after death, only blackness. Someone who enters into the Light and sees loved ones looking like they did in human life will believe we retain human bodies in the afterlife. There is no way for the NDEr soul having a brief experience to know its initial impressions will be dispelled later as it transitions back into natural spiritual state. I know it only because I passed through the brief NDE stages described in others' accounts before I completed the transition and lived as a Light Being for a while. That fullness of experience naturally gives me hindsight that others lack.

Why is there such a difference between what psychics see about the afterlife and what NDErs report?

Before I died, I totally believed in psychics and mediums. I have just enough psychic ability myself to know that psychics can access information about other people, even information not consciously known by them.

I was surprised that everything I learned and experienced in the afterlife demonstrated to me that psychics, mediums, and channels are not in fact communicating with anyone in the afterlife. I have no idea where they are getting their information other than from reading the person sitting in front of them or from the channel's own belief systems. Don't get me wrong—I do believe that gifted psychics can read other people. But based on my own afterlife, I do not believe our loved ones in the afterlife communicate through any intermediary. Rather, they respond directly to us through various ways that we can learn to recognize.

Why Should You Believe My NDE Account?

Even if we accept that NDErs have firsthand knowledge of the afterlife, why should anyone believe your NDE account when it is so different from what others experienced?

A YouTube viewer asked me this question. My answer is that I do not feel my job is to convince anyone. My intention in coming back to human life was to share the Knowings I received in the afterlife with anyone who would listen. I am merely a messenger—but a messenger with firsthand, personal experience with death and the afterlife. I also have significant training in language skills, as part of an extensive educational background, and a wide range of life experiences from which to draw analogies. I believe my background helps me describe the indescribable.

At the time of my death in 1994, I had practiced law for seventeen years in a very prestigious, highly competitive 270-attorney Midwest law firm. I was primarily a litigator, trained to persuade. I have always loved education and was rewarded for my efforts. I was a National Merit Finalist in high school, where I graduated magna cum laude. I have a Bachelor of Science degree magna cum laude with a dual major in biology and chemistry, a Bachelor of Arts degree magna cum laude in psychology, and a doctorate degree in jurisprudence. My first twelve years of primary education were in Catholic schools. In addition, I attended a Methodist college for six years, during which time I studied religions of the world. I traveled extensively in North America and Europe. I spoke French and a little German before my NDE.[4] My Source-designed character traits include some talent for art and music. I earned a private pilot's license in 1999 and a private investigator's license in 2001. I tell you this not to brag, but to give you an idea of the scope of life resources I bring to the task of putting Knowings into words for you.

I believe the Knowings I accumulated from living so long in the afterlife during my NDE surpass sources such as (a) philosophers who theorize with no personal knowledge of the afterlife, (b) people who have no firsthand memories of the afterlife themselves but claim to channel words from one or more unknown beings whose credibility cannot be tested, (c) psychics and mediums who claim to be in contact with loved ones in the afterlife who usually have only personal messages to convey, and (d) religious leaders regurgitating ancient literature.

Most important, I have gone deeper into the afterlife and experienced things no other NDEr has written about because their visits were much briefer than mine.

The best test of what is credible for each of us personally is what rings true when we read it because we remember knowing it before we came into this human life. Use that as your guide as you read this book.

How can you be sure that your near-death experience was not simply a vivid dream?

In 2014, I had an NDE-like dream and can now answer this question in detail.

I dreamed I was in the Light with a group of Light Beings standing at the edge of a black void. The Light Beings were luminescent, humanoid-shaped, and had no facial features. They wore long, flowing white robes that pooled around and under their feet. Naturally, with my warped sense of humor, my first thought upon seeing this was: "I wonder if they realize they are standing on their robes and if they move they'll fall over?" My mother, who also died in 1994, came from behind me in the dream and crossed to the area where I was standing. She had on patterned shorts and a matching shirt-type top, like shorty pajamas, and was very young looking. She passed by me and crossed the void in front of me to reach a rectangular opening where other Light Beings awaited. The opening was similar to the open back gate of an 18-wheeler and had a flap-like label hanging from each side. I cried out and asked my mother to take me with her. She turned around and said: "There are two types of people. People like me who can come and go from the physical world at will. And 'corporate' people like you and those with you. Corporate types have to live out their physical lives no matter how painful or distressing. That's just how it works. Stay with Patty and Ann." I woke up literally suffocating. My nose was totally congested and I was having a major asthma attack. My heart was beating a mile a minute. The dream and inability to breathe scared me.

This sounds like an NDE account, doesn't it? I was in physical danger of actually suffocating, so having an NDE was possible. But here is how I knew this was a dream rather than an NDE:

(1) The area I was standing in at the edge of the void had partial walls that did not seem real. In my NDE, when I manifested physical environments they were absolutely real, as real as any human experience.

(2) Light Beings do not wear clothes. More important, my mother wouldn't be caught dead wearing shorty pajamas.

(3) The void kept morphing between appearing to be outer space and appearing as an open chasm. This void was nothing like the comforting black void I felt in my NDE.

(4) The opening I watched my mother go into morphed as well. Sometimes it looked like the open vertical doors on the back of an 18-wheeler truck. Other times the dimensions changed to a horizontal rectangle. Sometimes it looked like a tunnel. Nothing I saw in my NDE morphed when I tried to see it clearly. The closet thing to morphing in my NDE occurred when my five Light Being friends became visible after I saw five horizontal bands of Light. I couldn't tell whether the Light Beings came out of those Light bands or the Lights had been all I could see of my friends while they were at a distance. But still, my confusion as to the Light Beings' origin wasn't anything like the morphing in my dream.

(5) What my mother told me does not square with what I learned in the afterlife. There may well be Light Being parts of Source that do come and go from the physical universe at will. And my mother might be one of them. But a Light Being soul does not have to stay in a physical body if the life it has chosen is not producing the experiences desired. Living a human life is a choice, not a prison sentence—even for a corporate type like me.

(6) My mother's name was Patricia Ann.

(7) During the day, before my dream, I replaced my computer wallpaper with a picture of my high school friend Patty and me. I had also looked up an e-mail from my friend Ann to retrieve some

information she had sent me. I recognized the flap-like labels hanging from the opening my mother entered as those displayed on the credit-card machine at my local post office. Recognizing elements or events from earlier in the day in human life is a big clue that you are experiencing a dream rather than an NDE.

(8) I recognized my dream as one of the three phenomena humans call dreams that I learned about in the afterlife. Some scary dreams are actually communications between a Light Being soul and its body warning the sleeping body to wake up and take care of a problem in physical life. Inasmuch as I was suffocating, I believe this was just such a warning.

(9) I was scared during this dream. I was never scared during my NDE.

(10) There was no feeling of unconditional love in this dream, as there always is during an NDE.

Did your doctor or nurses know that you had died? You said you were alone when you died. Did the medical personnel come into the room and resuscitate you?

The radiologist and radiology technician knew after the fact that I had been unconscious. But, I didn't tell them I had died. I didn't talk much at all for a while after the NDE.

I was alone when I died because the radiologist and radiology technician left the room to get mammography films developed. My body revived spontaneously as I reentered it. Medical personnel did not resuscitate me. By the time I came back into the body, the radiologist and technician were back in the room looking at my mammogram films and drawing a diagram for the surgeon to use as a road map. When I finally got enough control over the body to say "I passed out," the radiologist called for a nurse, who came in and took a series of blood pressure readings. The radiologist and technician realized I had lost consciousness because I couldn't remember who they were. It took a half hour for my blood pressure to come back up to normal after they called the nurse. A finger stick also showed I had an extremely low blood sugar reading. The radiologist created an incident report about this that I obtained from the hospital.

More information about my NDEs can be found in chapter 21 of this book and in my other three books.

3

Source's Nature

BEFORE MY NDE, I BELIEVED IN A MALE GOD IN THREE parts: Father, Son, and Holy Ghost. I believed God, like humans, responded favorably to flattery and worship, punished sinners, and intervened in our lives if we prayed effectively enough. That belief system was shattered when I experienced God in the afterlife.

During my NDE, the only identification used for God was "the rest of us," which doesn't make for a very good name. So I adopted "Source" as the name for the God I experienced after reading that name in other NDE accounts. The Source I came to know is an amorphous Energy field with no physical, or gender, characteristics at all. My understanding is that Source is the same entity our religions call God, Yahweh, Allah, the Supreme Being, the Creator, and other names.

Early in my afterlife, I received huge downloads of Knowings about the differences between humans and Source. Humans think Source thinks and acts like a human. It does not. In fact, I learned that human innate character traits are often, by design, the opposite of Source's nature. Extensive descriptions of Source appear in chapter 2 of *BACKWARDS*, *BACKWARDS Guidebook*, and *BACKWARDS Beliefs*. That material characterizes a Creator so different from the traditional humanoid God that my readers and YouTube viewers posed many questions about Source. Following are some of them.

Where did this Energy field called God or Source come from?

I never asked this question directly while I was in the afterlife. I did, however, get a hint or suggestion about Source's origin. The vague sense I got was that it may be either part of a larger entity or one of several such entities. This information was very hazy, so I wouldn't rely on it. I couldn't tell at the time I was inside Source whether I could not understand its origin or ultimate nature, or I hadn't focused enough on the topic to get a clear answer.

Is Source the only God or Energy field? Or are there many levels of reality or universes that each have their God?

Source is the only entity I encountered in the afterlife and it is the Creator of the universe. My impression during the entire afterlife experience was that there is only one universe at a time. I was informed that Source imagines physical universes one after the other, but not simultaneously. If my impression is accurate that there might be other entities like Source, or that it is part of a larger entity, then there might be other universes as well.

Is there a God Central, that is, a being, essence, or central processing unit, like a CPU in a computer?

Yes, there is. I experienced it as a "core personality" or "core entity." Think of it as you would a novelist who has his own personality, which is his core, and then he creates book characters in his mind who have their own personalities. With Source, its own innate personality and character traits are its core. And we are the book characters in its mind. That is why my Light Being friends referred to Source as "the rest of us." They meant the collective consciousness of Source, within which we all exist as mental characters.

While I was in the afterlife, and after I received Knowings about it, I thought of Source as a Collective Being because it is composed of its own identity and zillions of mental characters with their unique identities. This appellation isn't technically correct because Source is not a being. And its mental characters have no more substance than the book characters in the novelist's mind. But using the term *Collective Being* is the best I can do to describe with words an unfathomable entity. The nature of Source is so vast, and so foreign to human nature, that I got the sensation I was witnessing what my psychology degree program would have called an immense multiple personality disorder. And, like a human with multiple personality disorder, Source can present itself as its core personality or as one or more of its zillions of mental characters. But, unlike a human, Source can also present itself as all personalities at the same time.

Please understand that Source is not literally *divided* into a core personality and mental characters any more than a novelist is. There can be no real division within one mind. I use the concepts of a core personality and mental characters within Source in much the same way the Catholic religion uses the doctrine of Father, Son, and Holy Ghost within God. Though the tri-part deity concept always confused me as a child, I can see now why the Church created it. The limitations of language force us to segregate and label complex ideas, like different aspects of Source's immensity, with words that tend to imply separation. I hope assigning the words *core personality* and *mental characters* to Source's mind does not confuse any of my readers into thinking we are separate from Source. We are in fact parts of Source.

What color is Source?

Source has no physical characteristics and is invisible, so it has no color. NDErs see the Energy field emanating from Source as a brilliant white light because early in an NDE we still perceive as humans do. I discovered in the afterlife that the white color is actually many different hues that all reduce to white to humans' limited eyesight. I knew the names of the different hues while I was in the afterlife. I don't remember the names now, but I do recall they were not in the English language.

Nanci, are you saying that merging into Source was not a visual event but rather the experience of Source? Are you saying that you did not "see" Source?

Correct. I felt Source, but did not see anything humans would identify as a being or discrete entity. Source has no visual appearance.

It consists entirely of Energy.

I learned in the afterlife that while we are in physical form, or have recently passed over into the afterlife, we "see" Source Energy as the Light. The Light is an aura or corona of Energy that Source radiates that has no physical appearance. Humans interpret this Energy as light because that is one of the ways humans perceive energy. Once we make the transition out of human perceptions in the afterlife, we no longer see that Light. So, while I was inside Source I "saw" nothing of its nature. However, the experience was very much a visual event. With my mind's eye, I beheld Source's life before and during the Creation of the universe. It was like watching a million panoramic, high definition brilliant color movies in my mind at the same time.

You said: "With human eyes, we perceive Source's Energy as physical matter." You do not mean this to be literal, but only an analogy, don't you?

I mean it literally with respect to the universe. The whole universe is Source's thought Energy, its imagination, made manifest. These manifestations are what humans perceive as physical matter.

Does Source have a sense of humor?

Yes, Source has a sense of humor. We ourselves would have no funny bone if Source didn't have a sense of humor because human animals are incapable of wit. It takes the creativity, imagination, objectivity, joy, and humility of our true nature as parts of Source to give rise to laughter and mirth in our lives.

Clearly humans were designed to enjoy humor as evidenced by the fact that laughter results in beneficial physiological changes. You have probably heard the Reader's Digest slogan, "Laughter is the best medicine." It takes the complexity of the human body to display humor in all its glory. Humans can laugh out loud, smile, snicker, guffaw, and, as my favorite T-shirt says, "Laugh[ ] so hard tears ran down my leg."

Our own eternal/spiritual personality, as well as the personality of the human we inhabit, determines what we find funny. Finding humor in irony and well-crafted jokes comes from our Light Being personality. When the human personality influences our behavior, we laugh at practical jokes, naughty words, and situation comedy revolving around bodily functions. The TV show *Two and a Half Men* is a perfect example of comedy directed at the human personality.

Does Source ever say to one of its mental characters, "You were great! You were so funny, so clever, so bright, you cracked me up!" while to another one He's thinking, "You were totally shallow, you did nothing, you accomplished nothing, you stood for nothing and went nowhere. Congratulations. Now get away from me!"

No. Source never does anything even remotely like this. Only a human would think and act this way. Source lacks the capacity to form judgments—including the human judgments described. Because the purpose of creating the mental characters/Light Beings is to garner experiences in the physical world, all experiences meet Source's purpose. We can never fail to accomplish our true purpose.

Never does Source say, "Get away from me." It couldn't banish part of itself even if it wanted to. All Light Beings are part of Source's own consciousness. The terms *mental characters* and *Light Beings* are merely my way to describe the individual personalities Source imagined for itself to experience the universe. We are never separate from Source no matter how much it might appear to humans that we are.

Can Source have preferences?

As far as I know, everything in the universe is Source's preference. It makes no distinctions. Nor does Source have judgment as part of its makeup. So, no, I don't think Source prefers one thing over another, one person over another, or one outcome over another. Preferences are part of judgment, which is a human characteristic.

You said Source has extreme curiosity. Do those of us who share this trait get it from Source?

Yes. Source's mental characters—us—have personalities that are a combination of Source's innate traits and traits it can only imagine.

Some of us got curiosity. Others got different Source traits.

I was surprised to learn in the afterlife that Source is tremendously curious. I could feel its curiosity like an itch it couldn't scratch and a giddiness I have always associated with children. Curiosity is what drives Source's interest in experiencing absolutely everything it can imagine, even things we find repulsive or painful. This aspect of Source is explained in more detail in *BACKWARDS Guidebook*, as it is a very hard concept for most of us to grasp. Think of it as being like the child who is told not to touch a stove because it is hot and will burn his skin. Then he touches the stove anyway. The child might intellectually recognize the warning inherent in what his mother said, but still be curious about what "burn" means to him.

You also wrote that Source created variety out of curiosity. How can an all-knowing God be curious? He already knows everything.

Source's curiosity revolves primarily around how various circumstances and emotions *feel*. Source knows intellectually all there is to know in our universe. Yet Source is curious about how experiencing all that goes on in the physical world feels in all of its variety of sensations. Think of it as the difference between reading a textbook about flying and actually flying an airplane. Source already has the "book knowledge" of aviation and created the universe to feel the physical and emotional sensations of piloting an airplane.

I have read that the afterlife is spent where there is no past or future, just an eternal now. If this is true, then it seems that Source would know about outcomes because they have already happened. What do you think?

I likewise noted a lack of "time" while I was in the afterlife. I also experienced that all topics of Universal Knowledge are knowable in the now. It's all a matter of focus. Whatever we focus our attention on in the afterlife exists in our "now." Even if we focus on thousands of events, there is no linear sequence to them. For example, when I recalled all of my other physical lives and the experiences I have had in non-physical eternal life, all the memories were in my mind at the same time. I could focus on particular events in one discrete lifetime but those events would not feel like they were in the past, present, or future as compared to other lifetimes. Timing concepts just don't exist in the afterlife.

I did not get the impression that Source does in fact "know" all outcomes in advance. My understanding of Creation, as I witnessed it through Source's eyes, is that Source created the processes that govern physical matter, but then the processes play out in their own unique ways. In other words, there is no destiny or preordained outcome. Events manifest on the fly. Source's innate curiosity is about how the outcomes of these events *feel*.

If Source is all-knowing and powerful, why would it need to experience human life?

Source has no *need* to experience human or any other physical life. That is a choice Source makes in order to feel what life is like as different imaginary creatures and things. Creating us to experience physical life is Source's way of exploring its own senses and imagination. It's sort of like how a baby plays with her fingers and toes, and learns to recognize herself in a mirror, as she gains familiarity with her body.

I can accept that Source is very emotional, but having curiosity implies having all emotions (I think). Can Source experience grief, fear, hatred?

Source cannot experience grief, fear, or hatred of its own innate nature. These emotions are not part of its core traits. But Source can imagine them. That is partly why it created all of us mental characters and the manifested physical world within which we interact. The universe was created so that Source can experience emotions foreign to its innate nature.

Maybe Source, being highly emotive, does experience giddiness and also anger and judgment?

Yes as to giddiness and (righteous) anger. No, the core personality of Source does not experience judgment. Judgment is a purely human character trait that Source imagined. It is not an emotion, although emotions often lead to snap judgments for humans.

How can electricity or an Energy field *feel* or *know* love?

Of course it is hard for my readers to believe that something I describe as an immense Energy field can feel love. We have been trained to believe energy is not alive. Human senses limit and define our awareness of life. For example, humans cannot perceive life in rocks, water, and stars, but these inanimate objects may well be inhabited by Light Being souls. Humans have been indoctrinated to recognize life only when it comes in plant, animal, or humanoid form. Most NDErs project that expectation into their experiences and manifest humanoid heavenly beings. I experienced Source as an Energy field with self-awareness, personality, emotions, and everything else that defines being alive. It's not an inert element, for instance, like what we think of as electricity, although I do use electricity as an analogy to describe Source. My intent is to make it clear that Source is not humanoid.

You state in a YouTube video clip that unconditional love is more akin to a force field, and in reality is not actually an emotion. This has me a bit confused, as you have stated in your books that Source is a highly emotional entity. Is there a way to reconcile these statements?

Naturally my reader thinks that love has to be one of Source's emotions, rather than something akin to a force field. My statement sounds bizarre from a human perspective. While we are in human bodies, we think like humans using only their limited range of experiences. But afterlife Knowings assured me that Source's unconditional love is more like an Energy field than an emotion.

When we NDErs go into the Light, as we say, we feel unconditional love. That Light is the outer fringe of Source's Energy field. What we NDErs feel is literally Source's Energy field, which we identify as love because it is similar to the emotion of love we feel as humans. But unlike human love, which is a reaction to a stimulus, Source's unconditional love is not given in response to anything we do. Source's unconditional love exists as part of its innate nature as pure Energy. Love is simply what Source's Energy field feels like to someone used to being human. What we NDErs recognize as the feeling of love *is the effect Source's Energy has on us.* Source is, in effect, totally made of love. Its Energy sparks feelings of love in us the same way putting a finger in an electrical outlet sparks intense tingling and shock in our bodies.

It's interesting that you see Source as highly emotive. How do you know that when you were "merged with Source" that the emotive state wasn't just you–a part of Nanci, perhaps, that still had to be there in order for "Nanci" to return?

I knew I was not feeling my own emotions because I'd previously had the experience of merging with my five Light Being eternal friends and feeling their emotions as I sampled their lives, the same way they lived parts of my life during my life review. I therefore had experience in the afterlife differentiating between feeling someone else's emotions and feeling my own. Also, I'm an empath in human life. I've had a lifetime of experiencing other people's emotions and discerning what's theirs and what's mine.

I have read the theory that there is a silver thread that connects us Light Being souls to human bodies. The last part of this question reminded me of that theory. Nothing I experienced or learned in the afterlife supports this notion. Nothing ties us to human bodies except our will to be here.

Whenever anyone asks you how Source can find all the horrors of human life interesting, which seems to demonstrate a lack of compassion, you respond that Source has compassion but does not allow its own feelings to interfere with Creation. How is Source showing compassion when it allows us to suffer rape, abuse, and even murder?

Several readers have asked this question, which demonstrates that most of us do in our heart-of-hearts understand Source to be an unconditionally loving Creator. What we see in human life seems to belie that knowledge because we assume it means Source deliberately tortures us with horrors like rape, abuse, and murder by allowing them to occur. Our religions have taught us that Source is a controlling Creator. This belief is based on the fact that humans are controlling, and unawakened souls assume Source is just like humans. But Source is nothing like a human.

Source *does* feel overwhelming self-compassion, and deep love and gratitude, for all those parts of itself that suffer while engaged in this physical manifestation. I know because I personally experienced Source's emotions while inside it during my afterlife experience. My purpose in making the statement was to explain how Source can find the painful aspects of human life interesting. The core entity Source cannot experience pain directly; it must imagine it through its manifested universe. However, interest is not Source's only reaction to our experiences. Because we are Source, it suffers when we do. Our emotions are Source's emotions because Source is the only consciousness that exists.

Despite its compassion, Source the core entity does not *control* what its Light Being parts manifest for themselves in this earthly environment. As aspects of Source's own personality, we Light Beings have the same character traits and innate powers that the core entity of Source does. Source cannot change its own nature. Thus it cannot change the fact that its mental characters have the ability to manifest physical reality, including what happens on earth. We have free will to use that manifesting ability because Source has free will to use it. Source's core personality does not step in and take control over our manifestations. Though Source could exercise self-control, which is what would be required to control us Light Beings, doing so would defeat its creative purpose to experience all that can possibly be created in a physical universe.

More important, Source knows we have free will to stop the horrible things we do while encased in human bodies if we so choose. The core entity Source does not need to intervene.

We Light Beings, individually and collectively, have the power to create what happens in the earth manifestation. But, sadly, we resist awakening to our true nature and power. We can collectively change human nature because humans are manifestations. We need only agree at the spiritual level to do so. In the religious history I saw in the afterlife, I saw that major changes in mankind have traditionally been accomplished via Light Being-initiated changes to human DNA or huge downloads of Universal Knowledge, both of which appear to humans as evolution. We can change mankind faster if we awaken more of those of us inside humans to our true spiritual nature, and manifest humans to be less violent.

We Light Being souls have the power to take control over our human hosts' behavior so that their violence, greed, territoriality, and revenge do not craft our daily lives. We souls seem to be the ones who lack compassion for each other. We are the ones who refuse to take responsibility for how our bodies act. We individually refuse to train and guide our body so that his or her behavior is less violent and more loving. Humans are animals that can be trained just like you train your dog to refrain from biting people. More important, each of us can exercise our own free will to act more from our spiritual nature. It requires being present in the moment and consciously choosing a different behavior. Although human emotions may be instantaneous, behaviors in response to those emotions need not be.

We Light Beings can put forth the effort to heal our own eternal personalities, which have been influenced by the traumas of numerous physical lifetimes. We can also heal our host bodies' traumas accumulated throughout this lifetime. We have the power to self-heal as part of our manifesting ability. Healing old wounds will prevent those hurts from motivating present behavior.

If we truly want a world free of rape, abuse, and murder, the power to change it is within each of us. We simply have to wake up and use it.

You state that Source delights in its Creation and is always in a state of bliss, which souls experience after death. How can Source take any delight in our suffering?

It doesn't. I have never said that Source delights in human suffering. Source delights in having created the universe, a magnificent feat. This is a direct emotional response of the core personality of Source. But it does not "delight" in the suffering that takes place within Creation.

Source feels everything we feel because we exist solely within it. Its core emotional reactions are more indirect, objective, detached, or removed than the emotions we feel intimately while inside human bodies. Source's emotions are more like what we experience when we watch a movie and are grossed out by blood and guts, or feel fear when it's a scary movie. We may feel real horror during the fictional event, but afterward can look back and say our emotional response was artificial because we didn't *really* experience the event that triggered our emotions. We lived it vicariously. Similarly, nothing we experience in human life is real to Source. Therefore, it doesn't invest any more emotional energy into what happens here in its imaginary universe than humans do when they watch TV shows, movies, or virtual reality video games.

You compare Source's delight in Creation to watching a movie, but isn't He the movie, meaning He would experience human suffering not as being something "cool" but rather painful? Since He only experiences bliss, He cannot experience anything painful. So why would He choose to create pain and suffering in order to experience Himself?

I do compare Source's emotions about what happens in the universe, including what happens to humans, to the indirect emotional response humans get when watching a movie or a dream. Source has both direct and vicarious emotional responses, just like we do.

This reader is correct, however, that Source's mind is generating the "movie" we call the universe. I used the movie analogy simply as a way to show that Source can get emotionally engaged in what its various mental characters are doing while still knowing that none of it is real. This is explained more fully in *BACKWARDS Guidebook.*

My reader erroneously assumes Source experiences only bliss, which would make it illogical for Source to manifest a universe where other emotions it cannot feel predominate. Source has a wide range of emotions that includes everything any of its manifestations feels. Remember, *we* are Source, so it feels everything we do, including pain. Humans feel only what Source can imagine.

4

Creation

MY DEEPEST UNDERSTANDING OF THE UNIVERSE, Source, and our relationship to Source, came near the end of my NDE during a gradual awakening to deeper and deeper layers of Source's nature. The Knowings I received at this time revealed a comprehensive explanation of life, death, the afterlife, and just about everything else I could think to ask. This new cosmology shattered my religious belief that we are separate beings thrust out into a cruel universe by a fickle controlling God, and that we have to earn our way to heaven by following inconsistent rules of behavior dictated by religious leaders. Instead, I learned the entire universe, and everything in it, exists solely within Source's imagination. The intellect of the entity that created the universe is so vast that it can hold in present thought an entire physical universe and everything in it.

I was shown the simple folk nature of the Genesis account in the Old Testament. Part of that biblical account depicts very accurately how the universe began. Source thought "let there be" a physical universe in much the same way as Genesis says, "Let there be light." But, unlike the Genesis account, Source did not create specific stars and planets, much less land masses, seas, and mankind. During my NDE, I watched as Source replayed Creation in its memory. I was informed by Knowings that Source expended huge volumes of mental Energy to manifest the universe. Then it established rules or plans for how each part of that manifestation would evolve over time. Source created the principles of physics, biological evolution, chemical reactions, and gravitational forces, and intended their interplay to generate a wide range of stars, planets, moons, nebula, gases, and everything living and inert. I saw stars and planets form and die as Creation exploded. I witnessed the birth and extinction of millions of plant and animal species on solid matter and in gaseous environments throughout the universe.

Creation is the most astounding of Source's powers and has generated a host of questions from my readers.

Creation of the Universe

Is the process of Creation a sort of combination of Source and us Light Beings working together to create or manifest universes?

Not exactly. While I visually relived Source's memories of Creation, Knowings explained what was happening. Source is the sole Creator of the universe, which existed before Source imagined its mental characters/Light Beings to bring its awareness into physical experience. I did learn, however, that there are groups of Light Beings that help maintain the manifestation of the part of the universe that most interests each group. For example, I saw a group of Light Beings I call "All Those Who Have An Interest In Earth" and how they maintain the overall manifestation of what humans see as physical reality. So, though the Light Being parts of Source's mind help maintain the manifestation of physical matter, Light Beings did not work together within Source's mind to create the universe. The universe was created first.

You seem to be saying in your books that humanity is a manifested race that can exist on its own in the way that a dream exists. But can the dream continue without the dreamer?

Human Perspective. Some spiritual philosophies assume each soul manifests its own human body. Thus, when the soul leaves, the body dies. These philosophies are correct that humans are manifested, but not in their assumption that souls manifest them.

Source's Perspective. Humans are a manifestation created within Source's core mind. I learned in the afterlife that the entire species of human animals exists in the same way that every other part of the universe exists—as Source's thought Energy. Source's core personality/consciousness is the dreamer in this regard, not the souls inhabiting humans. Source is forever, so there is no possibility of there ever being a time "without the dreamer."

Am I missing the point that the human and Light Being are each a separate distinct entity, capable of surviving the absence of the other? Or is their merged relationship part of Source's relationship equation for their co-existence, *i.e.*, you can't have one without the other?

Human Perspective. Before my NDE, I believed God created my body and soul together specifically to be Nanci. This question hints at a similar belief. We have been indoctrinated with the ideas that we are human beings and souls are necessary parts of our bodies, *i.e.*, "you can't have one without the other." Some of us have been taught that souls provide the life force that animates humans.

Source's Perspective. Both humans and souls are Source's thoughts. Thoughts exist independent of one another. Souls are not the life force for humans. Humans are manifestations that exist regardless of whether or not Light Beings choose to inhabit them as souls. The Light Being characters in Source's mind exist whether or not humans populate any part of the universe. Humans and Light Beings are distinct thoughts within Source's mind but they are not distinct entities. There is only one entity—Source.

How did Source manage to imagine all the experiences human life can provide before man existed in his present form? We all know that it took hundreds of thousands of years of evolution to develop *Homo sapiens*.

Human Perspective. The theory that human life is predetermined pervades human religious and spiritual belief systems. According to this belief, God created all human experiences and parceled them out to individual humans according to a master plan for their lives. Creation is therefore concluded. I learned during my NDE that nothing could be further from the truth.

Source's Perspective. Source did not imagine all the potential experiences humans could have before present day man evolved. What humans today experience as physical life is manifested moment by moment by the Light Being souls inside them. We are the architects of our own lives. Life is a creative work in progress. It was not pre-designed by Source. Creation is not static; it is ongoing.

Our Creation

I also witnessed *our* Creation while inside Source.

Before I spent time in the afterlife, I believed I was a human being with a soul. I believed my soul was an integral part of the human body, like blood and bone. I learned in the afterlife, however, that I was completely wrong. We are not separate beings from Source. We are not beings at all. We are literally individual unique characters or personalities that Source imagined, similar to the characters that populate our dreams. I learned that Source created these mental characters as a way for it to experience what its manifested physical world is like, similar to how we imagine dream characters to experience our dreamscapes. For convenience, I call these characters "Light Beings." I adopted the term after reading NDE accounts in which the NDErs describe seeing Beings of Light in the afterlife. Afterlife Knowings informed me that these Light Beings are the mental characters in Source's mind that I was given information about.

"Light Being" is shorthand for Source's mental characters that carry its self-awareness, perspective, viewpoint, and point of reference into the physical universe. We are like the fictional personas spies or undercover cops adopt to infiltrate dangerous situations.

When some NDErs say, "We are all God," it makes me shudder a little. That seems perilously close to blasphemy. *Emanations* of God, maybe, subordinate *fragments* maybe, but to say that we are God, of the same substance and on a level with Him/Her/It, that just makes me feel spiritually nauseous. Why should I dare even contemplate this?

Human Perspective. I think my reader's nausea emanates from religious indoctrination. Our religions teach us to fear Source and to expect retribution when we do not make ourselves subservient to it.

Source's Perspective. It's true that we are Source—"of the same substance and on a level with it." But the words *fragments* and *emanations* are good characterizations of how much of Source's consciousness we each represent in comparison to the whole. That is, so long as we all understand that we are not separate beings at all, much less "subordinate" ones. We are simply Source's mental characters, trains of thought, personalities, daydreams, or roles to play within the universe. There is no reason for one thought in Source's mind to be or feel subservient to other thoughts. Saying we are Source is no different than saying book characters are the author or that dream characters are the dreamer.

Our Relationship to Source

What keyword(s) should I focus on and practice in order to realize our Oneness, return to the Source, go from ego to soul, listen to our soul, reconnect with God, etc. I don't know the correct way to phrase it, but how does one go from separation to Oneness/wholeness? I just need the keyword(s) that will open the door and allow God into my life and therefore Oneness. Is it being open, willing, focused, or what?

Human Perspective. Many religions and spiritual belief systems are tethered to a central belief that we are separate beings from the God who created us. They also teach, however, that we can return to God and heaven if we only do the right things. Theories abound as to what those right things are.

Source's Perspective. There are no magic words for experiencing Oneness with Source. Nor are any needed. We are already one with Source. We do not have to do anything to get back to that state because we are now within Source and have never left. This is the startling truth that was revealed to me as I awakened as Source after completing all phases of my afterlife. It was incredibly humbling to realize, and know it in my very core, that I have never actually been anyone but Source.

We feel as if we are separate because that is how we are designed as Light Beings. We rarely overcome that feeling while in the body. If we were constantly aware of our true nature, we would not have genuine human experiences. We would be like the characters in the TV show *Flash Forward*, who, having seen the future, change their present to try to force a different result. So, Source built amnesia of our true nature into the incarnation process.

We were created because Source desires to know experientially all that it knows intellectually, all that it could conceive of to know, and all that could evolve to be known through its own creativity. Source is extremely curious by nature and wants to have a vast range of experiences. So Source created its mental characters to have individual unique personalities, emotions, self-awareness, and the will to live. We are all, each and every one of us, simply Source pretending to be imaginary creatures similar to the dream characters we create each night. And, just as our dream characters get tucked away in our memories when we awaken from sleep, Source stores its memories of our individual personalities as Light Beings when we have run our course of living the illusion of separation. Until then, our job is to experience what it is like to feel separate. To experience what human life is like. Enjoy human life for as long as it lasts. We will become aware of our Oneness soon enough.

In *BACKWARDS*, you wrote: "And it is this truth—that we are literally part of the Source—that assures our ultimate return to it." Why do you think that conclusion logically follows? Here, impeachment of a part of a membership by the majority can certainly occur. Your argument is by no means obvious. I need something more convincing.

I actually didn't use logic to draw the conclusion that our return to Source is guaranteed. Knowings about Source's nature and ours implanted this truth directly into my mind. But, even applying logic, the conclusion is inescapable because: (a) we are thoughts in Source's mind; and (b) thoughts cannot actually leave someone's mind; ergo, (c) we figuratively return to Source because we never left its mind.

We experience only an illusion of being separate beings. We eventually wake up and understand that the separation was not real, that what we thought of as our individual identities are mere thought patterns or personality lines or characters in Source's imagination. And we are Source.

If the reader who posed this question is suggesting that some of Source's thoughts can collude to eject other thoughts out of Source's mind, relax. That cannot happen. This comment hinges on a belief that we are actually separate beings from Source, which is not the case. There can be no majority rule when there is only one consciousness.

I get your message and am relieved you do not entirely agree with Eckhart Tolle [*The Power of Now* and *New Earth*]. However, he and the entire Eastern philosophy seem to be about connecting and staying connected to our Source (God). Why do you disagree?

I do not disagree of my own accord. My mission is to share with anyone who will listen what I learned of Universal Knowledge in the afterlife. I learned in the afterlife that our connection with Source is built in. Humans and Light Being souls believe they are separate beings from Source. They are not. I see no reason to strive for something that already exists and that we will experience automatically when we fully awaken to who we really are.

What connection does our subconscious mind have to Source?

Human Perspective. I learned while earning my degree in psychology that the term "subconscious mind" was coined by French psychologist Pierre Janet. It means different things to different people, but is generally thought to be part of the human mind.

Source's Perspective. What we call the subconscious mind is part of Source's mind, with Source just pretending to be a separate identity from its core personality. Everything that exists is part of Source's mind. There is only one consciousness—that of Source.

The old concept was that people are walking around without

a relationship with God, and they need to ask God/Jesus to come into their lives, at which point they will be "born again." Do you think this is necessary?

My understanding from watching the history of religion on earth while in the afterlife is that nearly all religious precepts are manmade. They do not come from Source. The idea of needing to be saved is clearly of human origin because it is fear-based. This religious precept instills the fear that we won't get into heaven if we don't do what our church says. This is organized religion's attempt to assure its own continuity through control. You'd never get that kind of idea from Source because it is not true.

I learned in the afterlife that asking Source to come into our lives is unnecessary because *we are already in its life*. Our body/soul beliefs are backwards. My understanding is that the whole process of entering the afterlife and returning to Source that exists at the Light Being level of perspective is automatic, whether we believe in it or not. This is because the entire universe exists solely in Source's mind. There's nowhere else to go. We never leave Source's thinking. Thus, there is no possibility that we can end up anywhere else but in Source's mind, whether we ask for a relationship with Source or not. Think of it as similar to the fact that our own thoughts can't get away from us and end up in hell or on Mars. Our thoughts exist solely in our minds.

What is the reason for the "spiritual corporation" in the afterlife—angels, archangels, spiritual guides—if we are here only to gain experiences?

The idea of a spiritual hierarchy in heaven was created by ancient writers whose manuscripts are included in the Bible. These writers naturally gave heaven a kingdom structure because kingdoms were what they were familiar with from human life. The writers created heaven in man's organizational image.

I neither saw nor experienced angels, archangels, spiritual guides or spiritual beings (other than Light Beings) while I was visiting the afterlife or while I was watching Creation. Nor did I get any Knowings that indicate they ever existed.

If there are no spiritual intermediaries between us and Source, does this mean Source is somehow active in our lives, or is Source just an inactive bystander after we incarnate?

Remember, in ultimate reality we are Source's thoughts, not separate beings. There's no way Source could be an inactive bystander in our lives when it is doing all the thinking that creates our lives. But looking at it from human perspective, no, the core entity of Source does not routinely interfere in the lives of the manifestations inhabited by its mental characters/Light Beings. Because we are ultimately Source's own thoughts, there is no reason, in my opinion, for there to be spiritual intermediaries. How would one thought even act as intermediary between other thoughts in Source's mind?

You speak of physical manifestation as something Source wanted to experience through us. I know we are all One, yet something about the idea of our doing this as a service to Source (if this is what you are saying) contradicts many of the beliefs I have had. Are we One, or are we separate beings serving Source?

Human Perspective. The idea that we are serving Source comes from religious beliefs. Many of us have been told we must know, love, and serve God in order to be saved. Trying to get on Source's good side has always been a feature of human religions, starting with primitive humans leaving food and other treasured goods at locations believed to be frequented by a god.

Light Being Perspective. We Light Beings are not separate beings serving Source. We are not designed to serve Source; we *are* Source. Subservient roles are a concept tied to the Alpha, Beta, and followers hierarchy that exists in the animal kingdom. It takes two beings for one of them to serve the other.

Human manifestations were created to fulfill Source's desire to experience all that it could imagine. So, to that extent, humans serve Source. But they are not separate beings. They are merely creative thoughts, imagined creatures, similar to our own dream characters. Do our dream characters "serve" us as subservient beings?

Source's Perspective. There is only one entity in existence—Source.

Source cannot be subservient to itself. The idea of service simply does not apply.

Whether Source Controls Our Lives

I recently read a near-death experience book that portrayed the author's life as a series of events directed and controlled by God—a traditional religious belief. That got me thinking about how seeing the same events from a different perspective can make a world of difference. It can literally turn a victim into a powerful spiritual force.

Many humans believe God observes and manages their day-to-day activities. They think God decides on the good events we will experience and punishes us with bad events for transgressions or omissions. This viewpoint is chock-full of beliefs that we are cut off from our Creator, isolated, controlled by a being outside ourselves, and powerless to change because our lives are dictated by someone else. In essence, many believe we are victims of God's whims. While in the afterlife, I learned that such beliefs are the result of human fear and superstition. And with enlightenment, they can be corrected.

To Source, there is no reason to control what happens in the physical universe because the physical universe is not real. As an analogy, think of your own dreams. Do you consciously enter into the dream and control everything that a dream character does? Forcing some actions and vetoing others? Or do you just watch and see what happens, unconcerned about the outcomes because you know the dream isn't real? In the same way, Source manifests the universe, and allows us, its mental characters, to experience physical life without interference. To Source, everything happening in the universe transpires solely within its own imagination, and, therefore, has no permanent consequences. Just like our own dreams transpire solely within our own minds and have no consequences after we are awake.

The Knowings I received in the afterlife taught me a new way to view our Creator. I was shown that Source is all-loving and not controlling. We Light Beings have free will to pick and choose the events of the physical lives of the creatures we inhabit. We either allow the host body to lead its animal life with us just going along for the ride, or, we manifest into physical reality what we truly and deeply believe about human life and ourselves within it.

Because we are parts of Source, and we have the ability to control the actions and lives of the human hosts we inhabit (whether we exercise this power or not), Source in a very limited sense does control human lives. The difference between reality and the religious model is who has the power. In the religious model, God is an all-powerful external force and we are powerless. The religious model assumes that this external power directs and controls everything in the physical world. The reality I was shown in the afterlife is we are Source and therefore direct and control our own lives.

Was Gene Roddenberry's TV show *Star Trek* right when it portrayed superior entities testing and observing humans?

Human Perspective. Growing up in Catholic schools I often heard the phrase, "God doesn't give us more than we can handle." (I sometimes wondered whether the Church was aware of all the people who couldn't handle their suffering without the assistance of alcohol, pharmacology, and mental health professionals.) This old saw, of course, erroneously implies that Source doles out anguish to specific individuals. If so, there has to be a reason for it, doesn't there? As unawakened Light Being souls within humans struggled for generations to fathom the answer, they hit upon the idea that suffering was a test. If one passed the test—how that was judged no one knows—then the person would earn heaven.

Source's Perspective. The difference between the *Star Trek* aliens observing and testing humans, and the reality of Source, is that Source is not testing us. There is no reason to do so because there is nothing we have to prove to get to heaven. We are already there, though we are unaware of it. We have never escaped Source's mind, so there is nowhere to go back to when our bodies die. All that happens after the body's death is that we gradually increase our self-awareness until we realize we do not really exist as individuals at all; we are Source. When that happens, the illusion of separation is broken the same way the illusion of our dream characters is broken when we awaken from sleep. It might take hundreds or thousands of incarnations before that happens, like it did with me. I don't think it happens between incarnations.

If there is any testing and observing going on here, it is because *we* have chosen to test and observe ourselves. There is no one *out there* to do so. We are all inside Source challenging ourselves with difficult manifested lives.

P.S.—While I was watching the history of religion on earth during my NDE, millions of people were pointed out to me as messengers from Source about the truth about life, death, and the afterlife. I was tickled to see that Gene Roddenberry was one of them. This does not mean we should make *Star Trek* into a religion. Only tidbits of Universal Knowledge appear in its TV segments and one would have to know Universal Knowledge in order to recognize them.

If this is all Source's Creation, by thinking and dreaming, then what control do we have? Aren't we all then just puppets on a string?

Human Perspective. Humans believe they are separate beings from Source with no control over their lives.

Source's Perspective. No, we are not puppets. Although everything in the universe, including all thought, resides exclusively within Source's mind, part of that mind has created zillions of different and unique personalities. *We* are some of those personalities. We have control over our lives because *we are Source*, even though we can't remember that while we inhabit physical matter.

Each of us, as Source, has the very same ability to manifest physical reality. We co-create with the core entity of Source what humans perceive as reality. That is the control we have. We collectively have creative power over what happens to us in the physical world. We manifest our life events, consciously or unconsciously.

Again, the core entity of Source does not drive everything that happens in the universe. It created the forces that operate to produce those results, but the results are creative in nature and ever-changing. The real cause of the "puppets on a string" sensation is the failure of Light Being souls to take control over their human hosts, and humans failing to exercise self-control.

5

Light Beings

I DISCOVERED THROUGH KNOWINGS IN THE AFTER-
life that all of the intelligence, creativity, love, compassion, integrity,
humor, and other traits we cherish about humans do not belong to
humans at all! These are all characteristics of us Light Being souls that
show through the behavior of the humans we inhabit.

Each Light Being may choose to infuse part of its Energy, self-
awareness, consciousness, and personality into a human or other
physical matter as its soul. This Energy percolates throughout the
body. The Light Being soul experiences everything the body experiences but is not part of the body. For example, when I leave my body,
it is not like other loss of energy sensations I've had. It is nothing
like falling asleep, being rendered unconscious for surgery, extreme
exhaustion, or feeling completely drained of energy as with radiation
fatigue. In all these normal human experiences that make me feel
physically weak and out of fuel, I feel like I am still completely occupying my tired body. Getting out-of-body feels like my consciousness and personality literally escape the physical form. Once out, I no
longer receive physical sensations from the body. Nor do I feel as if I
am occupying any part of it. All of my consciousness exits the physical world, leaving a disconnected body behind.

Light Beings do not exist in physical reality. And they aren't really "beings" in the spiritual reality of the afterlife. Nevertheless, I

call Source's mental characters *beings* because when NDErs see them in heaven, they appear to be glowing humanoids composed of Energy and Light. I myself saw such beings during the early stages of my NDE. Later in my NDE, I learned that Light Beings manifest the ethereal visual appearance for newly arrived souls because that is what humans have come to expect—an angelic vision. Light Beings have no physical matter and, therefore, no real visual appearance unless they manifest one for a particular purpose. In essence, a Light Being is an individual focus of Source's awareness rather than anything resembling the beings NDErs see.

"Light Beings" is the term I use when Source parcels out bits of its self-awareness into physical matter to perceive the world from inside creatures and things. Source's awareness is so powerful that only tiny fragments can be interwoven into individual objects of physical matter. Think of what Source does with its Light Beings as comparable to what we do with our dream characters. Our mind mentally projects our dream, like Source's mind mentally manifests the universe. There may be other characters in our dream, but we participate and watch the dream as though we are inside only one of them. We see through its eyes and hear through its ears, looking out at the dream landscape and events. Just as in waking life we feel like we are inside bodies, and life transpires all around us, in dreams we have the sensation we are inside a character at the center of the dream's events. Source uses its mental characters/Light Beings to create the same sensation. Unlike our dreams, though, Source is not limited to viewing the universe from inside only one character. It uses Light Being souls to be inside every type of physical matter so that Source has the sensation of being within, and looking out of, all parts of the universe at the same time.

Light Being Characteristics

What's the difference between soul and spirit?

There may not be any difference, depending upon who is using the words. Trying to differentiate these terms is confusing, partly because we don't have well-known and universally accepted words for spiritual phenomena. Try to keep in mind that the words themselves are not perfect descriptions of the actual concepts, which to a large extent are indescribable. Certain terms are mere place holders, or shorthand ways of talking about a concept without fully describing it each time. Also, please understand that each person attaches his or her own meaning to words so that he/she has a way of communicating as best he/she can. I have chosen common meanings for both "soul" and "spirit," but others may use the words completely differently than I do.

I use "soul" to indicate the part of a Light Being's Energy, consciousness, personality, and self-awareness that it invests during incarnation into physical matter, including humans. Most people think of something inside humans when they hear the word "soul," so using this term is a good fit. I generally do not use the word "spirit" because it has too many different meanings, though I do use *spiritual* on occasion to denote non-physical life in general. When I refer to the parts of Source that inhabit physical matter as souls, or reside in heaven or the afterlife, I use the term "Light Beings."

Are you simply calling the Light Being soul "human?"

No. Light Beings are not humans. And humans are not souls. What we call a soul is part of a Light Being's self-awareness that has been reduced in scope in order to coexist inside a manifested human body. When I use the term "human," I mean only the manifested physical animal. I believe it is easier to understand the difference if you read my account of watching the Creation of the universe in chapter 2 of *BACKWARDS Beliefs*.

Why aren't Light Beings the same illusion as human animals?

This question deftly points out that discussing the differences between Light Beings and humans is splitting hairs, because they are both imaginary to Source. They are both merely thoughts. I have simply chosen to label some thoughts with names in order to discuss the Knowings about them that I brought back from the afterlife.

Human animals are manifestations of physical matter that inhabit Earth. They are perceived as real only by other manifestations. *Light*

Beings is just a term I use for Source's own consciousness and perspective divided into characters with different personalities. I know this is confusing because we are talking about different types of thoughts, imaginings, and illusions *within one mind* and putting labels on them to differentiate them. The distinction between a Light Being and a human is a matter of where Source has placed its focus of awareness—that sensation of being inside a being looking out through its eyes. Physical matter, including humans, exists within Source's mind but does not automatically have Source's self-awareness within it. In other words, if a manifestation is likened to a dream character, it would be someone other than us in our dream. A manifestation inhabited by a Light Being soul, on the other hand, would be like the character we play in the dream and from within which we view the dream.

Is there a difference between Light Beings and life-forms from outer space? If aliens are different, at what vibrational level do they function? I observed aliens that are extracorporeal, communicate telepathically, float instead of walking, have increased brain function, and can walk through our solid matter.

This reader's description of aliens certainly sounds like Light Being characteristics. Perhaps my reader saw Light Beings instead of aliens. True life-forms from outer space are physical matter manifestations, just like humans and the plant and animal species on earth are manifestations. Aliens appear as physical matter and they may be extracorporeal, communicate telepathically, have increased brain function, and float, but, to the best of my knowledge, they cannot walk through solid matter. Light Beings are not physical manifestations. They exist without physical matter. So, yes, they are different than aliens from outer space.

Although I learned in the afterlife that various types of Source's thoughts generally have different Energy signatures or vibration levels, the Knowings did not include a compendium of what type of thought has what type of Energy signature. So I do not know at what vibrational level aliens function.

Do Light Beings have personalities, or are all lumps and crevices of character ironed out flat?

Light Beings by definition *are* personalities. I use the term *Light Being* as shorthand to mean "a Source-designed mental collection of unique character and personality traits." We Light Beings have lots of "lumps and crevices" to our personalities. Nearly all of what we think of as our human personality is actually Light Being personality. Humans have very little personality—not much more than a domesticated cat or dog.

I heard you say in a radio interview that we've left part of ourselves behind in the Light. The person I am now has learned to play the guitar and the bass, learned homeopathy, has had a baby, and has been practicing Transcendental Meditation for years. How can I be anything like the "me" that got left behind in the Light?

When the body dies, the Energy that was the body's soul goes back to the Light and recombines with the rest of its Light Being Energy. This is what happened to me. Everything we experience in human life stays in our eternal personality and memory. So this reader's eternal personality and memories will always include playing the guitar and bass, knowing homeopathy and TM, awareness of what it is like to have a human baby, etc.

My reader is correct that the small part of her eternal personality that shines through her human host is not much like the rest of her Energy still in the Light. Our eternal Light Being personalities are far more complex, can express far more innate abilities, and have learned and experienced a zillion times more than the humans we currently inhabit will ever know. The part of the Light Being inhabiting the human is the limited personality, not the part still in the Light.

Can humans see Light Beings?

Sometimes. The characters within Source that carry its self-awareness into physical life look like Light Beings *only* from a human perspective, regardless of whether that perspective is experienced while a soul is in a human body or during the early phases of an NDE or death. A soul used to being limited to human understanding interprets the parts of Source's Energy I call Light Beings as glowing humanoid beings. If humans did not expect angels or celestial beings in the afterlife, Light Beings would not appear in those forms.

Some people perceive Light Beings in the physical world and interpret them as ghosts, glowing orbs of light, or silvery vapor.

Some people see Light Beings just before death. They can have any type of appearance, but often appear as the dying person's loved ones who are already in the afterlife.

Some NDErs see Light Beings as glowing angels or humanoid beings because these NDErs haven't moved very far through the transformation process. After we transform fully back into spiritual state, we no longer see each other in the afterlife as having a humanoid shape. We don't "see" each other at all. We know each other by feel.

Is there a connection between our Light Being and what we call electricity?

There is no connection, but electricity is a good analogy for some aspects of Source. Electricity is a type of energy familiar to humans. All energy is Source Energy. For example, when I revisited the afterlife recently without dying, I felt as though my body had been electrocuted with Source Energy. This was the only way I could describe the sensation in a way everyone would understand.

Before I found your books, I learned that souls are both old and young. Some souls are newborn. These various soul ages would explain the different types of humans here. But if all souls originate from the Source, shouldn't they all be on the same Source level?

Before my time in the afterlife, I believed I was an "old soul." I had read books claiming that souls have ages and are created in batches called "soul groups." I saw nothing in the afterlife to support either idea. Instead, what I witnessed during Creation was that all of the characters/Light Beings within Source were created at the same time, after the universe was manifested. I also learned that time is an artificial construct humans have created that does not exist outside human life. Consequently, there can be no old or young Light Being souls. There can be no batches of soul creation over linear time. Everything exists at the exact same moment in spiritual life.

All souls are indeed on the same level as Source in the same way that the dream characters in our dreams are all on the same level— they exist only as imaginary characters within one mind.

Does a soul choose a lower/higher level of consciousness before coming here?

It does not.

Human Perspective. Humans strive to find a way to create a hierarchy in the spiritual world because animals innately expect hierarchy within their own ranks. This is the origin of the idea that a soul could choose whether to have a higher or lower level of consciousness while inside a human.

Light Being Perspective. All humans are manifestations, and, therefore, have the exact same level of consciousness. The process of inhabiting physical matter automatically lowers the awareness level of the part of the Light Being Energy incarnating as a soul. The Light Being also divides its consciousness between the physical world and the spiritual world. This is a split in consciousness between two locations, not a lowering of the degree of consciousness in either of them. Nor is it a matter of individual choice. It is the way Source designed life.

Source's Perspective. All Light Beings are Source's own consciousness, and, therefore, are equally conscious.

Is the percentage of Light Being consciousness inside each human the same for all of us? Or do some humans have a greater or lesser percentage and, therefore, a greater or lesser sense of awareness?

I do not remember the percentage of a Light Being's Energy that stays in the Light versus the portion entering into physical matter as the soul. I *think* it varies, but I am not certain. I do remember that the amount of Light Being Energy invested in a human body has nothing to do with how aware the resulting human/soul combined person is.

If only part of our Light Being Energy is inside our human body, is it possible for us to occupy more than one body at the same time?

Before my NDE, I thought it might be possible for a soul to split and occupy two bodies at once. This supposition was bolstered by the fact that all my life I have had dreams in which I consistently have a different appearance and live in a different house. Although I was interested to know the truth about this topic, I learned nothing about it in the afterlife. My afterlife experience, however, was that I had incarnated into only one body. My life review consisted solely of Nanci's life.

Is it possible for *any* living or non-living thing to possess a soul?

Yes and no. Physical matter does not and cannot "possess" a Light Being soul. We Light Being characters within Source's mind can *voluntarily* choose to invest part of our Energy and awareness in any type of physical matter in the universe. A rock, horse, human, alien, and star all have exactly the same type of soul if a Light Being chooses to inhabit it.

Do Light Beings have certain powers that they have to learn about and learn how to make them work?

As parts of Source, we Light Beings have the same powers as Source but on a smaller scale. They are innate abilities. We don't have to learn what they are or how to make them work for us because we already know. Memory of our abilities is suppressed only while we are in physical matter.

It seems slightly counterintuitive that Light Beings are generally unaware that they are Source itself. The point is, if I know this fact from a human level of perspective, why don't Light Beings know this if they are supposedly at a higher level of perspec-

tive?

Light Beings' final goal is to reawaken to the truth that we are Source itself role-playing as different imaginary creatures and things within the physical universe. But the whole incarnation system would not be effective if we were not absolutely convinced that what we are experiencing in our lives "separate from Source" is "real." So, Source gives us mental characters/Light Beings amnesia regarding our true identity and purpose. We still have a layer of that amnesia in the afterlife, although ignorance of our true nature as Light Beings has been removed. I experienced this myself. In the afterlife, we believe we are separate identities from Source even though we no longer believe human life, or any physical life, is real.

We Light Beings continue to gain understanding of life as we move back and forth between the incarnation phase and the afterlife phase of eternal life. Just because a Light Being has full access to Universal Knowledge in the afterlife does not mean it completely and accurately understands everything it can access. A Light Being's individual level of understanding will depend upon where it exists in the progression from the incarnation phase to the phase where we are ready to awaken as Source. The closer we get to full awakening the more we understand. But full understanding does not occur until full awakening.

For example, if I had returned from my NDE following the early stage in the Light when I was bombarded with Universal Knowledge, before my eventual awakening within Source, I would have returned with very different messages. My religious beliefs would not have changed much. I would understand that I'm a spiritual being and not a human. But I would not understand Creation, or that we are actually Source, or Source's nature. My understanding of the information I received would be limited to what we souls understand while at the level of human perspective. If one of my loved ones on earth had communicated with me at that early stage of my afterlife, there is a high probability that even though I had unfettered access to Universal Knowledge, I would not understand it well enough to give my loved one the whole truth as Source knows it. My understanding of Universal Knowledge did not ripen until I completed the awakening as Source near the end of my NDE. This is the reason I do not trust messages people claim to have received by channeling one or more spirits in the afterlife. Who knows what that spirit's accuracy of understanding may be?

It is possible for us to intellectually learn the eternal truths at any stage of life, even without awakening as Source, just as this reader's question states she did. I returned to human life to spread my messages because I knew awakened Light Being souls would remember Universal Knowledge once reminded of it. But an individual Light Being's understanding of spiritual truths will vary and will not be perfect until it completes the experiential journey for which we were designed and reawakens as Source.

But if we are all part of Source, and not really ourselves, and our human selves are just an illusion, then my husband who died three years ago doesn't really exist as my husband anymore and my hope that we'll be together again someday is unrealistic. I don't find that comforting. Yet, you seem to have been very comforted by the whole NDE experience. Can you translate that into terms the living can understand?

The physical world and what happens in it is an illusion at Source's level of existence. But we Light Beings are really part of Source and we really exist at Source's level of existence as part of Source. We souls truly exist as ourselves in what we believe to be the physical reality of the human bodies we inhabit. The experiences feel completely real and we have real emotions about them. The only thing illusory about us is our belief that we are separate beings from Source and that we are humans.

The Light Being that was inside my reader's husband as his soul is eternal. *That* is the personality my reader loves, not the human body's personality. Her husband continues to exist as that beloved personality, with all its human memories, in the afterlife. My reader will recognize him as such when she gets there herself.

In addition, my reader is already with her husband in the Light because part of her Light Being Energy remains in the afterlife and in communion with those she loves. It's just the amnesia of incarnation that keeps us souls from knowing all this. When our host body dies, we—the Light Being Energy currently serving as soul—will recombine with the rest of our Light Being Energy in the afterlife. We will be whole again. And we will be able to communicate with our loved ones in the afterlife with all of our multiple simultaneous levels of awareness being conscious of it.

Light Being Life

Where does a Light Being reside?

Human Perspective. Due to NDE accounts, many of us have come to believe that Light Beings reside in heaven.

Source's Perspective. A Light Being is a constellation of character and personality traits existing only within Source's mind, just as characters in a novel reside only in a writer's mind.

If you saw only Light Beings, and not angels, in the afterlife, what were the Light Beings doing?

My Light Being friends welcomed me, communicated with me telepathically, watched my life review with me, shared their physical life experiences with me via direct merger into my Energy, and accompanied me to the afterlife stage when I awakened as Source.

What is the Light Being's role in the afterlife?

My observation of my five Light Being friends was that their role was to guide me through the various stages of the afterlife, starting right after I realized I was dead. They also participated with me in the stage of afterlife when we gather experiences vicariously through merging our Energy with that of other Light Beings. I merged into each of them individually, and all of them at once, several times. During the review of earth history, I saw Light Beings helping to maintain the manifestation of the Earth and tweaking the manifestation of human DNA. In addition, Knowings indicated that we Light Beings help each other while in the afterlife and assist in the crossing over process.

In later NDEs, I learned that Light Beings sit on councils that help guide the physical lives of souls with particular missions.

Could you please tell me how Beings of Light who are formless can recognize each other? Also, how does a Light Being recognize Source?

In our Light Being state we recognize each other by feel, not appearance. We retain a watered-down version of this ability while inside human bodies. For example, even in the dark we can sense whether a loved one or a burglar has entered our room at night. We feel the energy of the person's presence. During my NDE, I recognized my five Light Being dearest friends by how they felt to me—their Energy, auras, and thoughts. We are able to easily discern these features while in spiritual form. I recognized Source the same way—by feel. I remembered the feeling from when I was integrated with Source before choosing this human life. Don't worry about your loved ones' ability to recognize you, or you to recognize them, in the afterlife. It's not a problem.

Do Light Beings like to hear themselves being talked about?

Light Beings have no vanity and seek no attention. Those are human traits. During my time in the afterlife I observed that we Light Beings couldn't care less whether humans discuss us or what they say. Human life no longer interests us after we have left it, much in the same way that in human life our dreams no longer interest us after we wake up. Oh, we might remember a dream for a few days, and puzzle over its meaning, but very shortly the dream ceases to hold our attention. It's the same way in the afterlife. Human activities have about as much relevance to our spiritual lives as dreams have to human life.

Does the part of the Light Being still in the Light only observe the life of the soul or does it sometimes intervene in that physical life on behalf of the soul?

The part of our Light Being Energy still in the Light/afterlife does intervene in our physical life if called upon to do so. We souls can access Universal Knowledge and consciously manifest reality through the part of our Energy still in the Light. I recommend to all that we do so frequently and use those powers to improve our lives on earth and assist in consciously manifesting. We can also get guidance if we just listen to the part of ourselves living outside the influence of human life.

Why should Light Beings help humans prolong their time on earth? Why bother, since the afterlife seems infinitely better?

We Light Being souls prolong human life only if it is necessary to meet our spiritual goals. That is why no human can die before its time. Those that do accidentally die too soon have an NDE in which the Light Being soul learns it came home too early and should return to human life.

Labeling something as "better" is a human value judgment. Light beings do not judge which life is better, human life or afterlife. We have no concept of judging in our spiritual state.

Communication Between Body and Soul

Can we communicate with our own Light Being by talking or thinking? Will it respond? How does our acknowledgment of being a Light Being within a human body help us to advance if we cannot access our Light Being?

I want to clarify that I use the term Light Being to refer to us— you and me—in our true spiritual state as imaginary characters within Source's mind. Technically, we cannot *have* our own Light Being because we *are* Light Beings. It's like asking whether we can communicate with ourselves. Yes, we can talk to ourselves, just as humans do when they mutter to themselves going through the aisles at the grocery store. (Oh, am I the only one that does that?!)

I think this reader is asking whether human bodies can communicate with their on board Light Being souls. Yes, our bodies communicate with us through the language of physical matter, i.e., sensations, feelings, emotions, and other nonverbal cues. We can learn to attach words to these various cues by using the "Focusing" process steps listed in *Focusing* by Eugene Gendlin, PhD. But humans do not "advance" by accessing or communicating with Light Being souls.

Acknowledging and believing that we are Light Beings inhabiting human bodies partially removes the amnesia barrier that prevents us souls from consciously using our spiritual powers while incarnated. This not only helps us increase the happiness of the humans we inhabit, but also improve the quality of our human experiences by giving us more informed control over them.

If I need more courage and confidence to let go of the physical pain, fatigue, and anxiety I have learned to live with, suffer, and tolerate for so many years, will all I need be found in my own Light Being? Is that where I will find the courage and strength?

I need to reframe this question a little because it reflects our habitual thinking that we are human and that we humans possess our souls. We do not *have* Light Beings. We *are* Light Beings.

As parts of Source, we have the innate strength and courage to rise above physical life. However, in my experience, this takes sustained concentration that often eludes me. I find it far easier to temporarily shift my perspective from that of the human I inhabit to that of the Light Being I know I am. As Light Beings, we know that our true life is eternal and that no matter what we might experience here on earth, we will survive to glory in reunion with our Creator. With that one shift in mental perspective, I can reassure myself: "I am safe, healthy, and happy in this moment and no one can take that away from me." Then I can access the spiritual powers I have been telling you about.

I returned to this physical life to bring hope to my fellow human experiencers. To tell anyone who will listen that we can consciously manifest better experiences for ourselves. We need not suffer because we have the power to change our beliefs and, therefore, our lives because we manifest our beliefs into physical reality. We can heal our physical and emotional wounds. We can access Source's knowledge to understand that we chose these lives with all the pains and worries for a reason. We Light Beings chose this and do not want to escape it, like the human does. We want to be here because unconditional love compels us to bear whatever is necessary to support our quest as Source to understand the scope and limits of our powers, and to be here for each other as we do it.

To access our spiritual power, we must believe it is there. We must hold tight to the conviction in our heart of hearts that we are integral parts of the almighty Source we worship, that we too have innate powers, and that human life's sorrows are temporary. For those of us who have not had NDEs, this is where faith comes in.

There are times when the human feels depression, sadness, mourning, abused, etc. Is there a way I as a human can tap in to the power of the Light Being inside me and use it to relieve me of my miserable feelings?

This question likewise falls back on the habit of assuming we are the human part of the body/soul combination. We are not humans. The personalities we identify as ourselves are those of the Light Beings inside the bodies—the personalities Source designed us to be. We Light Being souls are powerful, not our bodies. Despite the millions of books and articles admonishing us to tap in to our higher selves, our souls, or our spirits, humans cannot access Light Being powers.

But not to worry!

All that we souls have to do to consciously access our spiritual powers while inside a human is get the human mind out of the way. Meditation works to do this. Putting the human to sleep works. A technique called Focusing™, detailed in the book *Focusing* by Eugene Gendlin, PhD, works. Mindfulness works. Concentrating on the moment works. Keeping the human mind busy with repetitive tasks that require some concentration—like jogging, mowing the lawn, washing dishes, etc.—also works to quiet human thinking. Once that is accomplished, the Light Being soul can exercise its powers of unconditional love and self-healing to relieve the body's miserable feelings.

With my stressful situation ongoing, I've been trying to tell myself that everything's going to be okay, using positive imagery and statements to try to manifest the experience that I want. When I'm doing this for myself, I don't feel that successful. But

it came to me that if I, as a Light Being, would talk to my human host as a coach/mentor/parent/friend, it might work better. This actually seems to work better for me because I think I'm helping someone else. So instead of telling myself, "Everything's going to be okay and the situation will resolve itself to everybody's satisfaction," I'm wondering if it's accurate/correct/appropriate for me to tell my human host that I'm going to take care of it by making sure that my manifestations will result in experiences that will not be frightful and will result in peace of mind and joy?

I know exactly what this reader means about talking to our host body as though we are helping someone else. That's how I have to do it too. I wrote a *Backwards Glimpse* newsletter article that addresses this very concept, titled "Our First Loving Relationship." In it, I point out that a human's first loving relationship is not with his/her mother. It is with the Light Being soul inside. The article appears in response to a question in chapter 10 of this book.

Our Ultimate Awakening As Source

Near the end of my time in the afterlife, I processed through denser and denser layers of Source's Energy field, gaining as I went along deeper understanding of the Knowings I had already been given. In the past, I have called this process "merger" back into Source for lack of a better descriptive term. That's why many questions in this book use the term *merger*. I learned from my readers that the word merger creates the false impression that two separate beings are combining. This is not what I experienced and not what I intended to convey. What I experienced was one Light Being character within Source's mind awakening to the knowledge that it is Source itself. There is no word that adequately describes the process resulting in this *aha* moment.

Further complicating my search for the perfect word choice is the fact that while I was undergoing this phenomenon I still had the Light Being perspective, which includes ignorance of the fact that there is only Source and that Light Beings are not really beings. Thus, I still felt as though I were a separate being from Source and was *learning* its thoughts rather than remembering my own. My descriptions of the experience are true to the perspective I held at the time each event was happening. It was not until after the full awakening that I was able to look backwards and see the process in a different light. In this book, I will use the term "awakening as Source" rather than "merger" because, ultimately, it is a better description of what actually happens from Source's perspective.

The best human analogy of this awakening process I can think of is what happens to our dream characters when we wake up. While asleep, we are aware only of what is going on in each dream, which we witness from inside one dream character per dream. Usually that character is the same as our human identity, though we may have different personality and character traits in the dream than while awake. When we wake up from sleep, the dream characters we portrayed still exist but are no longer uppermost in our minds. More importantly, we realize we are far more than the dream character. We are the dreamer with a rich life outside dreams.

Once a Light Being merges into Source, does he stay there or come and go?

I learned from my Light Being friends in the afterlife that I had been integrated completely into Source before I volunteered to come to earth this time to be a messenger. So apparently we can come and go after awakening as Source.

If Light Beings are not sure what the implications of merging into Source are, why aren't they more apprehensive about going ahead with it?

I am uncertain why this reader thinks Light Beings are not sure of the implications of merger/awakening as Source. Perhaps he thinks of awakening as the loss of one's identity, which sounds like a bad thing to him. Or perhaps my reader thinks any change should be approached with apprehension.

It is part of human nature to resist change. We are not humans. We are Light Beings and we welcome change as a new adventure.

The way my Light Being friends presented merger/awakening to me when I was a Light Being was that I would be rejoining "the rest of us." The very idea filled me with joy and a sense of homecoming. I was thrilled. Even though I couldn't remember exactly what to expect, I knew it would be something wonderful. And it was.

Light Beings aren't apprehensive about awakening as Source because fear is a character trait of animals. We Light Beings no longer feel fear in the afterlife. There is nothing to fear about experiencing the maximum degree of enlightenment and understanding and awakening to the truth that we have never been anyone besides Source itself. Our identity expands at merger. Nothing is lost.

You gave the analogy in your book that souls are like drops of rain. Each drop is a thing unto itself until it hits the ocean, then it disappears (i.e., souls are drops of rain until merging into Source as the ocean). The drop becomes indistinguishable from the rest of the ocean. If this is true, then there is no way that a drop can ever become that same drop again and leave the ocean to assist other drops as they're dying! Would you agree?

I do not agree this analysis is correct and logical when applied to water. Evaporation of ocean water results in rain. Who's to say whether the exact drop that fell as rain once won't do it again through the evaporation cycle?

Nor does the logic hold when applied to Source. My understanding, from living it, is that Light Beings still in the afterlife are the ones who assist souls in crossing over, not Light Beings who have already awakened to the realization that they are Source. So there is no need for anyone reintegrated with Source to assume its former Light Being identity in order to assist the dying.

When we awaken as Source, the Light Being character we played when we thought we were a being separate from Source becomes fully aware of its identity as Source. But Source remembers each character and can call one up again to incarnate any time it wants. That's what happened to me. My Light Being friends told me I had been fully awakened as Source before this life as Nanci. Then, Source thought about aspects of its personality that could be messengers to earth at this particular time, and, my Light Being character came to mind. Once Source focused its thoughts on the character I used to play, I again became the character/Light Being I once was with all that character's memories intact.

The more important point to focus on here, however, is that only the belief that we are a Light Being character separate from Source disappears. Ultimately, we are not merely one character in Source's mind. We are Source itself. We awaken to the realization that we have always been Source and never a separate being or even an identifiable character. It is similar to waking from a human dream and realizing we are the dreamer and not just the dream character through whose eyes we watched the dream. By awakening as Source, we have not lost an imaginary character; we have regained our whole self as Source.

Now, if you had said, "Source is like a stew and we're all vegetables. When we join Source we help make up the stew. But, we can always step out and be just a carrot again if we need to," that would make a little more sense to me. Does it to you?

I love this analogy. In my experience, we can step out and be just a carrot again after awakening as Source. I did it (became Nanci, not a carrot).

The biggest difference between a stew and what I actually experienced with Source is that stew has different vegetables in it. Source has only Source Energy in it. We are not different from each other as vegetables are. And, though humans can eat stew and leave out the carrots, for example, Source cannot leave any part of itself out of itself. (Also, we Light Beings don't get mushy if cooked too long!)

Suppose a Light Being that is about to merge with Source decides it wants to stay permanently separate from Source because it prefers to carry on experiencing life as a separate and independent entity. Would Source be cool with this?

This isn't possible because Light Beings are not in fact separate entities from Source.

Human Perspective. We experience human life as separate beings from our parents, siblings, children, and all other earthly creatures. So it makes sense to believe we are separate from Source as well. Our religions also tell us we can suffer permanent separation from Source and we believe it and fear it. So, from the human perspective, it does seem possible to stay permanently separate from Source. In fact, that fear is the origin of the concept of hell.

Light Being Perspective. We Light Beings think of ourselves as individuals and experience the afterlife as discrete consciousnesses. Therefore we believe we are separate beings from Source. Our experiences have taught us that we can enter into physical matter over and over again and experience what it's like to be various things and creatures in the universe. We know we only put part of our Energy into physical matter, giving us the sensation that part of our consciousness is separate from us. From Light Being perspective, it seems possible to stay permanently separate from Source in much the same way as parts of our own consciousness temporarily seem separate from us while inside physical forms.

Source's Perspective. Source knows it has imagined a physical universe that it has populated with all kinds of creatures and things. Source knows that it interacts *with itself* through all of the physical universe creatures and things by putting small parts of its self-awareness into them. Source has intentionally given its physical creatures and things, and its Light Beings who believe they are living in the afterlife, amnesia about who and what they really are in order to make the experience feel absolutely real. Source knows that when they are ready, the Light Beings that inhabit physical things and creatures, and believe they are separate from Source, will awaken to the knowledge that they are actually Source and have never been separate beings. They will realize that they are literally Source pretending to be separate individuals by self-imposing amnesia as to its true identity. This awakening does not occur until the Light Being is ready for it.

Ultimately, from Source's perspective, it is impossible for one of its characters to permanently separate from Source. Source's thoughts cannot leave its mind any more than one of our dream characters can leave our mind and live on its own in the world.

You said that when we are finished evolving we merge or dissolve back into the Light forever and take all of our memories and

experiences with us. When we do this, are we still ourselves? Do our individual consciousnesses and personalities survive merging back into Source or do they no longer exist?

Human Perspective. We believe we are separate individuals/consciousnesses from our Creator. Our religions have taught us that when we die, we go to heaven and live blissfully forever and ever amen—as humans. We are given the impression that we remain humans in heaven and continue to live human-like lives—only happier. Therefore, we believe we would retain all of our memories and experiences in our own individual minds. Thus, from the human perspective, it would seem as if we would disappear as a human if we awakened as Source.

Light Being Perspective. We believe we are spiritual beings who live in the afterlife as discrete consciousnesses/personalities separate from Source. We know that the afterlife NDErs visit is not a forever and ever heaven, but rather more like a blissful temporary state of being between incarnations into physical matter. Once we complete the transition back into thinking and understanding as a Light Being, instead of a human, we retain and can remember every moment of every experience from every physical matter incarnation, as well as from life in the afterlife between physical lives. We retain these memories in our individual expanded consciousnesses/minds. Light Beings eventually realize intellectually that they will awaken to their true nature as Source, and that Source is a Collective Entity composed of many, many personalities/characters.

Source's Perspective. There is only one consciousness. Humans do not have individual consciousnesses. The only consciousness inhabiting a human is Source. Light Beings likewise do not have individual consciousnesses despite their belief that they do. This mistake arises from the fact that Light Beings do not fully awaken until they have completed all phases of the afterlife (described in my books). The only consciousness within a Light Being is that of Source. All of the characters, creatures, and beings in the physical universe and afterlife that believe they are separate consciousnesses believe that only because Source has cloaked their thoughts with amnesia. When we are ready, we will *awaken* to the knowledge that we are actually part of Source's consciousness and have never been separate individuals. We will *expand* our self-awareness to know that we are Source itself. Therefore, there was never an "us" to "still be us" after awakening as Source. There were never individual consciousnesses to survive awakening as Source. All of our memories and experiences are Source's memories and experiences.

The personalities we had as Light Beings will continue to live on in Source's imagination, along with all of the memories of what we thought were separate lives from Source. Nothing is ever lost. But we will no longer believe we exist as an unawakened, amnesiac, separate Light Being or soul.

You talk about "dissolving" back into Source. This sounds scary to me. Do you just revert back to formless Energy and all personality and self-awareness ceases to exist? In other words, are you erased?

No. I think my poor word choice (merger) unintentionally created this scare. I was describing the process from a human perspective when I chose the word "merger." As Source, we are formless Energy but our personalities and self-awareness is not erased or dissolved into nothingness. The only thing that literally dissolves when we awaken as Source is the belief that we were ever separate from Source. The illusion of individuality dissolves, not the personality, self-awareness, or experiences we have had.

I think the reason your assertion about merging into Source would bother people is because if we're all part of Source and not individuals as we think we are, then our loved ones who have passed away aren't really with us in spirit as we might have hoped. Correct?

Human Perspective. It is human perspective that creates the illusion of separation from our deceased loved ones. "Dead" means "gone" for humans. Being locked into this narrow perspective is what separates us from our deceased loved ones. Why would anyone think that our loved ones aren't part of Source just like the rest of us are?

Isn't being part of the same mind more like "with us in spirit" than anything else you can imagine as heaven?

Source's Perspective. The misconception that we are separate individuals is what makes us think we are apart from our deceased loved ones. From Source's perspective, our loved ones are always with us. Everyone is everywhere all the time—simply because we are all personalities of one entity. Our loved ones are a mere thought away. We are not separated from them as personalities, only from their former manifested flesh.

Psychics, mediums, and others who have experienced after-death communications have been able to do so because they can break out of that human mindset and accept that everyone is everywhere all the time within Source. All one has to do is tune in to those who have left human life in order to experience them here and now.

Do we continue to have a sense of self within Source? I assume that all our experiences and memories are absorbed by Source, otherwise all our field trips where we collect data for the Creator are a waste of our time and His as well. But do we get to remember and enjoy everything we have collected?

Yes, we remember and enjoy everything we have collected in physical life, both in the afterlife and after awakening as Source. But our sense of self expands exponentially. In my experience, I became aware that "*I am Source.*" My sense of self as a Light Being disappeared because it was replaced with the knowledge that I am Source, not a human and not a Light Being personality/character in Source's mind. As Source, we remember everything we have experienced down to each and every moment and every drop of sensory input from every part of our eternal lives. These memories contribute to Universal Knowledge.

6

Soulless Humans

TO MY GREAT SURPRISE, I RECEIVED A LOT OF COR-
respondence and YouTube comments about footnote 30 in my book
BACKWARDS. The note reads:

> One of the more startling revelations during my life as a
> Being of Light was that not all human beings are inhabited
> by Light Being souls. Some are simply not chosen. Others
> may have been abandoned as hosts once the souls inside
> completed their goals or missions. This "knowing" is consis-
> tent with the Universal Knowledge I received about humans
> constituting a separate race or species of beings from Light
> Beings, as non-scientists would use those words, capable of
> living without us inside.

Humans that are soulless for an entire lifetime are extremely rare.
But all human bodies are soulless for part of their sleep cycle while we
Light Being souls get out-of-body and manifest a different physical
environment to enjoy. These manifested snippets of life are part of
the phenomenon we call dreaming. Some humans are soulless temporarily due to an NDE, other out-of-body experience, or coma. A
Light Being soul can also leave the body briefly during times of high
stress, illness, or injury, such as when the body is in shock. Have you
ever had the sensation when looking deeply into a person's eyes that

the lights are on but nobody is home? The Light Being soul that inhabits that body may have stepped out for a bit.

What follows are answers to specific questions I have been asked about soulless humans. Everything else I remember from the afterlife about this topic is on my CD titled *Soulless Humans*.

What Is a Soulless Human?

How do you know some humans are without Light Beings?

While I was in the afterlife, I was given the impression twice that my human body could be resuscitated and go on living without me inside. The way this information was presented, it seemed at the time to be a fairly normal phenomenon.

I'm not sure my friends and family would have noticed a difference had my body revived after the NDE without me inside. (Ha, ha.) One of my YouTube viewers claims that everyone thinks lawyers are soulless anyway!

If a Light Being does not inhabit a human animal body, would the animal body still be alive?

Yes. Manifestations have the degree of life that Source gives them. But remember, the entire universe exists only as thought in Source's mind. There is no life outside Source. I answer the question whether the soul animates the body in chapter 3 of the *BACKWARDS Guidebook*.

You write that a human being can live without a soul. The very thought of that freaks me out a little. Should it?

Human Perspective. It would freak me out too had I not learned about soulless humans as I basked in the unconditional love and acceptance of the Light. While we are in human bodies, we come to believe we ourselves are human. That is perfectly logical, given the limitations of five physical senses and the false validation they give us about our nature. We are used to feeling human. It's all we remember. Yet, our religious and spiritual belief systems convince us that "we humans" have souls that live on eternally. So the idea that there are soulless humans out there feels a little like the myth that there are zombies out there. We fear something less than human is mingling among us disguised as one of us.

Source's Perspective. Soulless humans do not occur very often and they are nothing to fear. Source is the artist and Creator of our universe. Source's creations in the physical world are considered in the afterlife to be "manifestations." They are not real. They are like dreams, virtual reality, or literature. Humans are part of Source's creative environment; they are some of the manifested players. Every dream, virtual reality game, movie, and novel has "extras"—characters that do not play a major role in the plot. Think of a soulless human as an extra in the plot of Light Being incarnations.

How prevalent are soulless humans?

I was not given a number or percentage in the afterlife. My impression at the time this idea formed in my mind was that a soulless body is a routine, albeit rare, occurrence.

Which people are not chosen to have a soul?

I was not given this information in the afterlife. Each Light Being chooses whom to inhabit, or not, based on factors known only to itself.

Are there really only a few million humans who are actually inhabited by Light Beings, while the rest just act on instinct?

I never said that "only a few million humans" have Light Being souls. My sense from my NDE is that soulless humans are the rare exceptions.

As for humans acting on instinct, that happens regardless of whether a Light Being soul is inside. Most of us souls who haven't awakened to our true nature have no idea that we can influence or control the behavior of our bodies. How many times have you heard bad behavior justified by claiming, "That's just who I am … ?" Most of us allow our bodies to do whatever they want.

The idea of soulless humans is a total contradiction to your

statements that we are all Light Beings. This is also contradictory to all other texts I have read so far on this subject. I certainly hope that you are wrong, because otherwise some of us do not have much to look forward to in the life beyond. Can you explain?

I think this reader is in human perspective when he reads the pronoun "we" in my books. When I say *we*, I refer to the individual personalities that we have been taught to believe are human, but are actually parts of Source's self-awareness, the parts I call Light Beings. When I refer to the physical bodies we inhabit, I call them "humans" or "human animals." I seldom use the term *we* when referring to our hosts because I know we are not humans. I use the collective term of *we* because I am speaking to my fellow Light Being souls, not human bodies. With this in mind, I do not see how my statement that a few human animals are not inhabited by souls contradicts the statement I make *to Light Being souls* that *we* are all Light Beings.

Do souls only enter humans before birth?

Yes, but they do so at varying times before birth. There is no uniform moment when we can say that a fetus has a soul. I answer this question in detail in chapter 3 of the *BACKWARDS Guidebook*.

Do they only exit humans when humans die?

No. As mentioned above, all human bodies are soulless for brief periods of time.

Once our spirit is inside a human body, must it remain there until death of the body, or can it leave (for instance, during sleep) and another spirit will come in to occupy that same body? For example, if the first spirit just wanted to experience childhood in that body, could it be replaced by another spirit who wanted to experience adulthood in that body?

I learned nothing in the afterlife that would confirm the human theory of "walk in" souls. I do remember part of what I learned about dreams, which includes the Knowing that Light Being souls leave the body at times during sleep and continue manifesting human life in

ANSWERS FROM THE AFTERLIFE

what we call dreams. But nothing contained in that Knowing indicated that another Light Being could enter into the sleeping human while its resident soul was out.

If a Light Being really wanted to experience a particular human childhood, it could merge its Energy into the Light Being that had lived that human lifetime *while both are in the afterlife*, and it would experience the childhood vicariously. I describe how I did this while I was in the phase of life that follows what we call the afterlife. (See chapter 21, "Life as a Being Of Light," in *BACKWARDS*.) A Light Being does not need to enter a physical body in order to experience a particular life. So I see no reason to do it.

I would think that, literally, a person without a soul would be a person in a vegetative state, because to do or say anything at all, somebody has to be doing or saying it, and that somebody is what we call a soul. Isn't that right?

Human Perspective. We have been led by religions and some spiritual belief systems to believe that the soul animates the body. Science, of course, does not agree. Neither do I.

Light Being Perspective. What I experienced in the afterlife convinced me that the soul does not animate the body. The Light Being soul consists of Source Energy—that is, thought Energy. But manifestations like humans also consist of thought Energy. Manifestations are alive and can act independently from the soul inside them. The "somebody" doing or saying something through the body can be either the human animal or the soul inside.

Patients in persistent vegetative states may have been abandoned by their once resident souls. It simply makes no sense to a Light Being to continue to inhabit a host that has stopped having experiences. So we may choose to leave these hosts, who then live on without us. But my understanding is that the vegetative state comes *before* the soul leaves, not as a result of it.

If a human being doesn't have a soul, is she then, so to say, "disarmed" from having Light Being abilities such as consciously manifesting reality and unconditional love?

Yes. A human never has these abilities; only the Light Being soul does. And only the soul can utilize these spiritual abilities, not the human host.

Is it possible to love a human being who does not have a soul?

Of course. Soulless humans have personalities and traits we may admire and love.

Could I Be Soulless?

Could I myself be without a soul right now? Was I born without a soul? How would I know?

You would not be having thoughts about spirituality, life after death, and your relationship with Source if you were not a Light Being soul. You wouldn't be asking this question. Human animals have no interest in spiritual life. A soulless human would not believe there is an afterlife, much less worry about going there.

How can you tell when somebody is soulless?

Normally we can't tell when someone is soulless if they are well and awake. Sometimes we can feel that the soul has left a body just before the body dies. The body simply *feels* empty to us. The lights are on but nobody's home.

My *Soulless Humans* CD compares a long list of personality and character traits that are different for a human and for a Light Being. This is not a laundry list of how to identify a soulless human from behavior. Yet it does give somewhat of an indication of whether a category of behavior is controlled by the soul or the host body.

How can you tell if someone's soul has left the body while he/ she is still alive?

Usually the body is asleep, unconscious, in a coma, or very near death when the soul leaves the body. We Light Beings may also leave permanently when the body goes into a persistent vegetative state. Just because a body is in one of these mentioned states does not guarantee that he/she is soulless at the time. There is no way to tell from observing the body.

What Happens to Soulless Humans When They Die?

When the human finally dies, what happens to the human's consciousness after death? Does it disappear? Or does it take a different path than the Light Being soul takes when death occurs? Do humans, too, have a chance to ascend or evolve, or come back to work on their own evolution?

A human animal's "consciousness" disappears from the manifested world when it dies. But it forever remains part of Source, along with all of Source's thoughts that form Creation. Even science recognizes that Energy cannot be created or destroyed. It merely changes form. Source redirects Energy once used to manifest the consciousness of a particular human who dies into manifesting something else in the universe. The manifested human is gone forever. But because the entire universe exists solely within the mind of Source, there is no actual loss. What happens to humans at death is similar to what happens to your dream characters when you wake up. They vanish or fade away.

No, human animals do not have a chance to ascend or evolve or come back to life. They do not have an afterlife or "path [like] that the Light Being soul takes when death occurs." *We* souls inside humans do ascend, in that we recombine with the part of us still in the afterlife. We souls do evolve in the sense of changing over time. And we souls do have a path to the afterlife, which is automatic upon death of our host bodies.

Where does the personality of the soulless human go when the body dies?

It disappears from earth but remains part of Source's memory. Please don't worry about this. The person we hold dear as ourselves is the soul part, not the body part. We may love our host's physical attributes now, but we no longer care about them once we leave the body.

Do we have a chance of reconnecting with a "soulless" person again after the human dies?

The chance that we will ever meet a human who has *never* had a Light Being soul is less than our chances of winning the lottery. But if a human animal truly has never been invested with a Light Being soul, its personality and identity cease to exist upon its death, except for within Source's memory. We can manifest that human's physical appearance in the afterlife, if we so choose. I do not know whether the manifestation would have the same personality as the human animal that died.

Are Soulless Humans Responsible For Evil?

Do soulless humans commit all the bad or evil acts on Earth?

No. Wonderful and loving people—including you and me—engage in horrendous actions from time to time. Because Light Beings lack the human trait of judgment, when they inhabit humans they have no compunction about doing horrific things just for the experience of it. Extrapolating from that, I would say that not everyone who commits acts judged by human standards to be "bad" is soulless. It may be the Light Being soul driving the body to act "badly" out of pure curiosity. I explain this in chapter 11, "Who's In Charge?," in *BACKWARDS*.

I often find myself thinking: "What is wrong with these people? Why don't they want to help anybody? Why do they only think about making money?" Maybe now you've explained it— they are soulless humans. They're just animals, and you should probably try to deal with them the only way they'll respond, namely overpowering them into submission. What do you think?

The behavior you describe is human nature. The people you refer to do have souls; they just let human nature run their lives. They are not soulless, just *clueless* about who they really are, and do not know that they have the power to control their bodies' instinctive behavior. It's hard to get inside another person's thinking to understand why they do what they do. But to them their behavior makes sense. Labeling someone as soulless, and overpowering them into submission, just because one disapproves of his/her behavior would be a human act of judgment and violence, not the action of a Light Being.

7

Animals

HUMANS ARE ANIMALS. BIOLOGICALLY SPEAKING, THE human species is classified as one of many in the animal kingdom, chordate phylum, vertebrates subphylum, mammalian class, and primates order. Humans share many of their characteristics with other animals in their classification. Nevertheless, some of my readers get offended when I refer to humans as "animals," a name they reserve to all the species man considers inferior to humans. The questions that follow are from readers concerned about man's relationship to these other animals.

Do animals also have a Light Being and animal aspect?

Yes. Their bodies are manifestations, just as humans are. The very same Light Beings who put some of their Energy into humans as souls do the same thing with other animals, plants, and inanimate objects. We each probably inhabited one or more plants and animals before entering into our current human host. When all my eternal memories returned to me during my afterlife experience, I saw that I had lived several lifetimes as various types of earth animals. I recall being a fish coming up to the surface of a body of water and gulping air. In this memory I could see the sun glinting off the water, shooting rays of color like a prism, and the underside of a boat gliding over me. I remember thinking the view of the sun was spectacular and soothing.

In your books, you make it sound as though when the world was being created, souls resided in the rocks and plants, then animals, because Source was creating and wanting to experience all these new things. Did that end once humans arrived, or can we choose to reincarnate into an animal if we wish?

I didn't intend to make it sound as though Light Beings abandoned incarnation into other animals and things once we decided to inhabit human animals. We did not. We just added humans to the list of interesting creatures to inhabit. There is no limit to the creatures, vegetation, and inanimate objects into which we Light Beings can pour our Energy and perspective as soul in order to experience the physical world for Source. We choose whatever interests us at the time. And it's *us* inside the plant, animal, or object—the same *us* , the same eternal personality that would at another time inhabit a human. Many Light Beings new to Earth choose plants and smaller animals for incarnation to get used to the environment and scope out what Earth is all about. Later, they may or may not decide to inhabit humans.

What part do animals of lower intelligence play in soul evolution?

If you mean spiritual evolution, then none that I know of.

Human Perspective. Humans erroneously believe they can determine the intelligence level of other animals, including other humans, based upon their behavior.

Light Being Perspective. Animals, including humans, are manifested with innate cunning and instincts that may appear to be intelligence. But by far the greater intelligence in them is that of Light Being souls. The intelligence level of all animals with souls is therefore the same. We Light Being souls are just as intelligent when inhabiting a plant or pig as we are when inhabiting a human or more advanced species on another planet. However, we are limited in our self-expression, and how much intelligence we can display, by the physical attributes of the species or thing we inhabit. For example, the fact that a rock may be inhabited by a Light Being does not mean it can speak or create an opera. The rock's chemical composition limits the abilities the soul can demonstrate.

Knowings informed me that we Light Being souls do not evolve in the sense that science uses the term. We do not go from biologically simple to complex. We are already as complex as possible because we are literally parts of Source—which is our definition of supremacy. The evolving/changing we do is more on the order of rounding out our experiential understanding of the physical world. In that sense, interacting with animals is part of our learning experience.

I often see a much stronger sense of mindfulness in animals than in humans, the ability to be present and not worry about the past or future. Are animals more highly evolved than humans with our convoluted thoughts and emotions, goal setting, and lack of being grounded with the earth?

I learned in the afterlife that earth animals cannot be anything other than present in the moment. They are manifested to be that way. It is not a sign of advanced spiritual evolution. We Light Beings are the souls of all animals, including man, and one can't get more highly evolved than being part of Source. Mindfulness or lack thereof has nothing to do with it.

Should we really feel bad about stepping on an ant?

It's not for me to tell anyone how to feel. But we assume the risk of being stepped on when we incarnate into an ant.

I figure animals are also part of Source and therefore it matters how they are treated. Is that right?

Everything is part of Source. There is only Source. So, if one believes that Source should be treated a certain way, then everything must be treated that same way.

8

The Purpose of Life

ONE OF THE UNIQUE ASPECTS OF MY 1994 AFTERLIFE experience is that my thinking progressively transformed from the human level of understanding, to Light Being awareness, to Source's own perspective. My understanding of the purpose of life changed dramatically as I advanced through these stages of enlightenment.

Human Perspective. Many philosophers, religious leaders, and spiritual gurus theorize purposes of life based on a deeply held belief that humans are the epitome of Creation, the sole reason Source created the universe. Or they believe humans are the only creatures in the universe who go to heaven. Some belief systems claim we earn our way to heaven by our actions here on earth. Like many others, I believed all of these human-generated theories and explanations of why we are here before I learned the truth during my NDE.

Source's Perspective. Knowings I received from Source on the purpose of life greatly surprised me. I learned human theories have nothing to do with why Source created the physical universe. Because Source has no one with whom to interact, it created the universe to enable itself to interact *with itself* in the guise of amnesiac mental characters. *We* are Source's mental characters. To use a human analogy, the universe is a highly complex, long-lasting, interactive dreamscape, and we are Source's dream characters.

Light Being Perspective. I learned in the afterlife that we Light Beings generally set one of three goals for a particular human lifetime: (1) we are interested in a unique aspect of life or a specific human trait, our chosen "theme," and select a series of hosts whose lives will provide different vantage points on that theme; (2) we agree with one or more other Light Being friends to incarnate with them to perform a specific task at some point in our friend's lifetime; or (3) we agree with one or more other Light Beings to incarnate with them to provide loving support as they face the challenges of physical life. No matter which goal we select, there is always the overriding objective to strive to remain true to our own eternal nature and personality despite wearing an animal's body with its own traits and personality.

The most complicated and time consuming goal is number one. If we have chosen to study a theme, we will incarnate over and over again into different lives from which we can observe (a) how humans behave with respect to that theme, and/or (b) how well we remain true to our unconditionally loving innate nature through the decision points and challenges of human life. Our study of the theme we selected is complete when we have lived lives that allow us to witness and experience all conceivable viewpoints and perspectives on the theme. For example, a Light Being may select the theme of laziness. It will then enter into many humans sequentially in order to experience not only being lazy but also laziness's effect on all those around the lazy person. In one life, for example, the Light Being soul will live inside a lazy man in an environment where laziness is frowned upon. In another, it may inhabit a lazy woman who neglects her children. In a third, the Light Being will serve as soul for a lazy person in a culture where everyone is lazy. In a series of lives, the Light Being may experience laziness that leads to poverty, wealth, abandonment by family, support by family, illness, great health, fabulous inventions, leaving no mark at all on the world, etc. Interspersed among the lazy lifetimes, the Light Being may incarnate into a lazy person's mother, father, spouse, child, teacher, employer, spiritual advisor, physician, welfare case worker, or any other person who comes into contact with a lazy person. The goal of all these lifetimes is to know human laziness inside and out from all angles, in all possible scenarios.

Goal number two may require only a few minutes or hours of

human life to accomplish. Two Light Beings may agree to incarnate together with one pursuing a theme requiring multiple incarnations and the other agreeing to perform one task that furthers its friend's theme. An example would be a soul that comes into human life to perform a life-saving surgery on its friend so that the Light Being friend can experience what it is like to survive a deadly accident. The remainder of the lifetime, before and after performing the surgery, has no specific purpose.

Like goal number two, goal number three may not require an entire lifetime to accomplish. For example, a Light Being may agree to incarnate for the sole purpose of mentoring a younger person during a time of career crisis. The time before and after the mentoring phase occurs may have no purpose other than just for the soul to experience human life.

Thus, I learned that much of what happens to us in human life has no real purpose at all. Humans want to give it purpose in an effort to understand and control life, to justify suffering, and to try to earn a reward for surviving that suffering.

More Knowings on the purpose of life appear in chapter 4, "What Does God Expect of Me?" and chapter 5, "What Is The Purpose Of Life?" in *BACKWARDS*; and chapter 4, "What Is The Purpose of Life?" in the *BACKWARDS Guidebook*. I also have CDs and DVDs that go into more detail.

Why Did Source Create Us?

I am having a hard time thinking that there is this Source that sent us to Earth just so he could experience what we go through. It just doesn't make sense to me and has shaken my entire belief system. I feel a disconnect. Why did you tell us this?

I'm sorry I shook this reader's belief system, but my motives are pure. I gave up eternal bliss to return to human life for the sole purpose of sharing all that I learned in the afterlife. My intent is to inform, not persuade, and certainly not to make anyone feel disconnected. More important, what I have written would not shake my reader's belief system if it didn't ring true.

I know how others must feel hearing that Source sent us to Earth only for the experience. It was easier for me to accept this truth because I received it while experiencing the overwhelming love of Source up close and personal. During those moments I was awakening as Source, I felt that all the suffering I had endured during Nanci's life was totally worthwhile. I was deeply grateful to have been able to experience physical life for Source after I felt its gratitude, acceptance, and mind-blowing love. Once I knew beyond all doubt that I am Source pretending to be Nanci, I was humbled to my very core. How could I not be grateful that, as Source, I allowed myself the opportunity and tremendous gift of relishing the sensation that I am a separate person. I learned the importance of extremes in Source's emotional life. I understood that my Light Being self could not reach the heights of ecstasy associated with Source's blissful existence had I not known the painful contrast of my human host's fears and suffering. I could not truly appreciate the depth and breadth of unconditional love without the background of rejection and judgment of my human life. I could not glory in the freedom of spiritual existence, had I not dragged this warm, heavy, clay-like body around for decades.

I hope something in this response helps bring my readers acceptance of their role as Source's eyes and ears in the physical world. But this may be one of those spiritual mysteries that has to be experienced at Source's level to be understood.

When does Source receive the experiences we have had for it in physical life? When they happen? When we end a lifetime, or when we return to Source, so it gets them all at once?

I do not remember any Knowings on this topic. It felt to me like I "uploaded" (to the core of Source???) Nanci's memories and experiences during my life review. I know that my Light Being friends knew nothing about the life I had just departed before they watched it in my life review. From the Knowings I remember about Source and Light Beings, I would say that Source's core personality receives our memories during the life review. But, because we Light Being souls are parts of Source's self-awareness, the Collective Being Source experiences what we do in real time.

I cannot believe that Source/God would find the same human dramas, repeating over and over again (just change the names), as being interesting. What's the purpose of Source experiencing yet another murder, or yet another broken heart, or the same boring aspects of human life over and over again?

This reader's instincts are right on the money. Repetitive human behavior is no more interesting to Source than it is to humans. What interests Source is how its Light Beings' unique personalities influence how they *feel* about common human events, not the events themselves.

Though the events may be the same, humans'/souls' individual and combined personalities and history make how we are affected by events unique. It's thrilling to Source to watch each soul's distinctive journey. Even when two humans/souls participate in the same event, their thoughts, feelings, sensations, and impressions are slightly different. Think of how a grandparent with many children and grandchildren is still interested in each new baby learning to roll over, crawl, walk, and talk even though the grandparent has seen it all many times before. It's loving the person having the experience that makes it interesting—not necessarily the experience itself. Source's tremendous love makes the totality of our mundane lives unbelievably interesting to it.

Source does not specifically intend to experience another murder, or another broken heart, and isn't particularly interested in humans' boring behavior. In fact, Source does not literally intend to experience *any* specific human behavior. Source mentally created a multitude of different imaginary characters/personalities—us—in order to see what we Light Being characters would create within the physical matter environment. Source did this to see how we would interact with various types of physical matter when we pour some of our Source Energy into it. Source is interested in the creative process of its universe, not the daily actions of one type of creature on a tiny planet called Earth.

If the humans we inhabit engage in repetitive, destructive, or pointless behavior, it is because of their nature as animals. Most animal behavior is repetitive and boring. Humans are also violent by nature. They will use physical or emotional violence when they don't get their own way. Hence more murders and more broken hearts. We souls can choose to allow our host bodies to act like the animals they are. Or, we can choose to train and control them. When we don't exercise our power to redirect human behavior into more constructive channels, we get the repetitive, boring, and violent acts we see in the world. Source does not intervene to force humans to act certain ways, or to force Light Being souls to exercise control over their hosts, because that would defeat the creative process Source designed into the universe.

Are We Here to Learn?

Aren't we here in this earth realm to learn lessons and be a teacher also?

In *BACKWARDS* I referred to "lessons" a Light Being "learns" through incarnation. I had no idea when I used those words that my readers would think I am endorsing a prevalent spiritual belief. Apparently many people believe the purpose of life is to learn lessons about how to be more spiritual or how to earn a place in heaven. They believe these goals can be met by modifying human behavior. For example, they theorize that we are supposed to learn how to stop fighting with our boss or spouse, how to "turn the other cheek" when someone hurts us, how to share, or how to show kindness and love to others whether they deserve it or not. These are not the types of lessons I meant.

We Light Beings have nothing intellectual to learn from human life because we innately have access to all of Source's knowledge, which I call Universal Knowledge. Our goal is to learn what being in various situations foreign to Light Being life *feels* like. We are here to face primitive human behavior, thoughts, and emotions. The lessons we wish to learn are more like those of an anthropologist: we study human behavior to contribute to Universal Knowledge about it. Learning how to better get along with each other in human life does not improve our afterlife.

There are, of course, those among us who have come here with the goal of helping other Light Being souls to remember who they really are. You could call these people teachers or missionaries. But most Light Beings are not here to teach anything.

Aren't we supposed to be learning how to love one another while we are here?

No. We Light Being souls instinctively love unconditionally because we are parts of Source's self-awareness, and Source is unconditionally loving by nature. Our only purpose for being here is to experience a different set of character traits, those of humans and other creatures and things. We exist in order for Source to explore its own senses, creativity, imagination, ability to manifest, and self-awareness.

I received comments like this question from readers who misinterpret the following sentence in *BACKWARDS*: "The purpose of life here is so much simpler than you might imagine: to learn how to love unconditionally despite the difficulty of the circumstances."[5] I see now that this sentence can be interpreted to mean we are here to *learn* unconditional love *from humans*. That is not what I meant, and I apologize for not being clearer. I stated this Knowing more clearly in *BACKWARDS Guidebook* when I wrote: "Part of our mission on earth is to demonstrate unconditional love while in human form, even in the most difficult of circumstances."[6]

I should have written that we souls are here to learn incrementally how to overcome human trauma and hardship enough to *express* our innate unconditional love through our hosts' behavior. We do not learn how to love from humans, or how to love other humans. Rather, we souls strive to learn how to express our unconditionally loving nature despite the challenges contrary animal drives and instincts impose. An example of what I mean is the trauma victim who loses both legs, and, instead of turning bitter like a human would, he expresses gratitude and love to his caregivers, family, and friends for their support. In this instance, the Light Being soul inside the injured man is taking control of his life and learning how to show its innate unconditional love despite the difficulty of being handicapped.

It sounds to me like love is a human attribute. Why aren't we here to learn love?

Love is not a human attribute. Our societies lump many human drives, instincts, traits, and emotions under the rubric of "love," including possessiveness, protectiveness, sexual attraction, lust, gratitude, and maternal and paternal instincts. Some loving behavior, of course, is generated by these human instincts and emotions.

But I learned in the afterlife that humans are just animals and do not have the ability to love unconditionally as we Light Beings do. All those unconditionally loving feelings we ascribe to humans are actually *our* feelings—the feelings of us souls inside. Most of the loving behaviors we think we see in humans and pets are acts they have learned in order to obtain the food, water, or play time they want. The only aspects of love we can learn from humans is *conditional* love—how to withhold love to punish someone who displeases us and how to condition showing love on someone else's compliance with our wishes. Using love to manipulate someone else is a human trait.

But what else other than love is there to learn? If there is anything to evolve to or learn it must be love or understanding. Right?

I know many religions and philosophies teach that we are here to learn unconditional love, to experience unconditional love, or to express Source's unconditional love within the physical world. Based upon my awakening within Source, these assumptions are not accurate.

Our Creator loves unconditionally by nature. It knew all about what love feels like before creating the universe. The whole point of creating physical matter is for Source to experience everything it can imagine that is *different* from unconditional love and its other innate traits. Source does not enter humans as Light Being souls to learn, teach, feel, or relate to unconditional love. We Light Beings do not need to learn an inherent trait we enjoy as parts of Source. We live unconditional love fully, in every way imaginable, outside these bodies. Learning love for a Light Being would be like learning to breathe for a human. It's automatic! We enter into humans in order to experience their very different lives, character traits, and emotions. Humans do not love unconditionally. We are interested in how human *conditional* love feels, and the conflict between unconditional love and human love that makes us feel we have an angel on one shoulder and a devil on the other.

As I was whirling in a cyclone-like motion back into my body after my NDE, my Light Being friends kept chanting: "Love is what truly matters. Love is all that matters." I tried desperately to ignore them so I could memorize what I had learned in the afterlife. At the same time, I felt very strongly that I was assigned two new missions on earth: (1) to tell anyone who would listen what I learned in the afterlife, and (2) to experience unconditional love in Nanci's life. For years, I thought goal number two meant I was supposed to *find* unconditional love in a human relationship. Finally, another NDEr suggested to me that it meant I was supposed to *give* unconditional love. (That's why I sign e-mails "UL," for unconditional love.) That comment triggered memory of a Knowing about another Light Being goal in physical life. I recalled that after many incarnations, we begin to remember a little of our true nature and are able to act more like ourselves through the bodies we inhabit. Our greatest challenge becomes how to feel and show our unconditionally loving nature while still inside a body driven by animal instincts and self-centeredness. We souls strive to meet this challenge every day because we want to, not because some God somewhere else expects us to do it. Remember, *we are Source.*

Through incarnation, Source and its Light Being characters are learning what it's like *not* to be Source, to experience emotions foreign to Source—hate, revenge, fear, possessiveness, judgment, boredom, pain, suffering, etc.—and to experience all possible situations and behaviors from all conceivable perspectives. All this leads to complete understanding in the form of Knowings. Life is a creative, imaginative process. It's about living vicariously through physical matter and witnessing how the contradictory character traits of the soul and body play out.

Are We Here to Evolve?

If the world of Light Beings is all unconditional love and knowledge, what is the rationale for them to inhabit human bodies in order to evolve?

This question lays bare the illogic of the belief that the purpose of human life is to evolve us souls to higher levels.

Light Beings do not inhabit humans in order to evolve spiritually. Light Beings do not need to evolve because we are Source. We define Source as the highest level possible. What higher status could we possibly attain? Human life offers nothing other than learning what human life is like. Basically, humans give us Light Beings the opportunity to try to be true to ourselves despite living life on a primitive scale, in a wild environment, among vicious animals. It's a challenge and Source loves a challenge.

But you say in your first book that the Light Being is learning and evolving. So there must be a purpose or a road that we all travel. I mean, evolving from what into what?

I believe this comment stems from the following sentence on page 64 of *BACKWARDS*: "My beyond death experience reminded me that we choose to come to planet Earth, to inhabit human beings, partly to assist in evolving them as well as our own soul Energies to higher levels of awareness." I did not mean to imply that human life evolves souls to higher *spiritual* levels. While inside humans, we souls evolve/grow in our awareness of the contrasts between human character traits and our own, and between human lives and our eternal lives.

Humans think life has to have a goal they can understand and accept. In other words, there has to be something in it for them as humans. But for Source, physical life *is* the goal—to experience emotions, sensations, and situations unavailable to a purely non-physical Energy entity.

Source is constantly evolving in the sense that its Universal Knowledge base changes as it acquires more information about its imagined universe. Universal Knowledge expands with everything that happens in the physical world. We Light Being characters within Source are evolving into more experienced personalities, not into something different from our innate nature as parts of Source.

Life is the road we all travel.

I have read that we evolve ever higher in frequency in human life by how much we learn to love. For instance, that frequency determines how much heaven you can experience or want to experience. What do you think?

My understanding and experience is that human life is on a level of extremely low Energy, frequency, or vibration, if you want to use those terms. Experiences here do not increase our soul Energy, frequency, or vibration. In fact, it takes a significant transformation process in the afterlife to raise the Energy level of the part of us that has been a soul back to a point where it can recombine with the part of us that remains in the afterlife.

The idea that we have to earn "how much heaven" we can experience is entirely human in origin. We all return to precisely the same spiritual state and afterlife. Like life in general, what we experience in the afterlife will be different for each of us based upon our individual eternal personalities, not based on what we did or didn't do in human life.

Let's say we come into this world to learn to stop dysfunction and abusive behavior against ourselves. Is that correct?

That idea is not consistent with the Knowings I received in the Light. It's more of a human perspective. Let's say, for example, that the human theme a Light Being decides to experience is abuse. That Light Being will incarnate over and over again into various bodies to experience abuse from all angles, in all scenarios. My understanding does not comport with the idea that this soul is supposed to teach its host not to be abusive or to learn how to stop allowing others to abuse its host. Its purpose is merely to experience abuse from all angles. If, in the process, the soul can bring more unconditional love into the equation, and train its host body to stop the abuse, that's laudable, but not necessary. Humans will always be violent and abusive by nature.

The human host, on the other hand, would definitely have an incentive to learn how to avoid abuse because it is painful and goes against the survival instinct. So the manifested human's goal might be to learn to stop dysfunction and abusive behavior in itself and others. Light Being souls can definitely help with that by taking control of behavior when the human's emotions would otherwise lead to abuse.

Are We Given Any Guidance to Meet Our Goals?

Doesn't our higher self know all about our purposes for each lifetime and guide us?

I don't know what is meant by the term "higher self." As you know, there are no universally known and accepted terms for spiritual concepts, so we have to define our own terms for clarity. In my terms, I would say the part of our Light Being Energy that remains in the Light, while the other part enters a body as its soul, does know what its purpose is and does try to guide its incarnated part. That's why I encourage every soul to try to contact its own Light Being Energy still in the Light to get that guidance.

I believe that what we are doing here is part of the plan that we made at the Light level, but we "forgot" it. This includes our contract and the many other contracts that we make with other beings on this earthly plane throughout time. Formalized religion has sometimes called this the Divine Plan. But it is more than that and, besides, we are divine, if you will. Do you agree?

I do. One of the points I am trying to make with my messages is that God/Source is not "out there" somewhere. We are parts of the collective entity Source. Our life plan is an inside job—not an outside job. Moreover, the core personality Source does not have a Divine Plan which circumscribes our lives. We Light Being parts of Source manifest our own lives, individually and collectively, as we go along. It is a creative process, not a life plan set in advance.

Is there any way of knowing or finding out which mission we chose in the afterlife to follow or complete in this life? Are there any failsafe indications?

We will remember the theme or other goal we chose for earth life when we return to the afterlife. I don't know of any failsafe way to find out while still in the body. Knowing our goals might interfere with the genuineness and spontaneity of the human experience.

Most of us souls have no "mission," only self-selected goals. Generally, if a soul has a mission, it will know what it is. Some NDErs remember being assigned a mission during their NDE. Other souls remember they have a mission and its nature despite the usual amnesia.

If we're supposed to have amnesia about past lives and who we really are, why did you come back to share the information? If we're really not supposed to remember, so that we can have authentic human experiences, isn't it better that we don't know the truth about our situation?

There is a lot of logic to this question. I have nevertheless felt compelled to share what I learned in the afterlife despite the logic. I returned to human life for the sole purpose of sharing Universal Knowledge and awakening unaware souls. I truly believe knowing Universal Knowledge can help alleviate suffering related to not knowing the reason for, and meaning of life, and what happens after death of our bodies. I am one of millions of messengers Source has given us over the ages to help us remember eternal truths. I understood at the time I adopted this mission that some Light Being souls would awaken upon hearing my messages, and others wouldn't. If my own life is any indication, despite awakening to our true nature, the amnesia of incarnation is so strong that even when we know the truth we are still often lulled into believing we are human.

How do I find out what my intention was for this life, whether I should be a doctor or a full-time scientist?

As I understand our purpose for coming into human life, it doesn't include choosing a career. We most likely did not come into human life with an intention to do a particular job. We Light Beings have no interest in social or economic standing in human society unless they pertain to the theme we are studying. Our purpose is to experience a certain human emotion, point of view, physical handicap, character trait, etc.—theme of human life—rather than experience anything as specific or human-interest oriented as a job. A particular job or profession may provide more or fewer opportunities for us to experience the aspect of human nature we came here to experience, or create the opportunity for us to perform the task or provide the support we promised, but that is it's only relevance to our purpose for being here.

9

Humans

I RECEIVED A WEALTH OF KNOWINGS ABOUT HUMANS while in the early stage of my afterlife. I believe the purpose was to impress upon me the fact that humans are domesticated animals and not the incredibly complex, intelligent, sophisticated beings they think they are. The Knowings showed me how much my body's animal traits had warped my personality, how the drive for success had damaged my ability to love. More Knowings highlighted the vast disparity between human and spiritual life.

One simple difference is time. While we inhabit humans we garner a lifetime of memories of people, places, and things we experienced, one after another. We cherish, or regret, our past. We anticipate, or worry about, our future. The march of Father Time feels natural to us. But linear time exists only during human life, not eternal life. There is no past or future in the afterlife.

Source designed animals to live according to repetitive patterns, such as the birth and death cycle, day and night, and the cycles of seasons and weather. Early humans noted the cyclical nature of life and marked the events of their lives according to those patterns. For example, an early human might say he hadn't spied a hawk for three moons, or it took him two sleeps to find elk to hunt. Naturally occurring phenomena provided universally understood measures of time. Since those early efforts, mankind has refined how it measures and marks time. We now have seconds, minutes, hours, days, and so on to fill. Time measurements became as arbitrary as those for feet, inches, meters, etc., once they were removed from the patterns of natural phenomena. Yet this is how humans now measure their lives.

Once we leave these bodies and resume life as non-physical beings, we no longer experience cyclical patterns of physical phenomena. Nor do we need artificial measurements of linear time. We always experience "right now," that is, the present moment.

I have stated in various workshops that for us Light Beings, spending a lifetime in a human body, no matter how many years long it is, corresponds to about one second. This is because linear time does not exist in the afterlife. One reader asked: "Do you literally mean that a human lifetime passes by that quickly to a Light Being, or are you saying that a lifetime just seems that short because we are immortal?" The most direct answer is, "Neither."

A human lifetime does not speed up for a Light Being soul in the sense of a linear progression of lifetime events taking only one second. Rather, the events, emotions, experiences, sensory data, and corresponding ripples through the universe of a human life can all be experienced simultaneously in our spiritual state. We don't compare the length of a human lifetime with eternity and judge it to be about a second long in context. Each life we live gets stored in its entirety within our memories as part of who we are, to be accessed at will. We do not measure who we are as parts of Source by any time parameters.

Because once we leave these bodies we no longer feel the weight of eighty years of living, we Light Beings have no qualms at all about incarnating just to perform one task for, or be there to support, another Light Being soul.

Wasn't one of the Knowings you gained during your astonishing NDE the surprising notion that we are composed of two beings while living on earth—a human animal and the soul—both of them having their own personalities?

To be clear, we (you and I) are not composed of two beings while living on earth. We are only one of those identities—the Light Being soul. For millennia we have identified ourselves as the wrong personalities because amnesia compelled us to think we are human. We are not *part* of the human. Nor is it part of us. We souls are Source's awareness inhabiting human bodies. It only seems we are human because we are not awake/enlightened enough to remember the truth. Eventually, over a series of incarnations, we remember a little more each time about who we really are, and we can use that knowledge to lead less animalistic lives.

Are there humans who go through life living nothing more than an animal life?

Yes. Many, many people live entire lives on earth as though they were merely human animals. They spend all of their time eating, drinking, sleeping, recreating, and procreating, with no thought of anything more in their lives. In addition, we all live this way from time to time. That is, after all, why we chose to enter into these animals.

Why Humans Are Different From One Another

You say there is only one mind and one consciousness in the universe, but what about the consciousness of each one of us?

Human Perspective. We have been absolutely convinced all our lives that human beings are the epitome of Creation and the afterlife revolves around what humans do or don't do. Logically, then, humans must have consciousness that survives death and goes to heaven.

Source's Perspective. Human beliefs are logical conclusions for a species Source designed to be self-centered, self-absorbed, and arrogant by nature. But they are wrong. There is only one consciousness and it belongs to Source. What we mistakenly believe to be our own individual consciousness is Source's. We just don't remember that fact because, as Source, we have chosen to have amnesia about our true nature while we explore the universe. Humans do have animal consciousness sufficient for them to survive, but it is not the same level of consciousness that I call Source's self-awareness.

Human consciousness is more like what most of our dream

characters have. Dream character consciousness is projected by the dreamer. But the dreamer does not experience the dream from inside all of the characters—only one. We live in dreams the same way we do in waking life—by experiencing everything from the visual perspective of looking out from inside one body. Our self-awareness is centered inside our human and dream character bodies. The other dream characters are more like interactive props because our self-awareness does not jump from inside one character to inside another as they interact. We watch the other dream characters as a third party. Source manifests humans to have animal consciousness similar to the dream characters we do not inhabit. It is not until Source actually enters into a manifestation, like a human, through the process of a Light Being soul incarnating into that human, that Source has the sensation of being inside the human looking out at the world.

Why are there so many different levels of consciousness in humans?

Human animals, which are manifestations, do not have different levels of consciousness. Any one of them can at times have diminished biological consciousness due to sleep, anesthesia, dementia, or drug use. Otherwise, all human animals have the same level of consciousness that Source manifested in them.

I think what this reader has noticed is that humans display behaviors that reflect different levels of self-awareness and awareness of others, and different degrees of control by the Light Being souls within them.

If human animals are all on the same level, as I understand you to say, and all souls are on the same Source level, why are there so many different types of people on earth? Some of them are very ignorant and do malicious things to other people and animals, nature, etc. Others are empathetic, wise, humble, and so on.

Judging solely from their behavior, humans *appear* to have wildly different character traits and personalities. This is not actually the case. Human animals are manifested to have identical character traits but some degree of personality differences. Each Light Being soul inside a human, however, is designed by Source to be unique. The wide range of behavior we observe in humans results from two different personalities and levels of consciousness inhabiting the same body—the human identity and the soul identity. The combination of human/soul personalities, the struggle and interplay between the two identities, and the conflict over which personality is going to dominate at any given time, creates the diversity of behaviors. I discuss this at length in the chapters titled "Who's In Charge?" in *BACKWARDS* and *BACKWARDS Guidebook* and identify which personality is responsible for various types of behaviors.

Why do humans have different physical characteristics?

Physical characteristics like muscle strength and beauty are determined by genetics. Source designed the biological systems that resulted in the evolution of the human species and allows that system to produce an infinite variety of combinations of physical traits.

Why are some people intelligent, some normal, and others below normal in intelligence?

These judgments are based on observable behavior and have no foundation in fact. Knowings I received indicated that all humans are manifested with the same innate animal intelligence that includes cunning, strategy, manipulation, and self-preservation. Many are also eminently trainable, through education, to use and expand upon bodies of knowledge accumulated by humans but provided by Light Being souls.

True intelligence exists only in Source. The genius, creativity, and intellect—giftedness—we think is human is actually that of the soul residing within. This intelligence cannot be tested and measured. Nor would it make sense to do so inasmuch as all Light Beings have equal intelligence as Source. How much of the soul's intelligence shines through human behavior depends upon its goals for this lifetime, biological factors, and its level of awareness of its true nature. For example, if the soul's theme of study is what it is like to be brain-damaged from playing football, little of its Source intelligence may be displayed in post-football life. The truly frightening aspect of intelligence is that, because we believe we are humans and want to further human goals, we allow the combined body/soul being to use Light Being intelligence in harmful ways.

Why are some people happy and others miserable?

Happiness is not a human attribute any more than it is an attribute of a dog, cat, or horse. Happiness depends upon the ever-changing interplay of human experiences and emotions with our eternal experiences and emotions. The more we allow our true spiritual nature to be expressed in human life the happier we will be.

Why are only some people allowed to be wealthy?

Source does not control the distribution of money on earth. Source does not consider wealth important in the least, other than as one of many potential human lifestyles to experience. We souls do not necessarily experience every type of human lifestyle, such as a life of wealth or poverty, if it adds nothing to our perspective on the theme we have chosen to observe. Our spiritual motivations are not affected by what humans consider to be desirable.

Innate Human Traits

Victims

I learned in the afterlife that humans passively believe that life happens *to* them. Generally, they feel unable to control their lives, and therefore see themselves as victims of circumstance. Often they blame Source for allowing evil into their lives. These feelings are natural; they are part of human nature. There is nothing wrong with perceiving oneself as a victim of bad luck and others' wrongful conduct, or even blaming Source for our miseries as though we ourselves didn't script every moment of our own lives. We enter into human bodies in order to experience human life, including its sense of victimization. However, if we are unhappy with being a victim, we might want to reconsider believing that we are nothing more than the body we inhabit. That belief cuts us off from the spiritual abilities that allow us to consciously manifest a happier life.

We can become enlightened and change our beliefs about life. Some of us may think we cannot change our beliefs, telling ourselves, "that's just who I am." Well, didn't we once believe in Santa Claus, the Easter Bunny, and the Tooth Fairy? Didn't we once believe that being an adult would be fun? That hard work would always be rewarded? That life is fair? Do we still hold these beliefs, or did we change them over time?

We can learn and believe that we are actually powerful spiritual personalities—Source's beloved mental characters—merely inhabiting a human body. We can accept that as part of Source we have the ability to manifest what our hosts experience as physical reality. We can awaken to the realization that we chose this life for its challenges. Light Beings with a lot of incarnation experience craft the most difficult lives because they seek greater and more demanding challenges. We chose these lives while we were in our full-power state in the afterlife, knowing that human life isn't real. We choose the lives we have because we *want* to see how we will react to pain, hardship, the death of loved ones, and tragedies of all types. We *want* to see whether we are able to bring more spiritual powers to bear this time than we did last life. Participating in human life for a Source mental character is like *Call of Duty: Black Ops II* for a human gamer. But, for us, playing the game is the goal, not individual events, the score, or winning or losing. Testing our mettle. Facing all comers. Looking fear, disease, poverty, loss, and death squarely in the face and being able to say to ourselves: "I did it. I lived it." During my life review, my Light Being friends were proud of me simply for choosing to become human. Just for taking on the challenge! They considered me a great success, even though I felt as though I had failed in many respects.

We get to control how our life progresses by choosing our beliefs about who we are. A victor in the rough-and-tumble and always challenging game of human life? Or a victim of bad luck and worse people? Victory is for those willing to believe they are winners just for taking the exciting risk of entering human life with the trials it brings. Victors accept the life they have chosen, yet may try to improve it through the use of conscious manifesting. Victimhood is the animal default attitude. Either choice is fine. Source doesn't care whether its characters overcome hurdles in a way humans would deem to be successful, or whether they merely experience facing the hurdles. What matters to us Light Beings is what we wanted to experience when we chose to incarnate.

Violent

Humans are animals and all animals are violent when threatened. It is a natural part of the survival instinct.

Human history is at a turning point. We can either decide to consciously swing the pendulum back toward responsibility, love, and peaceful coexistence, or let the human species self-destruct. In the afterlife, I saw that 2013 and the years shortly thereafter are part of the major transition into the Third (and final) Earth Epoch. I saw that during the transition period, each soul is given the choice to either stay on earth to effect change or return to heaven to assist in the transition from a more powerful platform. For example, I believe that the Sandy Hook shooting victims, as a group, agreed in the afterlife to come into human life at this time in order to go through that horrific experience together and burn into our consciousness that violence cannot be tolerated if the human species is to survive. They were sending humans a message that change is needed.

If we don't want our children to be violent, we adults must be nonviolent. If we want our children to be safe, we adults must make the world a safe place for them. We cannot teach children that violence is a solution for problems if we want them to be safe. We cannot show children that adults settle their differences through murder—in wars, law enforcement actions, the criminal justice system, and gangs—and then expect children not to emulate us. Children don't do as we say, they do as we do. If we want the violence to stop, adults have to start sending a crystal clear message through both words and deeds that murder is not an acceptable solution for any type of problem. The people who want to arm schoolteachers could not be saying any louder or clearer that the American way of life is to kill the other guy before he kills you. If this is not the message you want to send, take a stand now. Decide that in your own life, you are going to be peaceful. Peaceful in word. Peaceful in deed. Keep constantly in the forefront of your mind that you are part of Source, the Almighty, the All-powerful, the All-loving. Know deep in your heart that, though you currently inhabit a human body, you are actually a powerful spiritual entity, not an animal. We do not have to act like wild animals. We can take control over the bodies we inhabit and stop them from acting out innate violent tendencies. If we each take responsibility for controlling our own behavior, violence will stop.

Self-serving

How many times have you told your dog or cat "No!" without effect? Animals refuse to accept *no* as an answer because their driving motivation is self-satisfaction. Only behavior modification training will stop an animal from doing something unacceptable. The same is true for human animals, as every parent knows after going through the stage of saying no twenty, thirty, or fifty times to a young child who is begging for a toy. A human who has been trained to take others' needs and feelings into consideration will accept *no* as the end of the issue. An untrained human will not.

Some hear "no" as a challenge. They'll spend time and energy trying to figure out a way to turn prohibition into acquiescence in order to get their own way. Some try a more direct approach to get what they want. They try to manipulate others emotionally into giving in to their wishes, or they argue with authority figures in an attempt to prove their reasons for saying no are faulty. Forceful methods of manipulation, which I define as anything hurtful, include threats, intimidation, and physical or verbal abuse.

When the direct approach fails, some people will resort to indirect, sneaky ways of getting what they want, going around the person who says no. For example, an adult might go over the head of a supervisor who won't give in and appeal to someone higher up in the company hierarchy. Or a child may ask the other parent for permission to do something already denied by the first parent.

We, of course, are not humans. As Light Beings, we have the power to train our hosts to act from *our* true character rather than their own. We Light Beings respect one another. We love one another unconditionally. It would never occur to us in our spiritual state to try to bulldoze over someone who has denied us something. We can use our spiritual character traits to train our bodies.

Human Morals

Do humans possess any moral judgment?

Humans have plenty of judgment, which is an innate trait related to the survival instinct. They judge everything as either good or bad according to instinct and their cultural or personal beliefs at the moment. But as a species, humans do not have an innate sense of justice and fairness. Those traits come from us souls inside.

According to the Knowings I received in the afterlife, humans do not possess morals—an innate willingness to abide by a code of right and wrong—any more than horses or dogs possess morals. Humans are animals driven by emotions, cunning, and instinct. They have to be domesticated—trained—to fit within society. Remember, human babies have to be potty trained or they will relieve themselves like dogs. They have to be trained to wear clothes, use utensils to eat, sleep in a bed, and communicate with recognizable sounds. Humans have to be trained, using reward and punishment, not to hit others when they feel like it; not to engage in sexual acts in public; and not to lie, cheat, or steal. Humans are similarly trained to abide by cultural rules and religious belief systems.

What we call human "morals" is actually a hodgepodge of cultural traditions and superstitions. A combination of innate human character traits and domestication produces various community codes of *mores*—a word defined as the customs or conventions regarded as essential to or characteristic of a community. Humans adopt codes of conduct that reflect their core traits of competitiveness, possessiveness, superstition, and survival instinct. For example, the idea that one Hebrew god is more powerful than others in the pantheon reflects the animal kingdom concept of hierarchy based on strength.

(Light Being souls have no concept of competition or hierarchy.) The belief that gods demand worship is human superstition based on fear of punishment. (Light Beings know that Source has no use for worship.) The prohibition against murder, and the directive to honor one's father and mother, arise from the survival of the species instinct. (Light Beings are not concerned with survival as they are eternal.) The Christian Commandments against adultery, stealing, and coveting one's neighbor's goods and servants reflect innate human possessiveness. (Light Beings share.) Adherence to rules like these does, however, promote civilized conduct among what might otherwise be wild animals.

How does morality fit into our roles as Light Beings in our host humans?

Morality is something needed for human animals to get along, like law and order. Humans are innately violent and self-serving. So moral codes are needed to try to reduce the impact of those traits. We souls often need to take control over our host bodies in order to decrease the damage caused by humans running amuck without moral codes.

According to the Knowings I received in the afterlife, religions erroneously tell us that we have to follow a moral code to earn our way into heaven. This is not true at all. Morality is a tool for human life and has nothing to do with spiritual life.

What motivation is there to suppress our animal instincts and be nice?

From the perspective of the human animals we inhabit, there is none. Animals act instinctively, without regard for others' feelings and in complete ignorance of the consequences of their actions. For an animal to be "nice," it must be trained. You train a pet not to use your home's floors as a bathroom, or to chew household furnishings, or to wake you up at night to go out. You train your pet to respond to your commands. Reward or punishment is used to "motivate" the animal to adapt to the training.

Human animals must be trained the same way. Parents potty

train their children and teach them to share, play nice, and eat with spoons and forks. Parents train their offspring to behave in society, telling them not to throw temper tantrums, hit brothers and sisters, or demand to be the constant center of attention. These lessons are necessary because a human child is like a wild animal. Reward and punishment must be used to train children because they are not naturally motivated to be nice.

Unlike other animals, humans have the capacity to learn the cause and effect relationship between actions and consequences of their behavior. They can choose to be nice, in accordance with their training, to avoid unwanted consequences. Thus "good" human behavior is often motivated by the desire to obtain reward or avoid bad results, rather than an intrinsic desire to be nice.

Fortunately, we are not humans. We Beings of Light are innately nice because of our origin within and connection to Source. When we inhabit humans as souls we have a choice. We may sit back and allow our hosts to live purely animal lives, without interference or guidance from us. Or we can take control and train our hosts to act primarily as we wish, to live a life more congruent with our spiritual values. Knowings that I received during my NDE informed me that we can access our innate spiritual character and powers even while fully enmeshed in the physical world. This would allow us to "be nice" to one another despite the human emotions roiling just below the surface. Most of us Light Being souls follow a middle course. We alternate between allowing our host bodies to dictate our behavior and taking care (we call it exercising self-control) not to allow raw emotion to motivate our actions.

Can We Overcome Human Nature?

Nanci, if the host animal is so (1) adaptable to pain, suffering, disability, and failure etc.; (2) afraid of change; and (3) lazy, where does the courage come from to rise above it all?

Humans are marvelous creatures, but they do not rise above their animal instincts unless trained to do so. Human adaptability allows the military, firefighters, medics, police officers, and others to be trained to put the welfare of fellow humans above their own. Parents and schools train children to rise above human self-centeredness and share with others, show consideration, and endure life's inevitable hardships without lashing out. Schools and religions train us to delay gratification in favor of greater rewards later. Many belief systems instill a sense of service to others, and encourage us not to dwell in the all too human perspective of what is wrong with our lives. As adults, we sometimes forget these valuable lessons and thus fail to apply them. We might need a friend or loved one to remind us to shift our focus off ourselves and on to something greater, like a Supreme Being, loved ones, or service to the community, in order to rise above human nature.

According to the Knowings gained in your NDE, fear belongs to the human animal. You also found that we could utilize abilities natural to us in our spiritual state. Does this mean that we can transcend fear and the struggle for survival here on Earth?

Yes ... at times. But it would not be in the best interest of the human host to completely transcend fear, because fear is part of the human's survival tool kit. We are responsible for preserving the life of our human hosts while we inhabit them. Fear is a natural warning alarm that we must learn to heed when appropriate and necessary. It is healthier that we learn to transcend unnecessary or hyperactive fear, such as fears that do not really relate to life or death—for example, fear of missing a work deadline, fear of not being popular, fear of standing up for our rights, etc. For more information about fear, you can listen by telephone to the recording of my workshop, "How to Conquer Fear," which is available via www.BackwardsBooks.com.

Human Death

What happens to humans when they die?

The body decays and returns to its chemical components. The human life and personality end.

Is there a part of humans that survives death just like in the

case of beings who are inhabited by a soul?

No. I learned in the afterlife that no part of a human animal itself survives death of the body. However, all thoughts, including manifestations, exist eternally within Source's mind. Although humans die in the physical world, their existence continues as thoughts in Source's memory.

Is there a human mind, as Michael Newton [*Journey of Souls* and *Destiny of Souls*] describes, and what happens to that mind when the body dies?

"Mind" is another word that means different things to different people. As I recall, Dr. Newton equates the human mind with ego. It would take me an entire manuscript to dissect Dr. Newton's theories and describe how they relate to or contradict the Knowings I received in the afterlife. My overall opinion is that Dr. Newton used traditional human perspective to *interpret* everything he heard during regression hypnosis. I found little support for his interpretations in the Knowings I received in the afterlife.

There is a human mind, in the sense of animal intellect, and it dies with the body. However, every single thought, belief, opinion, event, and piece of bodily sensory input is recorded in soul memory for all eternity. So whatever one may believe exists in the human mind is not lost. Only the physical brain decays.

I still lack clarity on the transition of mind. My take on the reports from near-death experiencers is that the human mind expands upon death of the physical body. Is this true?

I can see how NDErs would interpret their experiences this way, using human perspective. I shared this mind-blowing sensation during the early phase of my NDE. Having transitioned far beyond this stage though, I believe a more accurate characterization would be to say that the soul part of our Energy *recovers* from the limited thinking we experience while in the body. We Light Beings have always had expansive thinking abilities. They are merely tamped down in the part of us that incarnates.

Does, or can, God (Source) intervene in earthly lives (manifested, real, projections or whatever) or is he too engrossed in the theater of it all to edit his own play in favor of some actor or action that might be beseeching him to intervene?

All "lives" are Source's. All humans are manifestations within Source's mind. You could say that Source is constantly manifesting human lives, and therefore, constantly editing them. When people ask for an intervention, they are essentially asking themselves to rewrite the scripts of the human lives they are experiencing.

Mental Illness

What is the place and relevance of psychology as it is currently conceived?

The Knowings I received early in my NDE on the topic of mental illness indicated that science and medicine completely misunderstand mental illness. The gist of the Knowings was that most of what doctors call mental illness is actually an expression of spiritual abilities that the person has been given no understanding of or guidance in how to use.

I got my degree in psychology in 1974, and the NDE in which I received Knowings about mental illness took place in 1994. So, I'm definitely not current on psychology's present parameters. But in the afterlife I was given to believe that, as of 1994, much of the treatment prescribed by psychiatrists and other therapists was damaging because it failed to take into consideration that there are two personalities in the body, only one of which has much capacity to change— the soul. Humans can be trained, so behavior modification therapies are excellent for solving behavioral problems. But humans are not capable of changing their nature, or of making major changes to their Source-designed personalities. The Knowings I received led me to conclude that there is a tremendous need/opportunity for therapists with knowledge about NDEs. I would like to see that knowledge, along with Energy therapies, integrated into psychotherapy.

Do you think it is possible that some forms of what we call

"mental illness" could be disharmonies between souls and host bodies?

We souls all have disharmonies with our bodies, but we are not all diagnosed as mentally ill. I retain only partial memory of the Knowings I received about mental illness. But from what I recall, I would say that the diagnosis of mental illness reflects a disharmony between scientific principles and Universal Knowledge.

Can you tell me more about what we have backwards regarding individuals with mental illness? I know from other books that these individuals are regarded as higher spiritual beings. Is there anything we can do to help them here on earth?

From my afterlife understanding, people diagnosed with mental illness are not "higher spiritual beings." But they are exhibiting more innate spiritual abilities than most human animals. From my perspective, there is no need for us to help them overcome their so-called illness. Perhaps they can help us. What we need to do is stop judging them and holding them to the infinitely lower standard of "normal" human animal behavior. In addition, we can make their lives easier by accommodating their behaviors within a safe environment.

I learned early in the afterlife that multiple personality disorder is actually just the normal functioning of the Light Being serving as soul. We are able in our natural state to experience at will any of our physical "lifetimes." We can also merge into other Light Beings and experience their physical lifetimes. It's just a matter of shifting focus. Souls who can achieve this while encased in a human body are exhibiting more spiritual ability, not less human ability. Source has zillions of personalities within it. So it's spiritually normal for one of Source's Light Beings to experience having more than one personality.

People we call savants are able to utilize more of their innate spiritual abilities than what is customary in a human body. I watched a woman on *Good Morning America* who is revered for her ability to remember everything she has experienced since high school. Her story inspired the TV show *Unforgettable*. Well, total recall is one of every Light Being's natural spiritual abilities. The woman on TV is unusual only because she is able to access this ability while in a human body.

10

Mating and Love

HUMAN LOVE, MATING, AND MARRIAGE ARE PHYSICAL world pleasures not replicated in the spiritual world. They are most often based on animal appetites and needs. But we can infuse our pair-bonding on earth with elements of our spiritual nature to enhance our happiness.

Our first human experience with love—our first opportunity to form a loving relationship with another—begins in the womb. No, not the mother-child relationship. The very first human relationship we form is with our host body.

The baby we inhabit is not us. It is an animal conceived of human parents via the miracle of fertilization and cell division. A baby is no more than that. The person you know as yourself, the personality you hold dear, is the spiritual entity that incarnates into the human. Body and soul are fused together to form one visible creature, but two identities are definitely present. And because there are two personalities, the basis for a loving relationship exists.

The foundation for this loving relationship begins before the human is conceived. While still in the spiritual state, we choose our parents as we preview the general parameters of the lives of the offspring they will produce. We seek specific physical or emotional traits, or cultural or environmental exposures, in our host to fulfill a quest for the experiences we need to round out our understanding of our chosen theme. In effect, we preview our chosen future human's life. That preview sparks empathy for our host as we witness his/her potential joys, trials, and tribulations ahead. And thus the seed of a bond of love is planted.

You *chose* this particular body to inhabit because of who he or she is and the experiences he/she will have during this lifetime. You *chose* this human while you were full of unconditional love for his/her strengths *and* weaknesses. You *chose* him/her knowing in advance generally how this life would unfold. How much more love can anyone show for a human? This is a higher love than even mother-child love, because you actually knew before the body's birth just how it would hurt and disappoint you, and chose it anyway.

My mother described less than beautiful people as having "a face only a mother could love." My understanding of that phrase is that mothers see beauty in their children that others do not. In a way, that same concept of a mother's love applies to how we Light Beings view human life. Where humans see ugliness, pain, and suffering, we Light Beings see beauty, courage, and strength despite adversity. It's all in the viewpoint we choose.

From the human perspective, our bodies have never known life without us inside. We are so completely fused with our hosts that their entire development has been influenced and shaped with our input. Our humans cannot help but love us, what they consider to be their souls, for we seem as much part of the body as its organs and limbs.

The wonderful and precious by-product of this duality of body and soul is that we can never truly be alone on this earth. There are always two in our life. There is always someone else intimately interested in everything that happens in our life. There is always someone who understands and shares our life, our joys and sorrows, our highs and lows. We have right within our physical grasp a human who loves us unconditionally. A person who will never leave us no matter what we do—until death do us part. Our hosts similarly have someone who sees all, knows all, and loves them anyway—us, the Light Being souls inside. All we have to do is put our arms around ourselves to know both body and soul's warmth and love.

If ever you feel like no one understands you, remember your duality. Remind yourself that you are really an immortal, unconditionally loving Light Being residing within an incredibly generous and accommodating body. You and your host are capable of understanding each other in a way no one else can—for you have shared all of your thoughts and deeds. If ever you feel unloved, remember the other with whom you intimately share your current existence. Allow the most intimate partnership you will ever have comfort you. Love yourself and your body.

Selecting A Mate

How do we find love on Earth?

I did not learn anything in the afterlife that would help our human hosts find love on earth.

But I did learn that we souls do not *find* love, we share it. Love is an innate character trait we have as parts of Source. All we have to do is open ourselves up to sharing it with others to find out what love is all about.

Human mating and marriage require a lot more than love. Both require trust, emotional intimacy, commitment, and honesty. Marriage, and often mating, requires an entire lifestyle change. Marriage carries legal obligations and rights unavailable in other relationships in our society. Therefore we logically should not use love as our only guideline for finding or choosing a mate.

Don't we each have a soulmate on Earth?

So many of us feel a part of us is missing that we have created the myth of soulmate to explain the loss. We believe someone is out there for us, someone with whom Source intends us to have a mating relationship, and that finding that person will fill the hole in our hearts, supply that missing part. I discovered in the afterlife that the sense of something missing is real, although the idea that it is a human soulmate is a myth. What we actually miss is the rest of our consciousness, personality, memories, awareness, and everything else we hold dear about ourselves. Only part of our Source Energy is invested into the human body during incarnation. The rest stays in the afterlife. And we miss feeling whole. I know this because I lived through it. As my life review was unfolding, I regained the rest of me, the part that remained in the Light during my incarnation as Nanci. Memories of my eternal life and all my physical incarnations returned. For the first time, I felt whole. That sense that part of me was missing disappeared.

There is no one person out there somewhere designated by Source, the universe, or destiny to be the perfect human mate for us. Animals, including humans, mate on the basis of instinct. Mating decisions are based on looks, pheromones, lifestyle choices, and the drive to meet both known and unrecognized psychological needs. Humans are initially attracted to each other mostly because of visual input and chemical reaction, not because they recognize potential soulmates on a spiritual level. There is no soulmate that is a perfect match for each one of us—with a few exceptions.

The exceptions are that some Light Beings agree in the afterlife, before incarnation, that they will find each other and become mates or form some other relationship, such as business partners, friends, neighbors, etc. These spiritual agreements do support the notion of a soulmate. But the relationships are formed to further spiritual purposes, not human ones. This situation is not typical and certainly isn't true for every one of us.

What more often happens is that we recognize someone we love in the afterlife when we encounter that Light Being incarnated in the physical world. The recognition is entirely spiritual, for we do not have human appearances in the afterlife. The recognition may take the form of an instant connection on a number of levels, or a feeling that the two of you just "click." This happened to me when I first met my friend Sydney. As soon as I saw her, I said: "I know you." She assured me we had never met, but we did form an instant friendship. Over the years, I was privileged to take Syd to various chemotherapy and radiation therapy treatments and to support her during her ordeal with metastatic breast cancer. I was with her when she left her body and entered the Light. I had just left the nursing home minutes before Syd's former body passed away. A couple of years later, I was also diagnosed with stage three metastatic breast cancer. I instantly realized that Syd and I had met when we did so that I could witness her courage—an example of strength and acceptance I would need to get me through my own battle. Although Syd could not support me with her physical presence, I often felt her love from the afterlife during my treatments. Sometimes I could hear her whispering in my ear. Several times I felt her presence in the radiation treatment room when I was most scared. I told my therapists that someone was in the room with me, touching my arm or leg. They assured me each time that it was impossible. Eventually, I proved Syd's presence when the therapists entered the hermetically sealed, lead-lined room after treatment one day and saw that someone had pulled my robe off me. There is no way I could have done it myself as my arms were strapped down in stirrups.

The only way to find a soulmate, if you have one, is by accident. You must let go and just allow yourself to follow your Light Being instincts rather than human ones. There is nothing you can do to force or speed up discovering a soulmate, such as joining eHarmony.com or dating a million people. If you have an agreement with a soulmate to meet in human life, it will happen automatically.

We are often told: "There's more than one fish in the sea," or "If you can't be with the one you love, love the one you're with." If we don't have a soulmate, does it matter with whom we mate?

Sayings like these convey the message that all men and all women are interchangeable as mates. It implies people are fungible goods, meaning all are alike, so it does not matter which one you pick. This backwards mindset not only dehumanizes us but also robs us of our uniqueness as souls.

Each of us is sublimely unique in our thoughts, experiences, feelings, and memories. This is the whole point of Source granting us the gift of the illusion of individuality. We travel different roads, or if the road is the same, our experiences on it diverge. Our emotions whisk us away on a one of a kind journey of self-discovery and interactions. Multitudes of physical lifetimes during our eternal sojourns craft us into precious jewels. No two of us are the same—not even identical twins.

Those who parrot the age-old adage that suggests one mating partner can be substituted for another are looking only skin deep. They use only the shallowest standards to select mates, for any attempt to see beyond the obvious in a person requires too much effort. Dedication of time and interest is necessary to get to know another as the irreplaceable soul that he or she is, and to truly relate on an intimate interpersonal level. Emotional and physical effort is needed to rise above fear and chance feeling loved. Too often we look only to physical characteristics or financial status when making our mating choices. For example, some men attempt to replace a divorced wife or ex-girlfriend with a younger version with similar looks, as though women are cars. Some women replace a divorced husband or ex-boyfriend with any man who makes enough money, as though men are like jobs selected only for the salary. Treating one another this way constitutes acting out the basest of human animal instincts. We might as well sniff each other's hind ends to decide! Connecting solely on the physical level is the norm only in the animal kingdom, among creatures deemed to be below us in evolution.

It is time to remember that we are each minute reflections of our Creator and that Source intended each of us to be valued for our distinctiveness. To truly connect with each other on a spiritual level, and find the type of mate we seek, we must look deeper than physical attributes.

Unconditional Love Does Not Mean Being a Doormat

Every once in a while someone claims online that I am not a spiritual person, or that my NDE is not credible, because I assert my legal rights to copyright protection when necessary. These critics seem to think that a true NDEr is always sweetness and light, and never stands up to someone who attacks him or her. That view is not the understanding I gained of unconditional love in the afterlife.

Unconditional love applies to a person—not a behavior. We can love a person unconditionally and still hate some of his or her behaviors. The key is that we do not come to *hate the person* because of the behaviors. We do not judge the person unworthy of our love because of their hateful acts. That is the type of unconditional love I learned about in the afterlife. Unconditional love is love that does not judge a person unacceptable and unlovable because that person makes mistakes, even egregious ones.

We innately possess and show unconditional love while we are in the afterlife. But we souls are presently living human lives, not spiritual ones. We are capable of feeling emotionally hurt while in these bodies. As guardians of our bodies, we have the responsibility to protect them from harm, just as we do our children and pets. That responsibility gives us the right to stand up for ourselves and our bodies and to refuse to endure the hurtful actions of others. Loving someone and accepting him/her unconditionally does not mean we have to suffer abuse at his or her hands.

So many times we say to ourselves, "He/she didn't mean it." Or, "I'm used to it. It doesn't bother me." Or we make some other excuse for someone treating us badly. We have been brainwashed into believing that we have to stay in an abusive marriage, job, friendship, family, or any other type of relationship if we love the abuser. We have been taught to understand and accept their bad behaviors and inure ourselves as best we can to their harmful effects. We believe this because our religions and cultures teach us to "turn the other cheek." That is a human concept of love based on dominance and submission—not a description of unconditional love.

Unconditional love allows us to love the perpetrator but escape his or her hurtful behaviors. We can leave the abusive marriage, job, friendship, etc. We can stand up for ourselves within those relationships and say: "I love you, but I will not allow you to treat me that way anymore." Then, if the abuser is unwilling to change, we find a way to avoid the behavior, up to and including leaving. Perhaps Al-Anon says it best: that we should practice "detachment with love." We can detach ourselves from being in the line of fire of abuse and love the abuser from a safe physical or emotional distance away.

Why do you say in your workshops that humans are not capable of unconditional love?

Let me make clear at the outset that humans are capable of love—what animals call love. But *unconditional* love comes from the Light Being inhabiting the human. Human love comes nowhere close in comparison.

I learned in the afterlife that their nature leads humans to seek out and/or construct an environmental and behavioral "comfort zone," a set of known values wherein there are no surprises and therefore no unexpected threats to survival. The comfort zone of early man might have been a particular cave, well-known hunting and feeding grounds, a safe water source, and predictable weather conditions. Once Source, in the form of Light Being souls, began infusing its awareness into early humans, the comfort zone concept began to increase to epic proportions reflecting the new intelligence, curiosity, and creativity.

Soul infusions brought new and complex emotions to an animal previously known only to express fear, anger, protection of self and kin, and sexual appetite. Humans for the first time experienced joy, as shown in the impulse to create beauty in drawings, artifacts, and music. They felt love over and above the animal version inherent in mating and family bonding. The Light Being souls' level of awareness brought a wide range of new emotional experiences connecting actions with feelings. In other words, human/soul beings began to *care*.

Once humans cared what happened to them emotionally, an entire universe of potential threats descended upon them. Caring how one feels about an event has the potential to turn every action, reaction, interaction, and happenstance into emotional pain. The comfort zone concept works well to protect humans from death and serious injury. But when humans began to perceive emotional threats, they reasoned that the same comfort zone concept should work well internally. Humans became emotionally guarded as a species.

Emotional guarding entered mating relationships. It infiltrated parent-child bonds. The more frightened a human became, the more the need for a comfort zone grew. The souls' gift of unconditional love and acceptance was strangled by animal self-protection.

Generations of humans applying the comfort zone concept to relationships has resulted in a subconscious drive to make our loved ones the same as we are. Sameness carries no threat. The human logic is: If my spouse and children are the same as I am, and I know what *I* would do, then I will know in advance the potential threats they may pose to my emotional well-being and can successfully guard against hurt. I will be protected from any undesirable emotions and, therefore, will be content. Woe to the spouse or child who refuses to be the same, for the frightened spouse/parent will exert every available influence to restrict them to sameness. Human need for control joined forces with comfort zone needs and created the human desire to control everyone in the comfort zone. That is why humans cannot feel unconditional love without us souls inside them.

Does unconditional love exclude any form of discipline?

No. Feeling unconditional love for someone does not mean you have to accept bad behavior. All it means is that you love them despite the bad behavior. Discipline is necessary in human life for society to function smoothly. Our job as parents is to train our young ones to fit into human society, which will necessitate behavior modification training. Our job as souls is to try to help children learn about themselves as spiritual beings. That may involve a parent assuring a child that his or her love is constant and is based upon knowledge that the child is part of Source, and that the child's behavior will not destroy parental love. At the same time, however, the parent may have to teach children that discipline does not indicate a loss of love, only that the parent will not accept certain of the child's behavior choices.

Sexuality

Are homosexuality and gender confusion sins?

Human Perspective. Federal courts have recently reached contradictory decisions about the validity of statutes permitting same-sex marriages. Very few religions condone these marriages. Some political groups claim marriage can only be entered into by one man and one woman. This human bickering does not reflect Source's attitude at all.

Light Being Perspective. I learned in the afterlife that humans have erroneously allowed discovery of the X and Y chromosomes to convince them that human gender consists of two narrow polar opposites: XX (female) and XY (male). Knowings I received during my NDE explained to me that human gender is more like a spectrum, with nearly unlimited points between XX and XY.

I learned that the X and Y chromosomes are not the only DNA components that determine gender in humans. Many more chromosomes influence not only physical sexual characteristics but also attractions and behaviors. No one is *purely* male or female. Every human body exists somewhere on the gender spectrum.

Knowings also taught me that sexuality generally arises solely from biology. The human race, like several other species, is destined by biology to have a certain percentage of homosexuals in it. There is nothing an individual can do about it. It is pure biology. More important, instances of homosexuality is Source's own design because Source designed biology.

I also learned that sexual preference can be influenced by partial memories of previous human lifetimes. These memories usually take the form of a vague impression rather than specific events or facts. For example, a man may be attracted to other men because he has a vague impression from former human lives as a female that his sexual preference is male. The same phenomenon explains gender misidentification and the desire to have surgery to change genders. These behaviors arise from memories of the soul inside the human body. They are spiritual in origin—not the influence of the Devil.

Source's Perspective. I was convinced in the afterlife that Source forms no judgment whatsoever about the sexual or mating behavior of manifested creatures, including humans. Animal behaviors create a wide range of experiences for Source, which is the goal of manifesting an entire physical universe to explore. So, from Source's perspective, same-sex marriages are a matter of manmade laws and carry no spiritual implications.

Does sex impede our spiritual progress, offend God, or condemn us to hell?

Fear-based religions have created the concept of sex being bad.

Sex is a normal bodily function. We inhabit human animals to live as they do. Humans have sex. It's biology 101. What can make sex less than beautiful is the same with all other conduct—showing a lack of respect for the other person, violence, subjugation, and other hurtful behaviors.

There are no sexual "sins" against Source. So long as our host's sexual behavior is not destroying another person's serenity, there's no problem from Source's perspective. Here is an example of sexual conduct offending others: On a trolley car in San Francisco, I witnessed a young woman with her head in her boyfriend's lap, performing oral sex. Everyone around them just pretended not to see. I felt this was a sin against everyone else on the trolley. I found it offensive that this couple would perform a private sex act in public, with others watching. This, of course, is human judgment. Source would not be offended.

There is no hell, so there is no way our hosts' sexual conduct could condemn us to hell. Sex is one of the reasons we choose to incarnate. It does not exist without physical bodies. So there is no sex in the afterlife.

P.S. An NDEr I once met related his NDE account this way: During his NDE he met Jesus. Jesus asked him whether he was ready to come home to eternal bliss. He asked Jesus: "Do I get to keep my [genitals]?" When Jesus said no, the NDEr decided to return to his body.

11

Evil

BY FAR, THE QUESION I RECEIVE MOST OFTEN IS: "HOW can Source allow evil to exist in the world?" To understand Source's perspective on human life, as it was presented to me in my NDE, we must first understand the nature of so-called evil and why it exists.

What is evil?

I learned in the afterlife that evil is not a force in the universe. Nor is it the influence of a mythical Satan. Evil is a human concept, encompassing just about everything in the world humans don't like. Declaring something "evil" is a judgment call. It means the person or group labeling the thing *evil* has determined emotionally or intellectually that the thing is physically or morally harmful. Determining what is morally corrupt can be done only within the confines of a specific person's or group's principles, based on religious or spiritual beliefs and life values accumulated through experience and indoctrination. Holding the opinion that something is evil is a uniquely human experience, for being judgmental is an innate human trait. Humans are extremely judgmental, and often inconsistently so. Individuals and groups assign the designation *evil* on a relatively random basis.

Humans judge only their own animal behaviors to be evil. They do not condemn animal behavior in other species. No one calls a tiger mauling its prey *evil*. Nor do we think our pets are evil when they chew up our furniture or kill rats in the garage. Violent and predatory behavior is expected of lower-status animals. But humans do not consider themselves to be animals, or accept their evil behavior as the animal behavior it is, despite biology's classification of humans as mammals.

Humans collectively hold different attitudes about violence and killing committed in different contexts. Many readers complain to me about Source allowing Hitler to kill an entire race of humans. Many condemn killing innocent children and abortion. Yet humans lobby for legislation that allows state governments to put the perpetrators of certain crimes to death. Some people find it permissible to torture prisoners of war in the interest of national security. Politicians congratulate themselves on their patriotism when they send young soldiers off to war to kill and be killed. And, frequently, humans see no contradiction between these two sets of values. The concept of evil is a floating one, riding the tide of human rationalizations and fears.

In sum, "evil" exists in the world only because humans have indiscriminately labeled some events and behaviors with that word. When humans change their opinion about a behavior, it ceases to be evil. We have seen that happen throughout history, including the rise and fall of Prohibition, the proliferation or closing of gambling casinos, the use or censorship of profanity on television and nudity in movies, and recent legislation on medical marijuana. Evil is truly in the eye of the beholder of the moment.

When we are in the afterlife, we are no longer judgmental. We do not label actions or events as good or bad. We are able to objectively recognize that humans are inherently violent and self-serving. So we accept human suffering as a fact of life, in much the same way that humans observe wild animals and acknowledge that violence and the suffering it brings is the law of the jungle.

If Source is only pure Light and love, then its thoughts can only be pure and loving. Then how can this world consist of any evil whatsoever?

This question does not reflect an accurate representation of

Source's nature. Source's zillions of unique personality divisions fill Source with every imaginable experience. Therefore, Source knows what humans call evil by and through those of its parts living within the earth manifestation. "Darkness" exists in Source by virtue of the fact that much of the universe has such dim illumination that it appears black to human eyes. Remember, the entire universe exists solely within Source's mind. Source does not judge its thoughts of the universe, or any of its other thoughts. It does not label some thoughts "pure and loving" and others "evil." All thoughts are equally interesting and valuable to our Source.

Who is responsible for evil in our world?

The truth is: humans are responsible for the evil acts in the world. Not Source. Not Satan or demons. Humans are violent animals. They use physical and emotional violence to protect themselves from real and imagined threats to their ability to get what they want, to amass wealth in its many forms, and to exercise dominion over others. Aside from natural disasters, humans are responsible for the horrors we see in daily life. Humans wage war, engage in gang violence, rob homes and businesses, sell and use mind-altering drugs, abuse children, rape, and murder. And humans alone are responsible for these actions.

No one actually thinks of himself/herself as evil while committing deplorable acts. The person always has a rationale that he/she feels justifies the violence, even killing. That reason may be, "she deserved it," or, "I had no other choice" than to place my own desires and interests above the safety of another, or nothing more than, "he was in the way of me getting what I want." A small percentage of humans are so emotionally damaged that psychologists classify them as either psychopaths or extreme narcissistic personalities who are completely unable to empathize with another person. These humans may not even comprehend that other people have value, or that they are anything more than objects to manipulate.

When our religions talk about God allowing bad things to happen to good people for various reasons, it reflects the belief that Source controls every action taken on earth. Or, they think Source should choose to stop events humans consider evil. Alternatively, religions ascribe horrible events to the influence of Satan or other demons. Both beliefs have the common core of deflecting blame away from the humans whose actions directly or indirectly caused the harm. Why is this? I learned in the afterlife that humans, like other animals, have the built-in character trait of refusing to take responsibility for the consequences of their own actions. That trait is then reflected in human-created belief systems. Source or the Devil is blamed for what humans do because humans cannot accept the reality that they are responsible for their own evil acts.

We souls living within these bodies are also responsible in part for what happens to humans. Most of us do not accept responsibility for our manifestations because we are unaware we even have this ability. We allow our hosts to act in hurtful and violent ways because we do not realize we can prevent it. Worse yet, we have become so acclimated to human nature through reincarnation that we allow our hosts to use our innate creativity and intelligence to conjure up new forms of violence.

But Source did not leave us without a means to stop evil. All of the evil acts in the world would stop today if we would collectively use a tool that is available to each and every one of us—our ability to control our own human body's actions. We see this power in action every time someone exercises self-control. We Light Beings inside humans are unconditionally loving, rather than violent, and we naturally take responsibility for our own actions. Each of us can choose moment to moment whether to allow our host body to act out in typical selfish human fashion, or opt to do what is best for all of us collectively. Each of us can decide whether to act out human knee-jerk reactions to people and events, or to train our bodies to withhold reaction until we have time to think through a better course of action. Each of us can allow human emotions to run our life, or we can strive for a more peaceful way of living. As Light Beings inhabiting humans, we have the innate power to control our bodies' actions.

We can tame our animal hosts only when we come to believe that we are separate intellects from them. We can retrain our bodies to act more benevolently only if we become aware of our own true nature as parts of Source, and then choose to act from our spiritual nature. We can change the reality we create once we choose to manifest consciously from unconditional love rather than unconsciously following human nature.

The next time you are tempted to blame Source or the Devil for the evil in the world, ask yourself whether you consistently exercise appropriate control over your body's actions, and whether your actions have caused intended or unintended harm to yourself or another that someone might consider to be evil.

If Source finds all kinds of human experiences interesting, does this include rape, murder, child abuse, etc?

Yes, to a certain extent. The experiences I had while I was in the afterlife showed me very graphically how a change in perspective totally alters how we feel about something in life. Right now, we are absolutely, positively convinced we are human beings and that this life is real. When we get to the afterlife, we will be absolutely, positively convinced that human life is *not* real. We will be amazed that we ever thought otherwise. This happened to me.

While we are souls inhabiting human bodies we most often see ourselves as victims. We may see violence against our own species as inhumane and intolerable and judge it to be unacceptable in God's eyes. This is a purely human perspective, which we erroneously assume Source shares.

Now, try to adopt a mosquito's view of life. As a mosquito, you have an insect's view of life. You may see using bug sprays and chemical fogging against mosquitoes as violent and intolerable and judge those acts to be unacceptable in God's eyes. This is purely insect perspective, which, as an insect, you have projected onto Source.

Going back to the human perspective for a moment, we know that mosquitoes carry diseases and toxins that raise red welts on our skin when they bite us. We judge it permissible to kill mosquitoes in order to protect humans. They are only insects, after all, and their deaths are not as important as human deaths. Humans assume Source shares this perspective. Do you see how changing perspective from human to mosquito, and back again, shows that your opinion about killing changes depending upon whether it is your own species being killed? And do you see how each species assumes that Source must feel the same way that it does about life? Each species has created Source in its own image.

Source, however, takes the Creator's view of life—not the human's or the mosquito's. Source knows that humans and mosquitoes alike are manifestations of its own creativity and imagination. They are not real. All human and mosquito lives exist solely as thoughts within Source's mind. They are merely thoughts. And thoughts do not suffer when we twist them, torture them, and ultimately kill them when we stop thinking them. You know this from your own thinking. It is only Source's infinite power that allows its thoughts to manifest as seemingly physical entities with lives that appear to exist apart from Source's mind. In other words, we Light Beings have been fooled into believing life apart from Source is real. But the core entity Source knows it isn't. I realize this is a very difficult concept to grasp. Even though I was in the afterlife for what seemed like a long time, I did not know or understand this concept until I awakened as Source. I was then able to see life from Source's perspective.

I know this is a very different perspective from what most believe about Source. That's why I came back to share what I learned.

Why did Source create humans to be evil?

The short answer is: Source did not "create" humans *per se*, much less create them to be evil. Humans evolved from less complex animals, and thus retain the predator vs. prey instinct. That's what gives them the qualities we souls think make them "evil." Reliving Creation in the afterlife, I was surprised to discover that Source did not create specifically identifiable places, creatures, or things. I saw Source expend the Energy that makes up the universe, and create the principles that govern how that Energy behaves, that is, what we call scientific principles and laws of nature. But Source did not directly create any end products, including humans. Humans evolved over time just like all other creatures, plant life, and inert objects in the universe.

We Light Being parts of Source inhabit humans because human

character traits fascinate us. For the same reason, from time to time we also inhabit some of the millions and millions of other creations throughout the universe. Physical creations are so extremely different from our natural state as parts of Source that we instinctively find them compelling. For example, being peaceful ourselves, we Light Beings find human violence and abusiveness mind-boggling. We are drawn to it like moths to a flame—even knowing the pain involved. We want to know human evil, understand it, and experience it. And then include what we learn about humans in the vast experiential database I call Universal Knowledge. Why are we inside humans? Simply because each of us chose to experience something diametrically opposed to our own nature. We are driven by the same Source-given curiosity that compels people to become rubberneckers at traffic accidents, watch horror movies, and read murder mysteries. The media motto, "If it bleeds, it leads," reflects man's facination with misfortune.

Who but an insane God would create physical reality to be this way?

Have you ever watched a TV show full of murder, like *CSI: New York*, or one focusing on rape and child abuse, like *Law & Order SVU*? Are the creators of these shows insane? Have you ever read novels full of violence, like those of James Patterson or Michael Connelly? Are these authors or the readers of these books insane? Are the people who watch these TV shows insane? Don't these shows and books prove humans find all kinds of human experiences interesting, including rape, murder, child abuse, and other horrors? Finding something morbidly interesting does not mean we *approve* of it.

But, you may say, TV shows and books are not reality to humans. They are products of creativity and imagination that allow humans to explore unacceptable subjects in a safe way. In the very same way that TV shows and books are not real to humans, physical life is not real to Source. All earthly manifestations are a product of Source's creativity and imagination and allow it to explore emotions it could not otherwise experience. This does not make Source insane any more than it makes humans insane for expressing violent imaginings in books and movies.

The universe is similar to a virtual reality game for Source. Source knows it is imagining this physical world, and the people in it, and that the pain its virtual reality characters feel is not real. But to make the human experience believable, and to feel genuine responses to events, Source gives its mental characters amnesia about the fact that they are actually Source itself pretending to be different characters. Right now, we see only the victim side of life because of this amnesia. After we leave these bodies and reenter the Light, we will wake up and know that human life was never real. This is an extremely dramatic change in perspective, and one that is very difficult to believe if you haven't experienced it, as I did during my beyond death adventure.

How do you reconcile the fact that you can't literally kill people because physical life is not real, with the fact that humans do experience enormous suffering, including death?

All of human existence is manifested and illusory, not just the physical appearances of it. I learned in the afterlife that human suffering isn't "real" either. The emotional experience *is* real at the human level, but at our spiritual level the experience is vicarious. Let me explain with an example. When you watch a particularly important football game, do you get angry at bad calls by the refs, excited by touchdowns, and annoyed by commercial breaks? Are you then angry, excited, or annoyed with respect to your own life? No. You are only reacting to the game, and your emotions fade when the game is over. Similarly, when a woman cries through the ending of a chick flick, is she actually suffering in her own life? No. She empathized with the fictional characters for a while but forgets all about her crying after the movie ends. In much the same way, we Light Being parts of Source inside humans empathize with the lives of our human hosts. We suffer what they suffer—but only while we are in their bodies (and during the short time of the life review). My own experience in the afterlife was that all the pain and suffering I endured in Nanci's body disappeared. In fact, Nanci's entire lifetime was revealed to be artificial, like having a dream or playing a role in a virtual reality game.

As for suffering at death—that is optional for us souls, though maybe not for the humans we inhabit. We can choose to endure the death process, or to get out of the body before it dies. Many near-death experience reports come from people who got out of their bodies to avoid the pain of dying or resuscitation.

The most important point to remember is that much human suffering could end tomorrow—if we would only choose to end it. We souls have the power to stop our host bodies from hurting themselves and others. Why don't we? Because most people are not aware they even have this option. Most people truly believe they are human and cannot escape human emotions and motivations. That is why it is so important that we awaken each other to our true nature as parts of Source. Once you know that you are a powerful spiritual being, and not a human animal, you can believe you have the power to control your host body's behavior. Expressing more of our spiritual nature through our behavior would increase the amount of unconditional love in our human lives and consequently decrease the suffering.

Aren't some behaviors inherently bad?

Human Perspective. One of my YouTube viewers writes: "I am happy with the idea of not labeling people as being evil or not evil, but it is a whole different ball game to say that some of these acts in themselves are not wrong." Of course human societies deem certain acts to be intrinsically wrong.

Source's Perspective. I understand completely how incredulous the viewer is because I felt the same way when I learned about unconditional love in the afterlife. But I learned something else that helps me understand why people act in ways I consider unacceptable: there are a million different perspectives in the universe and they are all true for those who hold them, at the time they hold them. For example, humans have a completely different perspective on life and the afterlife than Source. My writings and talks generally reflect Source's perspective because that's what I learned in the afterlife. The fact that human and Source perspectives are different, though, does not make either of them wrong.

Source understands humans' beliefs about evil and right and

wrong—but does not share them. We Light Being souls are not expected to retain Source's perspective while inside these bodies. We share human perspective now, which is completely valid while we experience human life. It is why we are here. But just because Source does not judge human behavior at Source's level of existence does not mean we have to accept violence, killing, rape, torture, or abuse without judgment at the human level of existence. We souls experience the consequences of violence in the physical world and have a right to do what we can to prevent it. Punishing offenders may be an appropriate control measure. Adopting religious and personal values about right and wrong behavior may also be appropriate. But insisting that Source share human judgments is not going to change Source's unconditionally loving and non-judgmental nature. What we can change is our desire to project human nature and beliefs onto Source.

To be clear, Source does *not* say torturing or killing another human, or any act of violence, is "right" or "okay." Source simply does not condemn itself/us for what we do in the physical world—just like you do not condemn yourself for what you do in your dreams. Do you think you are evil when you hurt someone in a dream? Or have a nightmare full of murder and mayhem? No, because *to you* it isn't real. You are not the character you portray in your dream; you simply watch the dream through the character's eyes. The same is true for Source: it/we are not the human characters we portray in physical life. We are parts of Source's own consciousness participating in the manifested world in much the same way we participate in our dreams. My experience convinced me that Source is unconditionally loving by nature. That means it loves and accepts us, both human manifestations and Light Being souls within humans, despite what we do in the physical world. That's what unconditional love means.

How can Source allow this cruel earth behavior we have toward one another?

Source does not *allow or disallow* cruel earth behavior. Source does not judge or control its manifestations' behavior. Compare the situation where you tell a child not to touch the hot stove because it will hurt. The child understands what "hurt" means but touches the stove anyway. That natural curiosity comes from Source. Would you call the child who touches the stove anyway and gets burned "cruel" to its body? Or would you say his curiosity got the better of him? It's all a matter of perspective.

Much of our suffering results from mindless risk-taking by adults who do not think through the possible harm to themselves or others that could result from their actions. Even if they are aware of the potential consequences, it is human nature to assume "it will never happen to me." Take, for example, the car driver who always spends morning rush hour drive time talking on her cell phone or drinking coffee. Any moment her driving could prove deadly. Do we consider distracted driving cruel, or merely foolish? Or, what about the man with a sexually transmitted disease who refuses to protect his partners from exposure? Is he cruel, or lacking in self-control while in the throes of passion? Cruelty is not only in the eyes of the beholder but also a matter of intent. The curious child, careless driver, and reckless Romeo do not intend to harm anyone. They are simply irresponsible. Does that make them evil?

Source "allows" humans to act in ways they call evil only in the sense that it created human nature. Light Being souls allow evil only because most of us are asleep at the wheel. We have not awakened to the realization that we have been unconsciously manifesting merely animal lives.

Is exercising free will effective against evil?

As the Almighty, Source has full freedom of choice. We parts of Source who inhabit humans retain our ability to exercise our independent free will while inside these bodies. But untrained humans do not act contrary to their innate animal nature. Do you remember the fable of the scorpion hitching a ride across a stream on the back of a frog, only to sting the frog halfway across and drown them both? Earth animals, including man, are violent and self-serving by nature. This nature cannot be changed. But behavior can be controlled.

We Light Beings can impose our will upon the being we inhabit to control its actions. We do it all the time without characterizing it that way in our thoughts. We call it "self-control" and assume our human is exercising it. We call it "restraint" or "exercising discretion" and assume the human mind has made a decision not to act out. In all three instances the Light Being soul inside the human is exercising its free will to control its host's behavior. Human nature is essentially overridden by spiritual nature in these instances.

Both Light Beings and humans themselves can control behavior through training. Souls can train their hosts to eliminate certain behaviors through repeated acts of free will. That's how most of us overcome bad habits. Battling addiction—the ultimate test of control—requires a constant spiritual effort of imposing Light Being free will over human physiology.

Parents have a duty to train their offspring in how to act in the world, how to get along with others, and what conduct is acceptable and unacceptable. But behavior training does not stop there. School systems and various interest groups train their members. Humans can be trained more easily than other animals to do just about anything. Physical, mental, and emotional training are the backbone of societal structures as diverse as military special forces, police forces, firefighters, and street gangs on one end of the spectrum to sororities, social cliques, religions, and athletic teams on the other.

Both spiritual free will and behavioral training can be used to eliminate evil in the world. It is the widespread failure of both that allows violence and selfishness to run rampant. The exercise of free will could be increased if more of us souls would become aware of our true spiritual nature and powers, and if we could come to realize that we can use our powers while inside humans. And humans would be better behaved if our training institutions would take more responsibility to train out violence and selfishness. Parents must take their training roles more seriously, too, and if they don't, society must step in to fill the gap. Our cultures must remove the violence in TV, movies, books, games, videos, and social networking media, all of which tell young people that violence and self-centeredness are acceptable forms of behavior. We each have the power—both body and soul—to stop evil. It's time to stop complaining about evil and personally do something about it.

As Creator of the physical universe, isn't Source ultimately the root of all evil? If humans aren't actually real, then the evil of humans is still Source, which still makes Source capable of what we consider to be evil. Right?

As appealing as this logic is, it is based on a false premise. The fact that manifested humans experience evil in the manifested world does not make that evil real. Source is the only reality. Everything else is imagined by Source. More to the point, saying that Source is capable of *imagining* evil acts is not the same as stating that the core entity Source is capable in its real life of *committing* the acts that humans call evil.

Everyone reading this book has imagined murder, rape, incest, and other atrocities at some time in his or her life, whether while watching TV, reading a book, or dreaming. Does that make each of us personally capable of committing murder, rape, incest, and other evils? No. We can safely let our imaginations run wild in dreams or creative outlets because we know that our own character and will-power prohibit us from acting out imaginary events.

The entire universe is Source's imagination run wild. But the fact that Source can imagine human animals doing horrendous things does not make Source evil. While watching Creation in the afterlife, I saw that Source had to manifest the physical universe in order to be able to experience acts, thoughts, emotions, and events that it is totally incapable of experiencing directly due to its innate unconditionally loving nature.

Moreover, Source is an Energy field with no physical presence that could commit evil. Nor does it commit evil acts through its imaginary physical creatures. The core personality Source does not guide, direct, or control the daily actions of each and every creature in the universe. That would defeat the purpose of using the universe as a creative outlet to see what Source's imaginary creatures can produce. Source is capable of observing what humans call evil, and that is all it does.

Much as we might hate to admit it, at the physical universe level of existence, humans are responsible for the evil in the world. Human societies decide what behaviors are and are not labeled "evil." Humans commit the acts they call evil. And we souls let it happen. The solution to the problem of evil in the manifested world is to awaken souls to their true spiritual nature so they can better control their human hosts, and provide better training in self-control from birth throughout a lifetime. So they can better indoctrinate humans in the cause and effect practical truth that they are responsible for the consequences of their behavior. So they can show care and support for parents who grew up in abusive homes in order to break the cycle of abuse and violence in some families.

12

Religious Beliefs

I WITNESSED IN THE AFTERLIFE HOW FROM OUR VERY
first moments on earth, our beliefs are shaped by fear. The spiritual
truths we Light Beings know so well before we come into human life
are hidden by the veil of amnesia that drapes over our minds as we
enter physical life. So, while inside humans, we combat our fears and
ignorance of Source with myths and superstitions passed down from
human generation to generation. These eventually form the core of
religions. The Old Testament story of Samson and Delilah reflects
man's ancient love affair with myth as a teaching method. Delilah
was accused of robbing Samson of his great strength by cutting his
hair. We know now that strength is not dependent on hair length.
This is a myth, and like much of religious literature, is not meant to
be taken literally. We believe man is more sophisticated today than
in Samson's time. But do some of our beliefs still have an element of
superstition in them?

*Does the alignment of planets at the moment of our birth create our
personality?* The theory this belief was originally based on is that the
stars and planets are gods whose breath vapors create permanent personality traits when a baby first inhales. In fact, astrology has nothing
to do with personality, for stars and planets are not gods, and they do
not breathe vapors into babies' mouths. I was taught in the afterlife
that our personalities are eternal, designed by Source specifically for

us, and rounded out by millions of experiences in spiritual and physical life. Human personalities, on the other hand, are manifested to be the same, but are influenced during life by environmental factors and the eternal personality of the Light Being soul within.

Can we ward off negative energy by imagining we are surrounded by a bubble of white light? The Knowings I received in the afterlife indicated there is no such thing as negative energy. All Energy is Source Energy and, therefore, cannot be negative. However, I have encountered several humans I call "Energy Vampires" because somehow they drain me of energy when I am in their vicinity. I might classify this effect as *negating* energy, though it is not a negative energy.

If we inadvertently think about something we don't want, will saying "cancel, reject" in our minds prevent the Universe from delivering the unwanted thing to us? I learned that this superstition is based on the mythical Law of Attraction. The nature of the spiritual ability to manifest what humans perceive to be physical reality was drilled into my mind at various points in my afterlife journey. As parts of the Creator's consciousness, we Light Beings create our own physical reality. We are the power, not the physical universe, which is itself a mere manifestation.

Perhaps it is time to take the superstition out of some of our beliefs.

Consciousness After Death

The Bible tells us that when we die, we have no recollection of anything. Is this true?

Actually, it's the exact opposite. All near-death experiencers who have had a life review during their NDE state they had total recall of their just passed lives. I did. In addition, while in the afterlife I remembered every moment of every one of the hundreds to thousands of physical lives I have lived.

The Bible says we completely lose all consciousness after death until Jesus Christ descends from heaven and raises the dead from their graves. Is this true?

This belief is inconsistent with what I personally experienced, Knowings I was given in the afterlife, and what other NDErs experienced. NDErs prove consciousness continues after demise of the body. Exhumations of the dead prove bodies decay over time, eventually leaving only a dust-like substance. There is nothing in graves that can be reconstituted and raised into heaven. Moreover, heaven is a spiritual state of existence, not a physical matter place that could support the weight of human bodies.

Prayer

Does prayer work?

Human Perspective. I was taught as a Catholic school student that we are powerless and must get down on bended knees and beg God to intercede in our lives if we want something. This was called prayer. I learned in the afterlife that this type of prayer is based on fear, and mistaken beliefs about Source, and does not work.

Light Being Perspective. I was shown in the afterlife that we are not powerless. In fact, we are literally parts of Source's consciousness. It does not get any more powerful than that. Each of us mental characters/Light Beings within Source has the power to change our own physical reality. There is no need to pray to a greater power because we already *are* that greater power. We would be praying to ourselves. Instead, what we can do is take control mentally and form the intention to consciously manifest our lives in accordance with our spiritual goals. Then, to get more bang for our buck, we can ask our loved ones in the afterlife to add their intentions to our manifesting. My experience is that this type of "prayer" works.

We may be convinced by experience that supplication type or gratitude-based prayer works because sometimes we get what we prayed for. Actually, prayer focuses our attention and intention, allowing us to consciously manifest. When we feel our prayers have been answered, it is because we manifested the answer ourselves, perhaps with the help of our co-creator loved ones who have focused their intentions with us. When our prayers are not answered, it is because what we requested does not further our spiritual goals, or we did not have manifesting intention at the time we prayed. I know this isn't a popular answer, but it's the truth as I understand it from being in the afterlife.

Source's Perspective. The core entity Source does not take control over the lives of any of its manifestations with or without prayers to do so. There is no need to, because Source considers anything and everything its Light Being mental characters experience in the physical world to be part of the creative process it intended.

Do spiritual beings, like deceased saints, hear our prayers?

Human Perspective. One reason to assume praying to a saint is important *to the saint* is because performing miracles is a prerequisite to gaining sainthood in the Catholic Church. Therefore, some of us might believe prayers to saints will help them achieve sainthood designation and enhance their status on earth. There is no sainthood designation in the afterlife, only in the Catholic Church.

Unawakened Light Being souls project the human concept of hierarchy into the afterlife and assume some residents there, such as "saints," are more powerful than others.

Light Being Perspective. All Light Beings have equal power. In general, Light Beings in the afterlife do not listen for souls' prayers. I received Knowings in the afterlife that once we complete the transformation back into our spiritual level of awareness, we understand that human life is not real and thus give it no further thought. Light Beings are also aware that physical life is manifested. There is no reason for Light Beings to listen for our prayers because each of us has the power to manifest our own lives as we see fit.

Can spiritual beings answer our prayers? Are our prayers as important to them as they are to us? Or do they think our prayers are silly or unnecessary?

Human Perspective. Our religions encourage us to pray to saints, angels, and other spiritual beings to intercede with a humanoid God on our behalf, on the theory that we are powerless over our lives and need intervention from an outside power.

Humans feel powerful when supplicants beseech them, and this makes requests for favors important to those being asked. Unaware souls assume spiritual beings are just like humans, and project human nature onto Light Beings when they think prayers are important to them.

Light Being Perspective. Light Beings do not have human nature and could not care less whether anyone prays to them. However, if we specifically ask for the attention of our loved ones in the afterlife, they will respond to the extent they are able. They still love us and will do everything they can to show their love. There are limitations, however. Some souls are not in a stage of eternal life when they can communicate with loved ones on earth.

More important, we may pray for an event or outcome not truly in our best interest. While we Light Beings are in human bodies, we are in the absolute worst position to know what is best for us. Our thoughts are colored by human instincts and character traits. Our desires aligned with human ones. So we may pray for something that in the long run will either harm us or contradict our reasons for being in physical life. I think it best to appeal to the part of us still in the afterlife because it has the perspective we lack and will assist us in manifesting only those events that will benefit us in our spiritual quest. I find that if I ask other Light Beings to help me boost my own Energy/power to accomplish a manifesting goal, it does seem to work. So apparently we can get assistance with our own manifesting. It's just that no one else is going to do it for us.

My experience in the afterlife was that Light Beings find human interests to be "quaint" or "primitive," but not silly.

Source's Perspective. One reader writes: "Basically, you're saying that all the praying people do, asking for this and asking for that, God's not really listening to any of this!" Not really. It's impossible for Source not to be aware of our thoughts because all of our thoughts *are its thoughts.* However, Source is not really listening for our wish lists. And Source the core entity is not a Santa Claus we can ask for physical gifts and get them. It does not intervene to change its Light Beings' physical lives.

When praying, are we just supposed to be clear and know

what we desire, or are we supposed to be clear and know that we already have what we desire?

This question seems to me to arise from instructions given in Law of Attraction books. But, I learned in the afterlife that it doesn't matter one way or the other what words we use or attitude we take. Praying is not necessary, if what we mean by prayer is asking someone out there—Source or the universe—to grant our wishes. We each have the power to manifest the physical reality content of our human lives. If something we have been trying to manifest does not come to fruition, then it makes sense to ask other Light Being loved ones to assist us with the project. That's asking for assistance to do what we are designed to do, not praying for something to be granted to us by an outside benefactor. And whatever words feel right to us are just perfect for the job.

Is prayer even relevant?

It can be. Prayer can boost manifesting because it focuses our attention and intention on creating a particular result. It can also be used to communicate with those who are no longer in the body.

Is prayer in worship of Source worthwhile?

No. I learned in the afterlife that Source has no desire to be worshiped. That is an unawakened soul-created myth resulting from the belief that Source is just like humans. Humans dearly love to be worshiped.

How do you explain all the miracles that God has performed in people's lives?

What we call miracles are manifestations of reality, the physical world result of the exercise of spiritual power. We all have the ability as parts of Source to manifest physical reality, and thus to perform miracles. Some manifestations are called miracles simply because those who observe them do not know or understand the physical world explanations for how they came about.

Jesus and the Bible

Why do so many people see Jesus, who may have gone by another name, during their NDEs?

None of my extensive research suggests that a lot of souls see Jesus during their NDEs. The only statistic of which I am aware was compiled by the Near-Death Experience Research Foundation, which found that only 21 of 302 survey respondents stated they saw Jesus, or a figure like him who might have gone by another name, during their NDE. I know two NDErs who report seeing Jesus in the afterlife as a family member in a previous life, rather than as a religious figure. One was married to Jesus and the other was his sister in timelines very different than the early first century AD.

According to what I experienced and received as Knowings, there are two possible explanations for an NDEr seeing Jesus. First, during the early phases of an NDE, we souls manifest into reality what we expect to see on the other side. If we expect to see Jesus, because this is what our religion taught us, then we may well manifest that apparition. But it is not enough for an NDEr to merely believe in Jesus for him to appear. The NDEr must intend to create Jesus's apparition. Manifesting requires creative intention.

Second, there are Beings of Light who come to comfort and assist us in the transition from human to Light Being life. They do whatever they feel is necessary to bring peace, harmony, and love to the newly arrived soul. So, they may take on the faces of the soul's loved ones, or that of a religious figure such as Jesus, as part of their job.

Technically, there is no historical evidence that Jesus ever existed, much less a drawing or painting of him. NDErs who see Jesus recognize an artist's rendering of the man, such as a painting or statue created from the artist's imagination or a biblical description.

You wrote that during your NDE you saw that Jesus did not exist as one individual person. Then who made up the story of Jesus?

No one made up the story of Jesus. Like all oral tradition, the Jesus story has been crafted over generations from a variety of sources.

It is part myths taken from other first century religions, part Judaism's rich oral history about the Kingdom of God movement, part oral stories about several individuals believed to have lived in Israel in the first century, and part imagination. Oral history gets seriously distorted as it is retold. You may have had the experience yourself while playing the game "Gossip" or "Telephone," where one person whispers a couple sentences to the next person, who repeats it, and it moves on down the line until the last person says what he or she heard. Most times the end message is very different from what the first person actually said. Humans simply have poor ability to retain and repeat verbatim what they hear. I have read in medical texts that humans retain only about fifteen percent of what they hear. This poor human memory of the spoken word, and time, is what created the Jesus story, which was oral until committed to manuscript forty to seventy years after Jesus's assumed date of death. The passage of time, and retelling after retelling, simply crafted an oral history of epic proportions.

Add on top of this oral history the Catholic Church's historic efforts to edit material to fit its own needs. An example is the Mary Magdalene story. One Pope mistakenly referred to her from the pulpit as a prostitute. Rather than admit that a Pontiff, who is deemed to be infallible when it comes to Church dogma, made a mistake, the Catholic Church rewrote that part of biblical text to make Mary a prostitute. These events are well documented in scholarly research.

If you are struggling with my memories about Jesus, please understand that what I offer is what I remember from my afterlife experience. It is true for me, but may not reflect your present truth. I don't want to dissuade anyone from a belief held for years—a belief I shared before I had my 1994 NDE. Perhaps doing research on how the Bible was created might give better direction on answering this question than I can. There are many good books by biblical scholars, both those who believe in Jesus and those who don't, which explain how the various versions of the Bible were compiled.

Is Jesus Christ my savior and without accepting him I have no hope of entering heaven?

No. I used to believe this. But, I learned during my NDE that no one needs a spiritual savior. All Light Being souls return *automatically* to the spiritual form from which we come. We all go to what we call heaven, whether or not we believe in Jesus. No messiah is necessary.

Is the New Testament of the Bible a hoax?

No. Many scholars have studied the origins of the New Testament in great detail and they will vouch for the fact that it's not a hoax. Having said that, however, they will also tell you they consider the Bible to be cultural mythology rather than historical fact. I recommend books by Burton Mack, PhD, Burt Ehrman, PhD, and a recent compendium titled *The Evolution of God* by Robert Wright, PhD. These scholars will put the Bible into historical literary perspective for you.

I encourage anyone searching for answers on this, or any, topic to do two things. First, go into deep meditation, emotionally separate yourself from the body you inhabit, and ask for the truth about Source *from Source*. And second, before putting further reliance upon any particular words in the Bible, read some of the excellent books that explain how the Bible was created and how many thousands of translation errors are in it, especially in English versions. All Bible scholars agree that the oldest versions of the anonymous manuscripts compiled into the Bible contain mistranslations of ancient Hebrew. None of the original manuscripts, or their source documents, still exist. So, read the Bible in light of all that is known about its compilation, and then decide how much stock to place in specific phrases, or the book itself.

Isn't the Bible God's words written by male humans under His inspiration?

During my NDE, I watched the history of how Christianity started and grew. I saw that the manuscripts that went into the Bible were written by males because at this time in history females were not taught how to read and write. No one knows what inspired the writers because no one knows who most of them are. It was a common practice at the time for writers to use the pen name of a revered person instead of their own name. Perhaps reading some of the excellent books written on how the various versions of the Bible were created will answer this question better than I can. I recommend *Who Wrote the New Testament* by Burton Mack, PhD and *Misquoting Jesus* by Bart Ehrman, PhD. Both authors are Christian Bible scholars teaching on the college level who seek out the most authentic versions of the manuscripts that were selected by the Catholic Church to include in the New Testament. Both of their books were bestsellers and are available at bookstores and on Amazon.

Much of the Old Testament was written in ancient Hebrew without vowels, spaces between words, capital letters, or punctuation. So translators basically had to guess at the words intended, kind of like on the TV show *Wheel of Fortune* where the contestants guess at letters in a phrase until they are able to decipher the whole phrase. The big difference is that Bible translators had no idea what the original authors were trying to say, unlike the *Wheel of Fortune* scenario where the phrase to be guessed is familiar to everyone. Added to the translation problem is the fact that handwritten copies of the originals were made by the few who could read and write, and those scribes made copying errors. The experts say the King James Edition of the New Testament was translated from a Greek version that does not match the manuscripts used for the Latin and other Greek translations.[7] In sum, what we read in English is not a very accurate record of the original authors' inspiration.

Basically, the fact that someone (including me) is inspired by religious beliefs to write does not automatically make every word they pen Source's words. Having merged into Source in the afterlife and obtained its knowledge firsthand, I can tell you that most of the information in the present day Bible did not come from Source.

13

The Death Process

MEDICAL RESEARCHERS INTO NDES, INCLUDING PHY-
sicians Raymond Moody, MD, Melvin Morse, MD, and Bruce Grey-
son, MD, have through patient interviews defined a series of uniform steps they believe NDErs take after leaving their bodies. I was
informed in the afterlife that these steps are built into the process of
crossing over and therefore are standard, though the order in which
we take them may be different than researchers suggest. I describe
how I experienced each step, and the Knowings I received about the
steps, in chapter 19 of *BACKWARDS*. That chapter also details the
transition process we go through early in our afterlife to remove human thinking and remember who we really are. There is no similar
research data available on the transition process because so few of us
return to human life after completing the transition. In fact, I am
unaware of any other NDEr who has done so.

**I've been reading in a couple of different sources about op-
tions when we pass on. These writers say that we have three choices: (1) to go to the light, tunnel, loved ones, Jesus, etc., but, if we
do that, the sources say, we will be in a temporary place where we
will still have to reincarnate; (2) to choose a void where we won't
be able to feel or see anything for a while until we feel ready or,
according to one source, may actually choose to cease to exist;**

and (3) to stay still and do nothing until beings come for us to guide us into a spiritual journey that does not involve having to reincarnate. Is this true?

It sounds to me like these writers have read a lot of NDE accounts and are trying to harmonize them by interpreting them as presenting the NDErs with different options after death. The Knowings I received, and my own personal experience having died several times, is that the crossing over process is automatic. We can choose to fight it, but we are only delaying bliss and healing. Why would anyone want to do that? Moreover, the options these writers describe are actually stages of, not alternatives to, the automatic crossing over process I describe in *BACKWARDS*.

(1) Going into the Light does take us to the temporary state we call heaven or paradise, the same state of existence NDErs visit. This is indeed the spiritual state from which we reincarnate. It is temporary only because when we are ready, we can choose to stop incarnating and move into the next spiritual state I describe in *BACKWARDS*.

(2) Until we feel ready for what? There may be a void in our crossing over, but it is temporary—only until we see the Light. We Light Being souls cannot choose to cease to exist. We are thoughts in Source's mind, particles of its own self-awareness. We have no existence except as Source. We will always be part of Source's experience and eternal life.

(3) NDErs and deathbed witnesses confirm that Light Beings may in fact come for us to guide us through the crossing over process. And some NDErs have taken spiritual journeys with Light Beings and returned to their bodies before entering the Light. But the Knowings I received about death refute the idea that we can go on a spiritual journey from which we will never have to incarnate. There is no need for such an option. We can always choose not to incarnate at any time in our existence. Some Light Beings have never incarnated. We have free will and total control over whether we incarnate. No one forces us to do it.

Everyone has a different NDE story, except for the rising up to the ceiling, watching the medical team go to work, and eventually

leaving the area and seeing the Light. Why all the inconsistency?

Not many NDE accounts include the scenario described in the question. Most NDErs do not hang around the area of their bodies to observe resuscitation efforts by the medical team.

Dying follows a progression similar to that of waking up. There are only so many ways a human can rouse from sleep. It can be a sudden snap to attention, a leisurely wandering out of any one of a zillion dreams to waking life, or a gradual dawning of consciousness. So, too, waking from human life to spiritual life follows a narrowly defined set of parameters. We can pop into the Light; travel through a tunnel, outer space, or a wildly diverse range of experiences on our way to the Light; or simply become aware that we have entered the Light. NDE accounts are consistent in this regard because the process is basically the same for everyone, with the minor variations NDErs describe.

Is it safe to say that if a person dies, it means his time was up?

Yes. In general, our bodies cannot die permanently before their lifecycle is completed and it is our time to return home to the afterlife. Obviously we can die temporarily before our time, otherwise there would not be thousands of near-death experience stories. Nearly all NDErs are told it is not their time to die, they are given a choice of whether to stay in the Light or return to their bodies, or they simply return automatically upon resuscitation of their bodies. Obviously there are exceptions to the general rule that when it is our time to die we do not return. I got the impression in the afterlife that it was my time to die permanently. And yet, here I am because I wanted to tell others what I had learned in the afterlife.

Could the soul have an exit strategy that does not involve the death of the human host?

It is possible. We have a sacred trust to take care of our hosts and usually do not abandon them unless the body is in a permanent vegetative state.

Can we find out in advance how we are going to die?

We know before we enter into human life how we will leave it—what our exit strategy will be. Once we pass through the veil of amnesia at birth, we do not retain that knowledge. Having it would most likely change many of our decisions in life and likely destroy the reason we chose our parents in the first place.

Does a person ever die and say, "Wait a minute, I wasn't supposed to die now, something went wrong, I preplanned to die in a plane crash?"

Although we come into human life with a planned exit strategy, the plan is always subject to change. We manifest our lives moment by moment, so nothing is ever set in stone. We may complete the experiences we intended to have by an early age and decide to return to spiritual life. It may take us more than eighty years to accomplish our goals, or only one month. Or we may decide to stay longer than planned in order to support another Light Being soul in his or her human life. Love can keep us here, as we have seen time and again with NDErs who return to human life to care for their children or other loved ones.

Do you have any suggestions as to how I can make my mother's passing smooth so she ends up in the "right place" after she goes?

There is no "right place" to go when the body dies. That is a human perspective that, happily, does not actually apply to us when our hosts die. We souls simply wake up where we already are—in the afterlife.

The same year I died, 1994, I had the privilege of accompanying my mother as she began her journey home. This is called an empathic NDE. While holding her hand, I was able to see what she saw as she got out of her body and went into the dark void to look for the Light. That's all I was privy to seeing, but the experience does help me answer this reader's question.

Based on what I learned in the afterlife and my empathic NDE with my mother, I would suggest the reader start out by preparing her mother for what she is likely to experience as she goes through the transition from human to eternal life. There's a chapter in both BACKWARDS and BACKWARDS Guidebook about the dying process that anyone can use as a guide. I hope this foreknowledge might stave off the fear of not knowing what to expect and prevent potential unpleasantness. For example, NDErs who had no idea what to expect after death, or who feared what they might experience, have reported their NDEs as unpleasant or hellish simply because they misunderstood the small part of the process they experienced. For example, often the first thing we experience coming out of the body is darkness. We have lost our physical eyes and it can take a while to adjust to spiritual vision. Darkness can be frightening, and lead the soul to believe there is nothing after human life. So it panics. That's what happened to my mother at her body's death. She didn't see the Light right away and panicked, flitted around the room a bit, and then got back into her body. Even the priest in the room was aware of these out-of-body movements and slightly recoiled when my mother zoomed past him in soul form. Therefore, if my reader would gently open a discussion about what the process might be like for her mother, that knowledge might take away her mother's fear as she encounters various stages. Tell her the darkness is temporary and to look all around for a pinpoint of Light and go toward it.

I want to assure everyone that there is no "wrong place" to go. All that happens when we leave these bodies behind for good is that we wake up to the state of awareness we had before entering into the bodies. But the awakening process does take time, in human terms, and it does have stages. The first stage is to accept that we are dead in human life but continue to live. If my reader can help her mother hope—if not believe—that life is eternal, this might help her mother acclimate after leaving her body.

Finally, if anyone facing death has any unresolved attachments to life, such as addictions, compulsions, emotional issues with a friend or family member, fears, leftover desires to do or accomplish particular things, it will help greatly if we assist them in trying to resolve them now, if possible. Doing so has no impact on crossing over, but it may bring our loved one the peace and acceptance that he or she needs to let go.

I am so sorry my reader will soon be facing the loss of her mother's physical presence. I know exactly what that feels like. But her mother will still be with her in non-physical presence. And my reader and her mother have always been together in the Light. We don't put all of our consciousness into physical bodies because some of it stays in the Light. So they are together there now always and forever.

14

Suicide

MY NEWSLETTER ARTICLE ON SUICIDE TOUCHED A
nerve with many readers. I wrote it partly to comfort myself, after
my brother committed suicide, and partly to comfort others like me
still traumatized by their loved one's final act. I discovered that many
readers held the same view about suicide that I learned in Catholic
school, which is that taking one's own life is a sin. My afterlife experience reversed my beliefs about suicide, which helped a little after the
loss of my brother. Clearly the loss of a loved one has a devastating
effect on body and soul, no matter what our beliefs about suicide
might be. Part of my conversation with readers on this topic follows.

**There is a commonly held belief by many metaphysical au-
thors that anyone who commits suicide will have to come back
and repeat the journey. This then brings into question, what exactly is considered to be suicide in the upper firmament? A person
in intense pain, suffering terminal illness, might head to Switzer-
land and engage in euthanasia. Is this then classified as a suicidal
act from a non-human perspective?**

Human Perspective. Humans generally have negative judgments
about suicide because they are judgmental by nature. Humans consider suicide to be the ultimate failure because it is diametrically opposed to their number one goal: survival. The Christian among us

may consider suicide a sin, an affront to God's plan for the timing of our deaths.

In typical human contradictory fashion, our cultures approve of a type of "suicide" where police, military, firemen, and everyday heroes knowingly sacrifice their own lives to save others. And suicide bombers are revered by fellow jihadists for their religious fervor.

Humans may believe suicide is wrong not because it terminates a life—our societies approve of killing people in many settings—but because it hurts the loved ones left behind. Friends and relatives may secretly see suicide as an intentional decision to hurt *them*, and may blame their deceased loved one for not having enough strength, courage, or love to keep living *just for them*. A purely self-centered view of suicide may also include guilt feelings because the loved ones left behind might have been unable to predict or stop the suicide and feel they should have. Humans detest feeling guilty and frequently seek to punish the ones who made them feel that way. In the case of suicide, humans have concocted punishments in the afterlife because they have no other setting for their revenge.

The idea that suicide is a failure or sin, and reincarnation the punishment for it, reflects purely human values. The metaphysical authors my reader references are unknowingly projecting human thinking onto the afterlife, where it does not apply.

Light Being Perspective. Survival applies only to the manifested physical body, not the soul personality inside it. Survival is never a concern to Light Being souls inasmuch as they are eternal because Source is eternal.

I learned in the afterlife that Source does not have a plan for when we die. When we Light Beings choose a human life to enter, we ourselves plan a potential exit strategy. That's right—we preplan our human host's death. As we all know, though resist acknowledging, all humans die. Humans are temporary beings manifested by Source in order to have various physical experiences. Death is one of the experiences we Light Beings cannot have in our natural spiritual state. So we are interested in death when we choose a human life. Our chosen exit strategy may be an accident, illness, or natural causes. But it is our choice, not part of any plan in which we have no say.

Knowings I received in the afterlife taught me that suicide is not judged—at all. It is acceptable from a spiritual perspective for someone to choose suicide as the means of exiting the human manifestation. Because suicide is not condemned, it makes no difference whether the person was physically ill or suffering at the time of the decision to end his or her life.

Our overriding innate nature as parts of Source is unconditional love. It can be an unconditionally loving act to release a human animal from unrelenting physical suffering via suicide or euthanasia. As a culture, we accept this for our beloved pets, but not for our own animal hosts. That is because humans themselves, not us souls within, make most decisions about how human life will proceed. And the overriding innate human drive is survival at all costs. Because souls have no survival instinct, we can accept suicide without judgment or regret.

How do you respond to NDErs who say they were told in the afterlife they would have to repeat all the suffering that led them to end their life if they committed suicide?

One reader asked this in response to my newsletter article on suicide, adding: "Sandra Rogers's NDE is a good example of what can happen when a person unjustifiably cuts short their life. After she attempted to commit suicide, she was given only two choices by the Being of Light. One choice involved being revived and living out the rest of her days. (This was the choice she chose.) The other choice involved remaining in the Light with the condition of having to re-incarnate at a future time to re-experience everything that led her to commit suicide in the first place. Sandra's NDE demonstrates that people must overcome their problems in this life or else face them again in a future life. In Sandra's case, committing suicide did not solve anything. If we delay dealing with these problems by committing suicide, we may only compound them."

I have read Sandra Rogers's book, *Lessons From the Light: Insights From a Journey to the Other Side*, and I think my reader is generalizing to reach the conclusion that what happened to Ms. Rogers is a universal consequence of suicide. Ms. Rogers does not claim her personal NDE experience revealed a suicide consequence that applies to all of us Light Being souls. She does state she had access to Universal Knowledge, but never claims it informed her that all suicide victims have to reincarnate and relive the same events that led to their suicides. Ms. Rogers describes a life review full of abandonment by her father, living with a drug-addicted stepfather, family financial and emotional crises, being removed from her home after a suicide attempt at age thirteen, suffering a miscarriage in the tenth grade, multiple rapes, her grandmother's suicide, multiple suicide attempts, and numerous other traumas. During the review, "the Light" told Ms. Rogers she would have to make a choice: she could go back to her body and finish out its human life, or she could stay in the Light. But, according to the Light, if she stayed in the afterlife, she would have to return to physical life sometime in the future and relive the events that caused her to take her own life.

The two choices given Ms. Rogers's were unique to her as a Light Being soul and may relate to her goals for incarnating. Because Ms. Rogers the soul couldn't remember its goals for this incarnation, the Light would have to tell it to return to human life because it had work yet to do toward its goals. We Light Beings may choose an emotion or situation that physical life presents as our incarnation "theme." We choose to incarnate into many different human lives that will present opportunities for us to experience our theme. In Ms. Rogers's case, perhaps the theme was suicide. Sandra Rogers's life gave the Light Being one perspective on the theme. If it reincarnated, it would choose another life that would give it another perspective on that same theme. The Light Being soul would repeat the *theme*, not the events of Sandra Rodgers's life. This would be *its* choice because of its chosen theme, not because suicides are condemned to repeat the same events that led to their deaths. If the soul's theme is suicide, it would enter into any number of human lives and commit suicide again and again under different circumstances to get a broader understanding of why humans do it. It would also eventaully incarnate as the mother of a suicide victim; or the wife, husband, other family member, or paramedic who lost the patient; or experience some other relationship to the event of suicide. But there's no way it could repeat the life of Sandra Rogers.

It is not possible for a soul to reincarnate and re-experience the events of a former life. The reincarnated soul would be in a new body, with new family members, new friends, new job, new health, new life, new everything. No two lives can be identical. In addition, because of the veil of amnesia, there is no way the reincarnated soul would ever know to make choices that lead to the same events that gave rise to committing suicide in her former life.

Ms. Rogers does not need to learn how to overcome her problems for any spiritual reason. My reader's assumption stems from his/her belief that human life is our one chance to "get it right" and earn our way into heaven. Knowings I received dispel that fiction. We enter into human life in order to gather believable emotions and experiences to satisfy our own curiosity as Source. We return automatically to what humans call heaven. There is no need to learn anything, or get anything right by human standards, to earn our way into heaven or paradise. We reincarnate voluntarily—again, out of our own curiosity as Source—not to give us another chance to "get it right."

Ms. Rogers's account shows she only got as far as the life review in her afterlife transition, which occurs very early in an NDE, and she was still trapped in the human perspective. Thus she wouldn't have yet received the Light Being perspective described above from which to view and understand the purpose of life.

If a person commits suicide, will it be held against him in the afterlife in some other way (besides having to repeat the life)?

I learned in the afterlife that suicide is a perfectly acceptable exit strategy from a spiritual perspective. There is no punishment attached to choosing it. There are no negative judgments made in the afterlife about it, except possibly by the soul itself during the life review. We do not go to hell for suicide. There is no hell. Nor do we repeat an incarnation as a punishment for how we lived a previous human life. As I said before: incarnation is a choice, not a punishment. We always make the choice ourselves and are never forced into any particular host.

However, the problem is that while we souls are inside a human body we are in the worst possible position to know whether suicide is our chosen exit strategy. While we occupy a human as its soul, we share human perspective by default. And, although humans do have a very strong survival instinct, they also have the fight-flight-freeze biological response built into the primitive part of their brains. It is possible for a human to want to commit suicide as a flight response to escape extreme physical or emotional pain. If so, it would mean the human chose to kill himself, not that the Light Being soul chose suicide as its preplanned exit strategy. In fact, it is nearly impossible while we are still in the body to know our preplanned exit strategy, which makes committing suicide an extremely difficult decision to make. For that reason, in my opinion, we should respect a suicide's courage, rather than condemn him or her for what is either a preplanned spiritual choice or a natural biological response to extreme pain. Based on my own dealings with cancer and other life-threatening illnesses, I believe it would take an extremely strong and courageous human and/or soul to overcome the body's intense survival instinct, look death in the face, and choose death over life.

One of my readers reports that George Ritchie, MD, author of *Return From Tomorrow* and *My Life After Dying*, allegedly learned during his NDE that the quality of afterlife a person initially finds after suicide is influenced by the motive for committing it. For example, according to my reader, in theory those who kill themselves to hurt someone else, or to get revenge, haunt the living and witness the consequences of their suicide; and those who kill themselves feeding their addictions become stuck in limbo. I have read Dr. Ritchie's books from the perspective of one who has been in the afterlife, and believe my reader's interpretation of the books to be inaccurate.

George Ritchie had an extensive out-of-body experience while he was a twenty year old Army private about to enter medical school. In 1943, Private Ritchie was in an Army base hospital with double pneumonia and a fever that topped out at 106.5 degrees. During his first out-of-body trip, Private Ritchie wandered around the hospital trying to find his clothes and duffle bag, and then flew very fast over the Texas landscape. When he returned, he found his body covered by a sheet like a dead person. He sat vigil with his body until a Being of Light, whom Private Ritchie assumed to be Jesus, entered his room.

Private Ritchie's life then passed before his eyes. The Light Being seemed to be judging Private Ritchie, and asked him several times what he had done with his life, though Light Beings do not judge. Most of the book describes Private Ritchie's second, more extensive out-of-body experience with the Light Being in tow. They visited various earth-like scenes that, in my opinion, were manifestations produced by Private Ritchie's feverish nightmares. He admits that the fever caused him to have nightmares after returning to his body. By his own account, these manifestations all took place before Private Ritchie entered the Light. Therefore, he was not in the afterlife and understandably interpreted most of the scenarios to be hellish. Private Ritchie admits that no Knowings or explanations were given to him about the scenes he witnessed, leaving him to speculate as to their meaning using human perspective. Because of his background, he attached religious meaning to them, believing the events he saw resulted from the souls' refusal to accept Jesus as their savior.

Eventually, Private Ritchie entered an immense void, which he describes similarly to the one I experienced, and glimpsed a brilliant Light in the far distance that appeared to him to be a City of Light filled with Beings of Light. Private Ritchie assumed it was where souls who accepted Jesus as their savior went upon death. Just as suddenly as the City of Light appeared in the void, it disappeared, and Private Ritchie was back in his hospital room. Consequently, Private Ritchie never entered the afterlife.

I read George Ritchie's books as mostly about his feverish manifestations after he left his body and before he viewed the afterlife from a distance. His description clearly reflects what it is like to be out-of-body. I learned in the afterlife that we can instantly manifest physical reality as soon as we leave our host bodies, without having to go into the afterlife to reactivate this spiritual power. I think that is what accounts for everything Private Ritchie saw before entering the void and seeing the Light, with the exception of the Light Being he saw in his hospital room, which I accept as true. I believe a Being of Light (not Jesus) appeared to him and accompanied him on his out-of-body manifested journey, ultimately steering him toward the Light. I believe Private Ritchie did not receive any Knowings to explain the visions he saw because he had not entered the afterlife, a prerequisite for getting Knowings.

Private Ritchie's pre-afterlife manifested visions were not Knowings received from Universal Knowledge and do not reflect the truth about the afterlife of suicide victims. The books tell us a lot about Dr. Ritchie's religious beliefs and fears, but nothing about the afterlife.

15

Ghosts and After-death Communications

SEVERAL OF MY READERS HAVE ASKED ME WHETHER ghosts are real. Ghosts *are* real. But they are not what we think they are.

Many believe ghosts are dead people whose spirits have departed the body but remain earth-bound, roaming around or fixed in one place, until they are made aware they have died or complete unfinished business with the living. Ghosts are allegedly captured on film as balls or streaks of light, outlines of a human figure, or see-through apparitions of their previously inhabited human form. Thus, they appear to still be part of the physical realm. This concept of ghosts reflects the limitations of human perspective.

Human Perspective. While we occupy human bodies as souls, we generally default to human perceptions and interpret everything in the context of what we have experienced in physical life. In addition, humans are designed by Source to be self-centered. So it is perfectly natural for them to see themselves as the center of the universe with everything revolving around them. In short, humans believe everything is about *them*. That viewpoint created the traditional beliefs about ghosts. Some spiritual writers think ghosts are still linked to earth because their loved ones are here. Many people think ghosts appear in the physical world because they believe the human world is the center of the universe.

Light Being Perspective. Once we get out of physical bodies there are no places, no physical locations. The concept of "place" requires three-dimensional physical matter boundaries. It just seems like ghosts appear in the physical realm because that is the background against which we see or feel them, but they do not. Ghosts do not exist in a physical matter place, even though some humans perceive them around us in physical scenery and, therefore, assume they dwell here. Instead of ghosts inhabiting our earthly realm, we Light Being souls occasionally see into their spiritual one.

Perceiving things outside of physical life requires focused attention, like a camera lens focuses. A camera lens will see a wildflower very clearly when zoomed in for a close shot. Distant things, like the sky and horizon, exist in the background but are not in focus enough for the lens to catch them in sharp detail. When the lens zooms out, it brings the background images into focus. The small flower is still there, but the lens blurs it out of focus when shooting the sky and distant horizon. The same perception relationship exists between the physical and spiritual worlds. The only reason we do not routinely perceive those who have left physical life is because our lens of perception is stuck on the near object—the flower, or in this case, human life—making the surrounding images so blurry they seem to disappear.

Source's Perspective. How can it be that spirits are there just outside our vision? Because Source is always all around us, just out of focus, and ghosts are part of Source, just as everything else is. We Light Being souls are surrounded by Source's other thoughts and imaginings. There is only one mind and the universe exists entirely within it. Only one consciousness: Source's. So all the characters created by and existing within Source surround us all the time. All our loved ones from all of eternity continue to hold us in their loving embrace, though we can no longer see them with human eyes or feel their touch. But we can learn to perceive them with spiritual senses by changing our focus.

We generally call those who think they can communicate with spirits in the afterlife *mediums*. But we can all perceive Source's mental characters from time to time, though maybe not on demand as professional mediums claim to do. Often we hear stories of brief communications from the dead, perhaps in the form of the sudden appearance of a fragrance, voice, or vision. Something we recognize as the presence of our deceased loved one enters our awareness. Through meditation or focusing on the now, we can train ourselves to raise our awareness to the spiritual level, where it is easier to receive these impressions.

Ghosts, then, are what I call Light Beings dwelling in the afterlife. They were once souls within humans or some other physical creature or thing. Now they live spiritual lives. They do not actually appear to us in the physical world. We see them in the spiritual world superimposed over whatever earthly background is also in the frame of our vision. There is no scenery in the afterlife to form a background to our perception of ghosts. That is why they appear to be located in an earth environment. Occasionally a Light Being's Energy is so strong it permeates the darkness of physical life and can be seen and photographed.

Ghosts

Why do people sometimes see apparitions/ghosts of people they don't know?

We don't have to know someone from human life to be able to see him or her as a ghost. NDErs see all kinds of people they don't know during their NDEs. We're just seeing other characters within Source's mind.

Should we tell ghosts to go into the Light?

Human Perspective. Ghost hunters, and some spiritual writers, tell us ghosts are stuck in the physical realm and need to be encouraged to move on into the afterlife. As discussed above, this is not the case. Therefore, it isn't necessary to tell souls to go into the Light, but it can't hurt. We have no way of knowing whether these Light Beings can hear us.

Source's Perspective. Once we leave these bodies we automatically rise to a higher level of awareness—what we call going into the Light.

The Light, or afterlife, is not a place. It is Source's Energy field and expanded levels of awareness. We only perceive the afterlife as Light while we think we are human because humans can only experience energy in a physical sense. Once we complete the transformation back into our natural spiritual state, as I did, the illusion of Light disappears.

Ghosts reside in Source's mind just like everything else Source imagined for this universe. There is nowhere else to go. Remember, nothing exists outside Source. Souls cannot get lost or caught between realms, as some of us fear. That idea applies human understanding of physical life to a spiritual world to which it does not pertain. So there's no reason to worry about ghosts. They are not really lost or existing outside the Light.

What do people see or sense when they communicate with dark entities or demonic forces?

I don't know. Based upon the information I received in the afterlife, there are no dark entities or demons, only superstitious humans whose Light Being souls are unconsciously manifesting what they fear.

After-death Communications

Can dead people really communicate with us from the afterlife?

Yes. After-death communications are real. They have been documented not only in the popular book *Hello From Heaven!* by Judy and Bill Guggenheim, but also by a group of psychologists working in V.A. hospitals with post-traumatic stress disorder patients.

We can communicate with our loved ones in spirit form because they, and we, exist solely within one mind. We are all characters/personalities Source has envisioned as portals to experiences in the physical world. Though our primary purpose is fulfilled within physical life, we continue to live and experience eternal life after we leave physical life. More important, our love for those we have developed emotional bonds with continues eternally. We can, and do, reach out from the afterlife to those still on earth to express that love. It's just harder to be heard above the chaos of human life.

Can I communicate with someone on the other side without going through a medium?

Yes. I learned in the afterlife that mediums are not actually in contact with souls or spirits in the afterlife. They are reading the information field of the person who asked them to contact someone on the other side. Because of their emotional bond with us, our loved ones in the afterlife are far more likely to communicate with us directly than through a psychic medium.

Can I contact my deceased loved ones directly? Would they be interested in making a connection?

Yes, you may be able to contact your loved ones in the afterlife, though there is no guarantee. As I am fond of saying: "Everyone is everywhere all the time." Because we are all One in Source, your loved ones are right beside you all the time, just at a different level of awareness. It's a little like how a patient under anesthesia is still surrounded by the surgeon and nurses but is unaware of them during surgery. While we are in human bodies, we are like the anesthetized patient vis-à-vis the rest of Source's mind. So, you can try to communicate with your deceased loved ones mentally, perhaps during meditation or another quiet time. Simply call them to you and wait to see if you get a response. You might want to read *Hello From Heaven!* by Judy and Bill Guggenheim to learn about the many forms of after-death communication, in order to recognize any communication back from your loved ones. Not all Light Beings are in a stage of the afterlife when they can communicate through the levels of awareness all the way down to human level. But give it a try—and plenty of time.

The easiest way for our deceased loved ones to communicate with us is in dreams. I learned in the afterlife that dreams fall into three categories, one of which is not really dreaming at all but rather out-of-body living. The other two categories are what I call filing and storage dreams designed to sort through all of the data we collected during the day and file it in the appropriate memory area; and body-soul communication dreams we souls use to alert our hosts to health and other risks that threaten their sleeping bodies.

We Light Beings do not need rest. Besides, it's boring to watch our host bodies sleep. So we use our spiritual power to manifest a temporary environment, based on Earth or some other location within the universe, populate it with people, and continue to live as usual within that manifested world/dream. It is during these out-of-body living episodes that our deceased loved ones can most easily appear and speak with us—once again taking on the human form we knew and loved.

To communicate through dreams, all we have to do is let go of skepticism. Before you go to bed each night, form the intention to be open to contact from your loved ones in the afterlife. Then go to sleep. Keep doing it until you hear something. Time does not exist in the afterlife, so it may take a while for your loved ones to realize you are open and waiting to hear from them.

How do you know the difference between a dream your imagination concocted and a real communication with someone in the afterlife?

I didn't learn about this in the afterlife, but I can tell you how I tell the difference. Watch for these factors: (a) the dream isn't about the deceased loved one, or features a location where you wouldn't expect to see that loved one, and suddenly the deceased loved one "pops" into the dream; (b) the deceased loved one simply stands or sits and talks with you instead of taking part in the action scenes; (c) the action stops so that you can have a conversation; (d) your loved one may look younger, healthier, or happier than you remember him or her; (e) you have a strong emotional reaction to the conversation or feel like something of great importance has been communicated to you; and, (f) you feel like something has changed within you when you wake up.

You may not remember your conversation with your visiting deceased loved one after you wake up because the human mind is designed to forget dreams. But you will have a lingering impression that something has changed. The change may be merely a calmness you didn't have before going to bed, or, it could be as dramatic as a sense of knowing now what to do in human life, a burning question has been answered, or sadness has been lifted.

I often mentally talk with my deceased husband. Does he hear me, or am I wasting my time?

Whether or not this Light Being hears my reader depends on his focus at the time. There are lots of things to do in the afterlife and many stages of existence. When we're there, we are no longer concerned with what happens on earth to our loved ones because they are also in the afterlife with us. Only one of their multiple levels of awareness/consciousness is experiencing human life, not the whole Light Being. So my reader's husband knows he is not actually separated from her. The Light Being part of my reader still in the afterlife can interact freely with her deceased husband while part of her awareness is still inside a human. This is much easier, and more rewarding, than trying to reach through layers and layers of reduced awareness to communicate with the part of my reader that is essentially asleep inside a human.

On your YouTube channel someone asked why we couldn't communicate with the other side more, and you replied: "We can. I talk to my parents all the time." Is this communication in the form of telepathy or something like it?

Communication with those in the afterlife can be direct via auditory, visual, or telepathic communication during awake or sleep time; or it can be indirect through signs such as smells, mysterious events (such as a penny suddenly appearing out of nowhere), or other things we notice that we clearly associate with a deceased loved one. Although I said I talk to my deceased parents all the time, I didn't say they spoke back to me or even that they always respond. Not everyone in the afterlife can communicate back to the human level of awareness, and those who *can* seem unable to do it anytime they want. I don't remember why this is the way it is. But my parents do seem to take away pain when I ask for their help in handling it.

Is it possible for a deceased relative to view what is happening on earth right now from their new perspective in the afterlife? Could a Light Being tune in to what I am currently doing in the same way we humans can tune in to a radio station or switch on the television to watch a show?

Yes, we Light Beings in the afterlife can tune in to the lives of souls still on earth. But I think it has to be either: (1) while we are still all or partly in what I call "human mode," or still think like a human does, before complete transformation back to Light Being perspective, or (2) when it's our job to keep tabs on those "in the field," as I call it, such as when we are on a council of Light Beings overseeing a missionary soul or have otherwise assumed the role of monitoring a Light Being inhabiting physical matter. I know from my own experience that once we get to a certain level of Light Being perspective, we no longer view communicating down to the human level of awareness as important because we know that all incarnated Light Beings leave part of their Energy in the afterlife, where we can communicate with it directly via telepathy.

What you say about souls not following up on what they left behind on Earth, that they're just not interested. Oy gevalt! Keep that one to yourself! Mamma mia! Believe me, nobody wants to hear it, that news is just devastating! Isn't that like telling me that when I die, I'm not going to be interested in how my daughter is doing?

The reason my reader won't be interested in what her daughter is doing on earth, once she is living in the afterlife, is because the rest of her daughter's Light Being Energy and consciousness is currently there in the afterlife with the rest of my reader's Energy. Parts of both mother and daughter exist in the afterlife at the same time one or both of them incarnates. They can communicate telepathically, love each other unconditionally, and carry on life eternally. It's a heck of a lot better than what we are experiencing now on the human level. In addition, mom will know from her renewed Light Being perspective that part of her daughter's Energy is "asleep" and dreaming/manifesting a human life that isn't actually real. My reader would not worry about her daughter's illusory human life any more than she cares now about what happens in a virtual reality game her daughter plays.

Do you realize you are alone, among all the afterlife chroniclers, in the assertion that souls are not hanging out with us, watching what we do (at least some of the time)?

I'm not surprised. Most afterlife chroniclers are writing about their human perspective beliefs, not personal experience gained while actually *in* the afterlife. This is one reason I thought it was important for me to return to human life to disseminate these messages. I may be the only writer who has actually lived as a Light Being during an NDE and can remember anything about what it was like.

I'm not saying that after-death communications do not exist. They absolutely do and I've had many. I'm saying that, in general, once a soul recombines with the rest of its Light Being Energy, and completes the transformation back into pure spiritual form, it does not hang out and watch what goes on in the physical world. There's no need to. All we Light Beings in the afterlife have to do is mentally contact that part of our loved one's Energy still in the afterlife via telepathy and talk away. This includes communicating with those who have part of their awareness invested in the physical world. Of course, a Light Being may want to communicate a specific message to the part of a loved one's Energy that's in soul form for the purpose of, for example, reassuring a loved one still on earth that death is not the end of all life.

I think the difficulty my reader is having with this concept arises from her belief that a person can only be here or only be in the afterlife. Not true. We are bilocal. Part of our Energy reduces its vibration to enter a body as a soul, but the rest stays in the afterlife and carries on eternal life as usual. The part still in the afterlife is fully capable of communicating with others at the afterlife level of existence.

My best friend died yesterday of cancer. When you say in your books that Light Being souls do not stick around on Earth, it makes me feel all the more alone, if that's even possible!

I'm so sorry to hear of my reader's loss. I know she must be grieving terribly. And I am sorry that my books have added to her heartache. Please know that the love we have for others will never die. All souls are eternal, and we are rejoined with our loved ones in the afterlife. We are apart from our deceased loved ones only in this temporary illusion of life. The other levels of our awareness are still in loving communion, though we may not feel that now. When my reader's grief diminishes some, I hope she will try to make contact through that loving connection. Grief can block our ability to be aware of after-death communications. So, when she is ready, I hope she will try to feel her best friend around her. Just because souls do not hang around earth does not mean they cannot communicate comfort to us from time to time.

16

The Afterlife

HUMAN PERSPECTIVE. SPIRITUALITY USES THE PHRASE
"go into the Light" for crossing over from human life to the afterlife.
Religions say we "go to heaven" or "go to paradise." These shorthand
phrases encapsulate a human frame of reference that does not literally
apply to us after we leave these fleshy casings. While inside humans,
we observe physical matter beings moving from one physical location
to another. So we assume physical relocation applies to us in spiritual
form as well. It does not. We do not "go" anywhere when we die; it
only seems that way from the limited human perspective.

Light Being Perspective. Early in my afterlife experience, I was
amazed to discover that I could simultaneously hold multiple levels or slices of awareness. I spent quite a bit of time exploring that
phenomenon. I repeatedly adjusted my scope of understanding up
and down from one level to another, observing the more restrictive
awareness spans from ever more expansive ones. I was totally present
and conscious at each and every awareness point—all at the same
time. My degree of understanding changed depending upon the perspective I explored, but my physical location did not. I remained in
the afterlife. Knowings gleaned from Universal Knowledge informed
me that everyone has the same experience in this regard. We Light
Beings can shift between levels of awareness, and, from a human perspective it would feel like we have changed locations. But we haven't.

Once we make the transition into full spiritual state, we no longer feel we are moving about as though inhabiting a human body. There is no physical matter in the Light. Nor is there physical matter in what we call heaven or paradise, despite some very convincing visual manifestations seen by near-death experiencers. Light Being life is entirely mental and emotional. We expand our depth of understanding, perspective, frame of reference, and degree of awareness of things unseen in human life. Where we *are* becomes a function of knowledge and understanding—our *beingness*—rather than a location within a physical matter matrix.

Once we complete all phases of the afterlife, and are ready to reintegrate into the whole of Source, we become aware that we have never actually been a discrete being at all. We understand and accept that we are personalities or characters within the only entity that exists—Source, Creator of the physical universe. As parts of Source, we realize that we could not possibly leave it, and have not, therefore, gone anywhere during what we thought of as a separate existence.

So I say we do not "go" into the Light or heaven when the body dies. We simply expand our awareness enough to perceive the Light and heaven that has always been around us, and of which we are part.

When I had my NDE and I returned to my body ... my most profound memory was being drawn back and weighed down by GRAVITY! I know I had expanded, but I sensed that I was "out there somewhere." So if we do not go anywhere, then what was that about?

I had a sensation similar to what this fellow NDEr describes while returning to my own physical host. I felt as if I was being sucked backwards toward earth by a huge cyclone. Many NDErs feel as though they are being pulled toward the Light, or through a tunnel or outer space toward the Light. In addition, I felt movement from time to time in the early stages of afterlife, especially when I transitioned dramatically from one level of awareness to another.

Apparently the expansion and contraction of awareness feels like movement to us souls who have crossed over, or at least we interpret it that way because we still believe we have human senses until we complete our spiritual transformation. Think about the motion terms we use to describe changes in consciousness. We "fall" asleep and wake "up." We "come back" to our senses after a head injury. We "float in and out" of consciousness after surgery. Inspiring music "raises us up." But we haven't changed physical location during any of these experiences.

Early in our afterlife, we still think and perceive as we used to do in human life, even though we are now Light Beings. We have to go through a transition in order to divest ourselves of the lingering human thought processes and attitudes. Until they process further through the transition, NDErs and new arrivals to the afterlife still feel as though they are moving about within a physical body. After completing the transition, we no longer interpret changes in awareness as movement.

Our entire existence, and everything we experience, is but thoughts in Source's phenomenal mind. Thoughts obviously do not move about or go anywhere outside the thinker's mind. And, because Source can hold an infinite number of thoughts all at once, it does not have to shift from thought to thought as we do while in human bodies.

What about NDErs who say they floated up to the ceiling, then went out of the hospital room, or even left the building? Isn't this proof of actual movement, especially since once these souls go into the Light they are no longer here on earth?

Yes, but it proves movement only at the human level of perspective, not at Light Being or Source levels.

I also had the sensation that I was at ceiling level during my NDE. After I had already spent some "time" in the Light, I looked down and saw my former body sitting upright in a chair in the radiology procedure room. But I knew for a fact I was still in the Light because during this experience I received Knowings explaining why NDErs think they are "on the ceiling" when they are out-of-body.

Human Perspective. With out-of-body travel, our visual perspective moves from place to place. Changes in visual perspective feel like movement, or are interpreted to be movement, by human standards.

For example, when humans watch a movie, their brains interpret changes in scenery on the screen as movement of the characters from place to place. Their minds fill in the traveling they do not literally see on the screen.

We use motion terms to describe other human experiences that are changes in visual perspective rather than physical location. We "go" somewhere else when we daydream. We feel as if we "went back" to the past while musing over our memories. And some of our dreams make us feel we were actually there in the dreamscape.

Light Being Perspective. I definitely felt as though I had left my body when I began my NDE. I actually saw Nanci behind me sitting in the chair while I stood in front of it. I saw her again in the radiology room chair while I was in the Light, and felt certain I was in a different location altogether from where my body sat on earth. I felt the excruciating grossness of squeezing back into a cold, heavy, wet body upon my return from the afterlife. These movements all felt completely real to me. And they were—from a Light Being's perspective.

All these movement sensations are valid and real from non-Source levels of awareness. I do not discount any NDEr's experience, or my own, with respect to the sensation of motion. But feeling absolutely certain of our sensory experiences does not change ultimate reality.

Source's Perspective. Despite the sensation of motion I had in all the instances described above, there is no literal change in location from our Creator's ultimate viewpoint. Thoughts do not travel within Source's mind. Our lives simply play out like movies in Source's mind, with all scene changes contained within the imagined plot. As Source's thoughts, we have not wandered outside its mind despite how real the sense of movement feels to us in human or early stages of spiritual life.

Since both beings, the soul being and human being, are forms of Energy that come from Source, wouldn't both beings return to Source at death?

My reader is correct that both body and soul are forms of Source Energy, as is everything else. All that exists is Source, and Source is comprised entirely of Energy. Everything remains within Source's mind and never leaves it. Thus, from Source's perspective there is no actual "return" to Source for either the body or soul. There was never any "leaving," so there cannot be a "returning."

From a human and Light Being perspective, however, the body and soul have different outcomes of the body's physical death because they are different types of Source Energy. One is a manifested thought and the other is the self-awareness of Source as a Collective Being.

Humans are manifestations—thoughts. Their consciousness and awareness terminate at death because the thoughts generating them have run their course. There is nothing left to "return" to Source. Manifestations are merely Source's temporary imagination. They have about as much consciousness and self-awareness as our own dream characters.

We souls, on the other hand, are parts of Source's self-awareness. Manifestations are imaginary, but Source's self-awareness is real and eternal. Our self-awareness is part of the essence of who we are, not simply thoughts we have.

Imagine you are eating an ice cream cone, a sugar cone of delicious, creamy, chocolate chip frozen dessert that melts as you eat it and dribbles down your hand. When you finish imagining that you are eating an imaginary ice cream cone do you still exist? Are you still conscious? Are you still self-aware? Was the ice cream cone you? Or was it just a passing thought you enjoyed for a while? The ice cream cone was your temporary imagination just as humans are Source's temporary imagination. Your self-awareness is real because it is not the ice cream cone's self-awareness. Your self-awareness is real even after the human body you inhabit dies because you are not the human's self-awareness. You are Source's eternal self-awareness inhabiting a human via the mechanism of incarnation of part of your Light Being Energy.

Now remember one of your dreams. In the dream, you had scenery and various characters that interacted within the scenery in the dreamscape. Your dream characters are thoughts. They are part of your mental energy, but they are not you. When the dream is over, you are still you. The essence of who you are exists independent of your imaginary dream characters. So too, Source's essence and self-awareness exist independent of its manifestations.

Having said all that, however, I have to admit that humans do *in a way* "return" to Source in the sense that all the thought Energy that constitutes the universe will eventually contract back into Source's Energy field. The manifested universe, including humans and other creatures that inhabit it, will eventually fold back into Source's core Energy. In other words, Source will stop thinking this universe into existence. When humans die, their Source Energy stays within the manifestation until the entire universe contracts back into the core of Source. Humans are like dream characters: they disappear when the dream is over although a memory of the dream is implanted in Source's eternal memory.

Not Like Earth Life

The afterlife is nothing like human life. There is no physical matter to it. No bodies. No heartbeat, respiration, need to eat or sleep. No pain. No gender or sex. No earthly scenery because there is no physical matter in the afterlife to create it. Because there's no physical environment, we don't move around from place to place. There are no places to move to and from. We do not go to school or work. There is no need to. We can access all of Source's knowledge by focusing our attention on accessing Universal Knowledge. Although we do not work to earn a living, we do help meet each other's spiritual needs. For example, some Light Beings serve as greeters for new arrivals.

The afterlife is a greatly heightened state of awareness and consciousness with no lifestyle built into it. I am aware that authors who have used regression hypnosis claim their patients regressed to life between lives, or the afterlife, but Knowings I received during my NDE convinces me otherwise. These patients' accounts do not comport with anything I experienced or learned in the afterlife. My understanding is that we cannot achieve the afterlife state of awareness without dying or having an experience that gets us out of our body.

NDErs appear to be able to revisit the afterlife more easily than others. But simple hypnosis is insufficient to transport a soul into the afterlife or to trigger memories from that state of existence.

Where do people get the idea that in the afterlife we continue to have bodies, wear clothes, live in houses, grow flowers, take care of animals, and go on with our lives as before except that there's no negativity whatsoever?

I think that comes from a combination of religious precepts and projecting human expectations onto the universe in general and heaven in particular. Humans think everything must be like them and their societies. I also think that religions, spiritual books, and accounts of NDErs who just barely entered the afterlife have created a false impression. NDErs, in particular, have reinforced the misconception that heaven has earth-like scenery, people, and music. These courageous people have truthfully told their stories in the only way they can, by using terms and concepts from earth life, without realizing that the earth-like images they encountered were mere manifestations and not accurate representations of the afterlife. It is completely natural to project human constructs onto the afterlife when physical life is all you know. But it is still inaccurate to me because I have gone way past the stages of afterlife other NDErs experienced. I can look back with hindsight and see how they got their impressions, for I too passed through the temporary stage of manifesting physical environments into the afterlife. Unlike other NDErs, though, I was given Knowings that explained manifestation of physical life and how and why I was able to manifest and feel a railroad trestle tunnel, a meadow, and a hospital corridor in the afterlife that seemed as real as Earth.

Is it true that in heaven there are glittering cities and rivers and beautiful flowers and trees and parks and libraries?

No. These are temporary manifestations that NDErs see very early in the afterlife because: (a) their human beliefs about heaven are based on earth life, so they manifest into the afterlife what they expect to see; and/or (b) other Light Beings help NDErs by manifesting what will comfort them, including the illusion of physical environments, because earth life is the only frame of reference an NDEr has until completing the transition back into spiritual state. Once we souls get far enough through the transition, we realize these scenes are just manifestations and are no longer fooled by them. So we stop creating them.

Is it true it never rains and every day is a sunny day in heaven?

No. There is no physical environment in the afterlife. So there is no rain or sun.

Is there beautiful music?

Not in the sense that we hear it with human ears. I heard no music in the afterlife.

Isn't it dreary to have no physical environment, no moving around?

Not at all. I found my time in the afterlife to be the most stimulating and fascinating experience of this lifetime. But a purely intellectual life does get old after a while, and we Light Beings itch to go back into physical life in order to feel something different. The saying "The grass is always greener on the other side of the street" applies to Light Being perspective as well as human perspective.

So there's nothing to see and nothing to do and no one to meet in the afterlife?

Not exactly. Once we have completely transitioned into Light Beings, there is nothing to see outside our minds unless we feel like manifesting a physical environment for a while. In the afterlife we see mentally, similar to how we can picture a scene or person in our minds now but with much more clarity and substance. And there is plenty to do, although it is of an intellectual and emotional nature rather than physical action. Free of the body, we can mentally visit anyone else in the afterlife at any time via telepathy. We can also merge into other Light Beings and experience the physical lives they have lived, without going through the whole process of being born into physical matter.

Is being in the afterlife a lot like being stoned on marijuana?

I have no idea what being stoned feels like. All I can tell you is that everything I experienced there was at an intensity I could never have imagined while in my body.

Early in the transition process, I felt the most blissful unconditional love. It was warm and accepting, and, had I eyes to do so, I would have sobbed with gratitude for it. I next felt incomprehensible excitement and wonder over the wealth of information—Knowings—suffusing my mind. I was given the answers to so many questions I'd had in human life and Knowings about a huge variety of topics that interested me in school. I was flabbergasted to learn that I could simultaneously hold multiple levels of awareness, each with its own parameters, with ever deepening degrees of understanding. The most astounding sensation, however, was when the realization dawned on me that my human life was never real. The afterlife wonders went on and on. I describe everything that happened to me in my three books.

Do we heal from the traumas of human life in the afterlife?

Yes. Many souls need a lot of healing after they return to spiritual form. Healing is accomplished through waves of unconditional love saturating the soul's Energy, the sure knowledge that the soul is accepted wholeheartedly regardless of anything it might have done in human life, and returning to Light Being state after the human way of thinking is washed away.

Will we regain our youth and never grow old?

Since we have no bodies in the afterlife, there is neither youth nor age. When people see their deceased loved ones looking younger, it's because those Light Beings temporarily manifested that physical appearance for the occasion.

When someone who was very judgmental and negative in human life dies, is he or she still that way in the afterlife?

No. Being judgmental is a trait of the human animal and we leave it behind with the body at death.

Reunions With Loved Ones

Will we see our loved ones again in the afterlife?

Yes, we will see our loved ones again, but they will be in Light Being form, not in the human bodies we were used to seeing. They will still love us. One thing I can promise you: love never dies. It is a universal constant because it is the basic nature of Source. The love we feel in human form is a tiny taste of how much love we'll feel after we get out of these bodies. And, there will be no pain associated with wholehearted loving when we are in the afterlife. No fear of loss. No grieving. We will know for certain that our loved ones are always there beside us, always have been, always will be. We will know for certain that Source loves us beyond anything we can presently imagine.

In heaven, will our loved ones throw us a big welcome home party?

If you expect and intend a big welcome home party in a manifested physical environment in the afterlife, that is what you will get. In the very early stages of afterlife, we each manifest our own unique transition experience, assisted by other Light Beings who wish to comfort us. So, if seeing our loved ones again in a big party would comfort us, and make crossing over smoother and easier, that will be manifested just for us. But we souls will get to a point when we realize the scenery is just a manifestation, and we'll be ready to move on in our spiritual transformation.

Will I run into people who have treated me badly in human life, people I swore I'd never want to see again, and all of a sudden be best of friends?

You may or may not ever again associate with the souls of people you once encountered on earth. Remember, the people you disliked in human life will not be human in the afterlife. They will not look like their human hosts. They will be Light Beings, like you, whose very nature is unconditional love. You may not be the best of friends in the afterlife, but you will feel unconditional love toward them. In our spiritual state we are simply incapable of holding grudges.

Reunions With Pets

Will we see our beloved pets again in the afterlife?

Yes. Though pets, like humans, will have returned to Light Being form. They do not remain animals in the afterlife, any more than we remain humans. If it is really important to us to see Fido or Fluffy in recognizable form again, we will. The Light Beings who once inhabited their bodies will take on their appearance for a little while to help ease us through the transition.

Will our pets be waiting for us at the Rainbow Bridge with happy tails wagging?

You'll see a Rainbow Bridge only if you manifest that vision for yourself, or with the help of those Light Beings assisting your transition. There is no rainbow bridge because there is no physical matter in the afterlife. There won't be any tail wagging either. The souls of pets are the same as us—Light Beings. Everyone in the afterlife is a Light Being regardless of any physical form they may have previously held. The souls inhabiting our pets still love us and may choose to welcome us back to Light Being life.

Levels of Heaven

Are there multiple dimensions in the afterlife? Are we destined for a specific level or dimension of eternity that matches our personalities and desires?

No. I do not think the words *dimensions* or *levels* are appropriate to describe the afterlife because they imply human value judgments and arrangement of Light Beings into some type of hierarchy. The concepts of judgment and hierarchy are unique to animal life and do not exist in the afterlife. Everything and everyone in the afterlife is equal.

Neither our human host's personality, nor our own eternal personality, predetermines the type of afterlife we will lead. Our eternal lives are shaped by our own choices, which may be influenced by our Light Being personalities, but we live moment to moment in the afterlife. There is no destiny involved.

But are there different levels of "development" or "status" in the afterlife, *i.e.*, would a spiritually and morally developed soul like Gandhi's or Mother Theresa's exist on the same level with a child molester or mass murderer? Is one life on earth as good as another, or does the effort of leading a loving and altruistic life have any effect on the position of the Light Being after death?

I realize that some religions preach that what we do on earth determines our degree of bliss in the afterlife. This precept could not be further from the truth.

The idea of hierarchies of development or status is purely a human concept based in animal competition, judgment, and survival fear. There are no higher or lower levels, no hierarchies, no comparison of one soul versus another in the afterlife. All Light Beings are equal in Source's eyes because we are all aspects of the same consciousness—its own. Also, you cannot tell a Light Being's degree of spiritual development, or anything else about it, from what its human host does. My reader's judgment about Mahatma Gandhi and Mother Theresa, which is based on comparing their human actions with those of others, is completely off the mark from a spiritual standpoint. All Light Beings are equally spiritually developed inasmuch as they are all parts of Source's awareness.

Different casts or statuses, like we have on earth due to race, religion, or socioeconomic status, do not exist in the afterlife. Nor do our deeds while inside human bodies affect Source's love for us, or the degree of bliss and acceptance we enjoy in the afterlife. What our human hosts do has nothing to do with the quality of our eternal lives. Each of us continues to enjoy our own unique personality and experiences in the afterlife. We do not all have the same way of thinking or the same degree of understanding of who and what we really are. But these are transitory differences in mental and emotional states, not differences in places, such as realms or dimensions. To my knowledge, we may all be at different points in our journeys for Source but it's similar to being at different stages of enlightenment while in the body. It does not affect our "position" as a Light Being in the afterlife.

I learned and experienced in the afterlife that there are different stages or phases of afterlife, just as there are different stages or phases of human life—infant, child, adult, and old age. These stages are not dimensions or levels. And we all process through all the stages/phases regardless of what our human hosts may have done or not done. What most religions call heaven or paradise is the stage we enter into after the death of our human hosts, and where we remain during the incarnation phase of our eternal lives. During my NDE, I started at that stage but quickly progressed into a phase in which we gather experiences vicariously by merging our Energy into that of one or more other Light Beings. At the vicarious living stage, we no longer have spiritual bodies or even beingness. We are points of consciousness only.

After being at the vicarious living stage for a while, I progressed to the next stage. I merged into my five Light Being friends to form a collective entity of six personalities. My understanding was that this stage was necessary to acclimate me to living as part of a collective being so that I could awaken to my true nature as Source.

In the next stage, I started a series of awakenings as I passed through the core Source's Energy field, corona, or aura. During this phase I learned that the separate identity I thought of as myself is actually one of many characters within Source's mind, that I am Source, that I have never been an individual being, and that at no time was I ever alone or separated from Source or its love.

What about the heavenly realms?

There are no heavenly realms *per se.*

Is there an astral plane?

I don't know what people mean by the term "astral plane." But there is no place outside the physical universe that could be called a plane of existence by any name.

Does a soul have more experiences before returning through incarnation?

Yes. We Light Beings live our normal spiritual lives between incarnations. While residing in the afterlife between physical lives, we Light Beings continue to explore various levels of awareness, we heal, and we reflect on and integrate the physical life we just lived. After the incarnation cycle ends, we move into a phase of existence where we gain experiences by merging our Energy into that of other Light Beings to relive the physical lives they have lived.

How common is merging into other Light Beings?

Merging Energy is how we gain vicarious experiences after we have completed the afterlife phase during which we incarnate into physical matter. It's very common at this later stage of afterlife.

What if someone wants to merge into you and you don't want them to?

My experience was that no one can merge into us without our permission.

17

Life Review

THE OLD SAW THAT YOUR WHOLE LIFE FLASHES BE-
fore your eyes when you face death is actually very close to the truth.
Near-death experiencers confirm that we do review the events of our
just passed physical life. But we do not face the life review alone.
Those NDErs who have had a life review report that a Light Being
accompanied them.

During the life review, we not only relive every moment of our
just passed human life, but also feel the ripple effect of the emotions
triggered in all those whose lives were affected by our actions and
inactions. We feel the joy and the sorrow.

My five closest afterlife friends, whom I did not know in human
life, participated in my life review. I replayed every single thought,
word, and deed, as well as all of my human sensory impressions from
my just completed life as though they were images floating on the
surface of a giant bubble that engulfed me. One Light Being stayed
inside the bubble with me. The others popped into and out of various events of Nanci's life and lived them vicariously. My sense from
feeling my Light Being friends' emotions was that my life review was
more to satisfy their curiosity than for my own benefit. They reminded me telepathically that I had volunteered to enter into Nanci's life
as a mission, and they wanted to know how I had done. I never felt
they were judging my performance; only that they were very curious

about how my life had unfolded. They lovingly chided me that they had been skeptical about the wisdom of my volunteering for this mission, because we all knew I never got along that well when previously incarnated into human life.

Purpose

Why do we experience or feel the pain we caused to others during the life review? Is it for the soul to learn lessons for when it reincarnates into another body?

We will not remember any of the life review during our next incarnation. So, no, its purpose is not to learn lessons to be used in another life.

The primary purpose of the life review is to change our perspective from the narrow one we have while in a human body back to the more global one we enjoy as a spiritual entity. We get to see the *why* of everything that happened in life—to understanding everyone's motivations, and put events into context, after a lifetime of feeling as though life is an unassembled jigsaw puzzle. We also see the repercussions to ourselves, as well as others, of all of our actions, so that we can finally find out whether alternate decisions or choices would have made differences in our lives. During the process, we adjust our perspective to one of unconditional love. Eventually, the life review comforts us and wipes out any regrets or self-condemnation for the pain we've caused ourselves and others.

If it's true we don't have separate identities, that our personalities were created by Source solely to fulfill its desire to experience its imagined physical universe, why do we need a life review where we take stock of our behavior on earth and determine if we met the goals we set for ourselves pre-birth? Doesn't the very concept of reviewing an individual life imply we really are separate beings?

Knowings informed me that the life review is not conducted to take stock of whether we met any predetermined goals. That is a soul misconception. The idea of pre-birth planning of various events in human life is a misunderstanding of the reincarnation process, caused by the all too human belief that human life is the pinnacle of existence and what we do in it affects our afterlife. I saw very clearly in the afterlife that neither is true.

The life review has no judging purpose. Source does not judge us. The Light Beings who support and comfort us during the process do not judge us. Near-death experiencers who report feeling judged during their life reviews are sharing how they felt about their just passed lives, not revealing Universal Knowledge about the purpose of the life review. The NDEr is doing all the judging. No one else.

After the death of our bodies, we have to wake up and adjust to the fact that we are still alive but in a much different form. A life review is part of that process. It allows us to see how dramatically different the spiritual trait of unconditional love is from human beliefs and values. We relive our human lives, and all of the repercussions of every act, to help us put our recent experiences into context with our eternal lives.

Human Perspective. For a soul—and we still think like humans at this stage—the life review can feel judgmental. Many of us have been indoctrinated to fear Judgment Day, so we expect to be judged when we reach the afterlife. Perhaps the newly arrived soul fears the Light Beings around it is judging it (which isn't true) or the soul is judging itself on how well it behaved in relation to its own human moral standards.

Light Being Perspective. From the spiritual vantage point, the life review presents an early growth step in transitioning into the Light Being perspective. It allows the soul to witness its just passed human life with the renewed Energy and assurance of acceptance that comes from being bathed in Source's love and Light.

Source's Perspective. From Source's perspective, the life review offers healing via the opportunity to place into context all that the soul experienced on earth, viewing it more globally and objectively. It is a chance to answer the question, "What did it all mean?" and to find closure and new direction. It is Source loving itself through an honest self-evaluation of what its mental character experienced and how that integrates with all that exists within Source. The impulse is similar to the human desire to understand and heal our "inner child" and integrate that part of us into our adult personality. The fact that our inner child is not really a separate being from us does not make us any less interested in resolving trauma suffered in childhood. The same is true for Source. It wants to heal itself of the traumas that earth life induced. The life review helps do that.

From human perspective, we seem to be separate beings. When I resumed Light Being form after dying, I continued to perceive myself as an individual. It was only later, while awakening as Source, that I was able to see life from Source's perspective. I then realized I am not separate from Source and never have been. Each perspective is real. Each is valid. Each disappears as the new one replaces it.

Source is keenly aware of how emotionally traumatic the transition can be from believing one is a human being to knowing one is a Being of Light, and from believing one is an individual Light Being to knowing there is only one entity and we have never been separate from it. The afterlife transition process has been lovingly designed to ease us into each new perspective on life as we awaken from the human illusion.

Bottom line: Yes, the life review concept does relate to our belief that we are separate identities from Source. It exists because Source loves all of its personalities so much that it wants to understand and assimilate their physical experiences. But the existence of this process does not negate the ultimate truth that *we are Source*.

Why would an NDEr judge himself during the life review if he has become a Light Being and therefore is no longer judgmental?

Humans are judgmental. Light Beings are not. After we recapture our memories of who and what we really are, and complete the transition back to our Light Being form, we are non-judgmental. But that transition occurs at different points in the afterlife for different souls. So, we may or may not judge ourselves during the life review depending upon how far we have gotten in the afterlife transition process, what we see, how we feel about our actions in retrospect, how many times we have been through the human reincarnation process, and our level of enlightenment. Many near-death experiencers report that they did not judge themselves during their life reviews. I know I didn't. The NDErs who did judge themselves did so from the human perspective only. Perhaps they had not gone through the part of the transition process that would have enabled them to accept the life review with unconditional love. Or, as several researchers suggest, perhaps their life reviews were conducted very early in the experience because they were supposed to return to human life and the life review was intended to guide their future behavior.

Isn't the fact that we experience the feelings of all those people we hurt in human life a kind of punishment for those acts?

Some NDErs who had a life review will tell you that it can feel like punishment. But it was explained to me telepathically that feeling all the emotions of those with whom we interacted on earth is not a penalty for bad behavior. We feel all the wonderful emotions we inspired as well. Because it is human nature to dwell on and remember the negative, some NDErs remember and report only the parts of their life review that upset them.

The life review part of the transition process helps us readjust our thinking and emotions from what we were used to while inside a human back to our natural state as Light Beings. Showing us the impact on all who were affected by our earth actions gives us a global context, rather than the self-centered one we knew in human life. Yet the life review comes very early in the transition process, while we are still used to thinking like a human and judging everything as a human does. And a human-minded NDEr could easily misinterpret parts of the life review as punishment.

Scope of the Life Review

How long does the life review take? Doesn't it take a long time to replay every event of someone's life?

Many near-death experiencers who had life reviews state that their entire human life was reviewed in a second or two. That is because there is no linear time in the afterlife. Everything exists in the eternal "now." Also, our mental abilities expand so greatly that we are capable of simultaneously remembering, analyzing, and understanding huge quantities of data. We can access everything about an entire human lifetime at once and know it intimately now, in the moment, with no linear sequence involved.

What if the person you hurt is very philosophical and instead of being devastated simply accepts the pain as a teaching moment—would you then feel his lack of emotions during the life review?

There are no emotion-free human interactions. The philosophical person has chosen to ignore the human's feelings and interpret the interaction from Light Being perspective. That is what you would feel during the life review, as well as the ripple effect of the feelings of all the other people who were touched in any large or small way by that interaction. For example, the philosophical person might have internalized the hurt and anger, and then released it unexpectedly on someone else. You would feel that release of emotion and how the recipient of it was affected by it.

If you did some minor thing to another person who totally overreacts to it, wouldn't it be unfair to experience the whole unwarranted response during the life review just because someone misinterpreted what you said or did and reacted badly to it? Do we have to suffer through all the misunderstandings others have had about us?

It is not unfair to relive these events and experience others' overreactions. One purpose of experiencing others' emotions in response to our actions is to show us that their feelings are just as valid as our own, from their perspective. The life review allows us to get inside another person's perspective, something we have trouble doing while in human bodies.

As for suffering others' emotions over every misunderstanding, I experienced this during my second life review. I did not pay much attention to the life review I had in the afterlife because, at the same time the life review was going on, I was remembering all of the other physical lives I had lived. These other lives were a lot more interesting to me than Nanci's. I had the second life review during meditation a few years after my NDE. During it, I experienced every single time I had unknowingly or unintentionally hurt another person and all of their thoughts and emotions about me at the time. I was overwhelmed by the sheer number of times someone had taken offense simply because they misinterpreted my actions or intentions. I clearly remember reliving a meeting at my old law firm when I accidentally kicked another attorney under the table while crossing my legs. During the life review, I saw and felt that he thought I kicked him because he wasn't paying attention, and he was very offended by it. As painful as reliving all those tiny insults was, it was a blessing to learn that our intentions count as much as our actions during the life review.

Does the life review include the feelings and consequences felt by the people who worked in factories to build the technology we own, or the people affected by the pollution from the factories where the products are constructed, or the consequences in the lives of the people who are affected by a forest having been cut down to be used for pulp for a newspaper or magazine that we purchase?

I remember that we experience the ripple effect of our actions during a life review, which does include what others did in reaction to our actions. But I don't remember if we experience the remote repercussions that this question entails.

Since all souls are merged, do all of them experience our life reviews at the same time we do?

No, all souls do not experience our life review with us. All souls are not mentally or emotionally merged until they awaken as Source. In the afterlife, we Light Beings still think we are actual beings and that we are separate identities from Source.

Councils of Light Beings

How do you explain the accounts of NDErs who say they went before a judicial body for their life review?

One of my readers, who occasionally sends me comedy monologues based on one of my newsletter articles, once wrote: "I would like to think that after you die, there's a committee you go before and the chairperson says: 'All right, all of you sit down and listen up! Harry? Melanie never took your socks! Joe? No one stole your college ring; it's right in the drawer where you left it! Marvin? If you hadn't been a drunk, Marjorie wouldn't have left you! That's it, now all of you, get out of here. Next!'"

Actually, the life review does accomplish that purpose, though without the humorous presentation. The judicial body scenario occurs only with those of us Light Beings who have specific missions to fulfill in human life. Most souls don't have a mission.

The NDErs who went before a judicial body in their NDE attended what I call a council meeting. I describe my two council meetings in chapter 10 of *BACKWARDS Guidebook*. Natalie Sudman's book, *Application of Impossible Things: My Near-Death Experience in Iraq,* is a brilliantly written account of her meeting with her council.

Some of us are here on a mission for Source. We have specific tasks to perform and goals to meet. Missionary Light Being souls are monitored and kept on track by a council of Light Beings in the afterlife. This is necessary because otherwise the missionary might never figure out what it is supposed to be doing and the task won't get done. Missionary Light Beings meet with these councils when necessary to get back on track. And the meetings do feel judicial. Mine did. During the first one, I was basically told to "get with the program" because I was not performing the mission I volunteered for when I returned to Nanci's body, that is, telling anyone who would listen what I learned in the afterlife. In the second meeting, the council made it clear that I had failed in my mission but that it would not be held against me. They gave me the choice of coming home without fulfilling my promise, or going back to Nanci's body and suffering for the rest of her life. Believe it or not, I chose to come back out of pure curiosity about what was going to happen on earth during the transition between epochs. I also felt honor-bound to fulfill the mission I took on when I decided to come back into Nanci's body.

18

Evolution

THE WORD "EVOLVE" HAS TWO DIFFERENT MEAN-
ings: (1) to change, develop, or work out gradually over time; and
(2) to change or modify into a different form. I primarily use the first
meaning of the word in my books. Yet the second meaning, Darwinian evolution, is what many people think of when they read the word
evolve in my books. Many also jump to conclusions about the value
of the end result of both types of evolution. Not all evolution results
in a change into a different form. And not all evolution/change can
be judged as better than what preceded it. Change is simply change.
My use of the word *evolve* in my books generated the following discussion with my readers.

**You repeatedly say in your books that evolution of both the
human animal and Light Being is ongoing. To have an evolution
there is a beginning point, and an ending point, benchmarking
the change and a new beginning. What would be some instances
of evolution for each?**

Human Perspective. I saw in earth history during my NDE that
a first species of humans evolved from lower life-forms during the
First Earth Epoch. The predominant current/second version of the
human species emerged during the Second Earth Epoch, after Earth
reterraformed following the events that wiped out the dinosaurs and

mankind. Today there exists a small number of new, third species human beings. The third species of humans evolved in the Darwinian sense via tiny DNA mutations in the second human species. These humans live among us and are outwardly indistinguishable from the second version. I learned nothing in the afterlife about the accuracy or inaccuracy of human scientific theories of evolution. And I do not remember the process by which humans evolved from less complex animals.

Humans also evolve in the sense of change and growth through education, training, and personal experience.

Light Being Perspective. Light Beings' evolutionary path starts and ends in the same state. Light Beings start in Source, end in Source, and exist only within Source because they are by definition undivided fragments of Source's self-awareness.

Human Spiritual Evolution

Twelve years of Catholic education taught me that God created man in his present form by divine design. While I was earning my Bachelor of Science degree in chemistry and biology, I was taught that *homo sapiens* evolved from less complex hominids. As I watched the creation of Earth in the afterlife, I saw that humans did indeed evolve over millions of years from less complex animal forms. I also watched Earth's future, until the planet becomes uninhabitable. Humans did not further evolve biologically into another, different lifeform. I never saw humans look radically different than they do today.

Humans will never evolve into spiritual beings, as I believed before my NDE. Humans are manifested animals that die and are gone forever. Some religions claim humans possess souls that evolve into spiritual beings if they have earned heaven. What we call souls are actually Source, and, therefore, already constitute the supreme spiritual entity.

Our religions have taught us that spiritual evolution of the human animal is necessary to gain eternity. It is not. Our religions teach us that we must perform certain tasks, live certain ways, or think certain thoughts in order to evolve enough spiritually to get into heaven or paradise. I learned in the afterlife that our religions are teaching us human-created myths in this regard. Humans do not enter the afterlife; we Light Being souls do. We souls do not have to evolve because we are already Source. Do we consider Source to be the height of spiritual evolution? If so, we Light Being souls are already there. Nothing more is needed.

Catholic educators taught me that humans enter the Kingdom of God in heaven in physical form. I learned in the afterlife that humans do not ascend to heaven or paradise. Human bodies do not become divine or glorified so that they may enter into heaven as physical matter. "Heaven" is not a physical place, but rather a state of mental awareness. There is no physical matter to it. Yes, I know other NDErs have seen physical places when they visited the afterlife. This is because an NDEr's soul can *temporarily* manifest earthly scenes into physical reality in the afterlife. But only that NDEr can see these places, which are manifested to comfort the soul as it awakens from human to eternal life. These manifestations would disappear if the NDEr remained in the afterlife longer.

It is our hosts' nature to assume humans are terribly important to Source's so-called "Master Plan," and to believe that incarnating into humans is necessary for our spiritual evolution. It is not. Incarnation into humans is a very small part of the experiences we may choose in the universe. And whether we incarnate, or how many human incarnations we have, has nothing to do with who we are or whether we have fulfilling eternal lives. Some characters within Source never incarnate, or never incarnate into humans. Yet they exist in Source the same as we who incarnate do.

You have said that anthropologists will never find the "missing link" between ancient humans and present-day man because humanity was completely eradicated from the planet and recreated. Where did the humans in each species originate?

I remember very little about human biological origins. While witnessing Source's memory of Creation in the afterlife, I saw that both the first and second human species evolved independently from less complex species. I can't recall the specific species. The third species of humans evolved in the biological sense through DNA mutations to the second version. There is no missing link that bridges the first human species to the second or third.

How did humans evolve?

I remember none of the Knowings I received about the process of human biological evolution. I recall only that Source built biological evolution via genetic changes into the process of Creation. No individual species was directly created by Source, only the evolutionary processes that would give rise to all species. I also saw in the afterlife history of planet Earth that a group of Light Beings collectively tweaked human DNA to produce less primitive versions of the species. This was done in order to make humans capable of holding higher Light Being intelligence levels. My impression at the time I observed this was that the DNA improvement was "for our benefit," meaning for the benefit of Light Beings who are interested in inhabiting humans. The Light Beings who upgraded humans viewed it as something akin to a writer editing characters in a novel to make the book more interesting.

Did the first species of humans reach ultimate enlightenment, or did they end for other reasons?

It is not possible for humans to reach ultimate enlightenment. They are merely physical manifestations. Only the Light Being souls inside can be spiritually enlightened in the sense of being awakened to Universal Truths. The first human species was eradicated by Earth terraforming events that destroyed them and their habitats. Try as I might, I cannot remember what those events were.

What did the first human species look like?

What I saw was very similar to artists' renderings of Cro-Magnon man.

Can we tell the state of evolution of humans?

Yes, with a DNA test. But if you mean can we tell the supposed spiritual development of a Light Being soul by observing its human host's behavior, then no. Human behavior tells us very little about the Light Being inside, especially in those cases in which the soul takes minimal control over its host. I do not think one can accurately assess another's spiritual status by the level of insight shown in a human life. Some animal personalities are too strong for the soul to direct much of its host's life. Some souls choose to allow their bodies to run their lives. Being in a human body jaundices our perspective so severely that we could not receive accurate impressions even if it were possible to judge someone's state of evolution. The human judgment-oriented attitude colors everything we perceive while in these bodies.

Light Being Spiritual Evolution

Light Beings evolve in the sense that they change how they think, understand, and perceive gradually over time. They become more enlightened, for lack of a better word. But they do not change into anything else. The number of physical incarnations a Light Being chooses to enjoy has nothing whatsoever to do with a need to evolve or to have a place in some type of human-created spiritual hierarchy. Incarnation is an individual choice, not a requirement for achieving what humans might judge to be higher levels of existence.

What is "Light Being mode?" An altered state? How can I attain it?

I sometimes use the term "Light Being mode" to describe the way we think when in the spiritual state in the afterlife. It is an altered state of awareness vis-à-vis human thinking. Because we *are* Light Beings, we have already attained Light Being mode. But to *experience* Light Being thinking while incarnated, we have to stop the flow of human chatter in our minds and view life objectively and with unconditional love.

Are souls or Light Beings at differing (higher and lower) levels of evolution in the afterlife?

Not in the sense most people think, and definitely not higher and lower levels.

Human Perspective. Animals are organized into hierarchies. Humans want to arrange everyone into a hierarchy, even in spiritual matters, so that they can make judgments based on comparisons. It is human nature to try to judge other souls' degrees of development by some standard that humans make up—such as comparing human hosts' conduct to religious precepts or a societal moral code.

Light Being Perspective. There are no higher or lower levels or degrees of spiritual existence. There are stages and processes, but no fixed order to them and no hierarchy among them. Source's mental characters/Light Beings are not arranged in any hierarchy. All thoughts, all mental characters, are by nature equal. There is no ranking in the afterlife. There are no higher or lower levels or degrees of status in the afterlife.

Right before a Light Being leaves Source, and after it reenters Source, it is of the same Source quality. So what necessitates its evolution from less than Source quality back to Source quality via incarnations, since a Light Being is a separate and surviving entity?

Human Perspective. Many of us have been indoctrinated to believe that reincarnation is necessary to achieve eternal spiritual life. That makes infinite sense to humans, and unawakened Light Being souls, whose only source of information may be ancient religious beliefs that assume the purpose of life is to earn heaven by raising human spiritual awareness high enough to break through the pearly gates. This unspoken religious belief may be the underpinning for my reader's question, as it assumes we lose "Source quality" when we incarnate so that we can earn it back again through human lives.

Humans believe they are real. At the level of manifested life they are. From human perspective then, Light Beings are separate and surviving entities after death of their host bodies.

Light Being Perspective. During the incarnation portion of our existence as Light Beings, part of our Energy is lowered in frequency or vibration to allow it to blend with the dense manifested physical world. Because "Light Being" is merely my word for fragments of Source's awareness, Light Beings by definition cannot be "less than

Source quality." Lowering part of our Energy to the density of physical matter does not negate our identity as Source. Incarnations do nothing at all to change our Energy vibration. Nor is reincarnation a vehicle for raising a soul's spiritual vibration. That is a myth.

Once we reacclimate to life in the afterlife, we realize that human life was never real. We consider it more like a dream, fantasy, or virtual reality game that only one part of our multiple levels of self-awareness enjoys while the rest of us stays "awake" in the Light. Thus, from a Light Being's perspective, we do not "survive" the death of manifested human bodies because those bodies were never real in the first place. One of our multiple levels of awareness simply wakes up from the manifested world.

My understanding in the later phases of the afterlife was that I had to raise my Energy in order to move to the next stage, and, ultimately, to reawaken as Source. I accomplished this Energy increase through afterlife experiences, not human ones.

Source's Perspective. I responded directly to the theory that incarnation makes us souls "less than Source quality" when I wrote the following in *BACKWARDS*:

> [T]he only difference between the Source and each of us is the amount of Energy, and therefore power, we have … Our relationship to Source is that our tiny little bits of Energy are *qualitatively the same*, but quantitatively less powerful.
>
> [A] Light Being also retains the dual nature of being *both* an individual point of Source awareness *and* an integral part of the Composite Being Source. Both exist simultaneously. They are but two different perspectives on one Being's multiple levels of self-awareness. Each Light Being—each of us— *retains its identity as the Source*, while simultaneously enjoying the opportunity to experience different types of existences as a discrete personality.[8]

Light Being evolution is intellectual, and results in changes in how we understand life and our own nature. We Light Beings believe we are separate beings from Source only because Source casts a veil of amnesia over us. We live many, many physical and non-physical lives in the belief that we are individuals, so that Source may garner genuine experiences as allegedly "separate" identities. Then, when we Light Beings have finished our journeys and reawaken as Source, we remember that we have never been separate beings and that we are, in fact, just figments of our own imagination. That is the extent of Light Being evolution.

Do you mean that by incarnating into dense matter on Earth, it affects our vibration frequencies and we have to keep incarnating until our learning brings us back up into the same frequency level with Source so that we can merge into it?

No. I think this question understandably takes my use of the word "vibration" literally. The question is premised on the common erroneous beliefs that: (a) our vibration frequency matters in some way, and (b) what we learn in human life raises our vibration. I have read spiritual authors who espouse both beliefs, which I too assumed to be true before my NDE.

During my NDE, I was told that only part of a Light Being's Energy and awareness is, in essence, put to sleep when infused into physical matter. I needed a word to explain how the "putting to sleep" process affects this part of our Source Energy. Since there is nothing like this phenomenon in human experience, and no other NDEr has written about it, I didn't have the vocabulary to describe it. My original manuscript for the first and second books used the term "Energy signature," which I got from the TV show *Star Trek*. My editors felt I should change it to something more universally understood. So I chose "vibration" without realizing that word has a fairly defined meaning among spiritual authors.

Imagine a sunbeam shining through your bedroom window. Its property is sunshine consistently from the moment the beam radiates from the sun, through the atmosphere, through your bedroom window, and down to the carpet where it is absorbed. Because of its innate physical properties, and those of the window, sunshine will be warmer close to the window and cooler at carpet level. It may also appear brighter or more colored at window level and weaker at the floor. Now try to attach descriptive words to the part of sunshine close to the window in order to discuss it separately from the part of the sunbeam hitting the floor. That's essentially the challenge I face in trying to describe aspects of Source's Energy at various points in its aura or corona.

The problem with the word *vibration* is that humans, being judgmental creatures, tend to establish a hierarchy among vibrations with some higher and some lower. And humans attach more value to anything "higher." That's not how Source Energy works. Source Energy does not vibrate at frequencies that can be measured like radio frequencies or the various states of energy we know on Earth. One manifested thing's or creature's vibration or Energy signature cannot be compared to another thing's or creature's vibration/Energy signature and any type of worthwhile comparison of status made. They are all just thoughts of the entity Source.

It is impossible for us to learn anything in human life that increases our Energy vibration. The idea that humans can learn and earn their way to heaven is a soul myth that I believed before my NDE. Knowings told me that humans created this myth by projecting human behavior characteristics onto Source. In human life, we make others earn our trust, love, or respect. So it makes sense to souls to think that Source requires us to *earn* heaven. The question then becomes how to do that? The most prevalent answer among religions is we must learn enough, or become enlightened enough, to raise our vibration up to spiritual level. But our Energy signatures are Source-given, and have nothing whatsoever to do with human learning. Incarnations have nothing to do with the process of awakening as Source, which is automatic when the time is right.

You have said that Source's mental characters evolve and return to Source at different "rates." Why do you think there are different "rates?"

It's not that I *think* there are different rates of change/evolution among Light Beings. This is something I learned from accessing Universal Knowledge during my NDE, although the word "rates" was never used. No words were used. Maybe "paces" would be a better descriptor, or simply "different points in eternal life." I received

Knowings that we Light Beings have unique lifetimes that may or may not include accessing a lot or little Universal Knowledge, may or may not include physical incarnations, and may or may not include living virtually through merger into other Light Beings in the afterlife and experiencing their physical lifetimes. All this afterlife activity may or may not enlighten us all at equal increments or "rates." We Light Beings change/evolve throughout our existence, not just while in human bodies, and we do it at our own individual paces.

Since separation of soul from Source is an illusion, and we are all One in Source, how can it make sense that any soul is evolving and will return to Source since the soul never left Source?

This reader has hit the nail on the head. It is only at the human and Light Being levels of awareness, blanketed in amnesia as they are, that we mental characters believe we have left Source's mind and are evolving back to it in the Darwinian sense. From Source's perspective, we are simply parts of its own personality in development, just like a child's personality develops as it grows into adulthood. From Source's perspective, the "return" consists of the Light Being character waking up to its true nature, when amnesia no longer works.

You mentioned that if we remember what we saw of our future during the previews before incarnation, it will alter our present. Won't that happen to us now that we know what we really are?

My best understanding is that knowing what we really are may help us create happier human lives, but the illusion of being human is so strong that we will mostly forget who we really are and act like humans.

19

Reincarnation

AT THE SAME TIME MY LIFE REVIEW WAS PLAYING OUT, I learned that reincarnation is real. Suddenly I could recall in detail the events of hundreds to thousands of physical lifetimes I had lived. This memory burst hit me the moment one of my Light Being friends joined me inside the life review bubble on which images of every moment of Nanci's life floated. The fact that reincarnation exists came as a surprise. My church never mentioned it. I grew up believing I was created to be Nanci the human, and that when I died my human soul would live on for the rest of eternity. It never occurred to me to wonder whether I existed before Nanci was born. My NDE changed all that.

One of the many points of radical difference between human and spiritual life involves time. Humans are limited to experiencing a linear sequence of events and, therefore, assume the afterlife is linear as well. This led humans to adopt the labels "past lives" and "future lives" when speaking of reincarnation. After we transition into the Light Being state, however, the perception of time disappears and no experience seems past or future or before or after. During my life review, I remembered the content of all my physical lives. They were all there in my present memory. I didn't have any sense of one being older than another, or coming before or after another. Every event exists in the present moment in the afterlife. It's as if everything that ever was, is, or will be is stored in the giant computer of Source's mind to be accessed at will. We usually do not consider data in a computer to be past data or future data. It's all just data, there at our fingertips. We have access to all of our eternal memories as Light Beings, and these memories are not layered in the linear time sequence that we experience when we inhabit humans.

Once my memory of all my other lives was restored, I could recall every single second of what I had done, seen, heard, tasted, smelled, felt, and thought in each life. All the events of each incarnation, and all the sensory input from the physical or non-physical forms I had taken, had been faithfully recorded, along with my understanding of how those lives had impacted and helped form my eternal personality. Although I accessed all of these memories at the same time during my NDE, I chose to relive some of them in a linear fashion as I focused on one lifetime and then another.

I learned just before my life review that before entering into Nanci I had completed the incarnation stage of eternal life some thousands of earth years before, and I had reawakened to my identity as Source. Then, Source asked (to use a human term) for volunteers (again a human concept) to incarnate on Earth during this time in history in order to assist with the transition into the Third Epoch. I volunteered. My five Light Being friends thought this was pretty ironic because they know human life isn't a good fit for me. This is primarily why my Light Being friends had been so curious during my life review to learn how Nanci's life had gone. They were still laughing about my having taken on this mission because it was obvious to them that I was ill-suited to undertake it. But free will truly exists. And here I am.

Selecting A Human Life

Human Perspective. While we inhabit these bodies, we truly and deeply believe that human life is the zenith of physical existence, the center of the universe, and Source's own special interest. This is only natural for human animals because Source designed them to be self-centered. Unawakened Light Being souls do not remember their true nature and so adopt human beliefs about reincarnation. From the human perspective, we expect that the reincarnation process revolves around human interests, such as how we will look, whether we will have talents, how wealthy we will be, whom we will marry, and what our jobs will be. Many spiritual authors have in good faith publicized this narrow viewpoint as fact.

Light Being Perspective. One afterlife Knowing I remember about reincarnation is that we first choose a human "life"—a unique confluence of heredity and environment—not the specific body we enter into. We next choose the parents who, because of their genetic makeup and lifestyle, will produce offspring likely to have the opportunities and life we seek to experience. We do not choose our parents based on what we observe of their behavior.

Surprisingly, the specific body we inhabit is far less significant to us than the parents we choose. In fact, if we enter into a child who is aborted or miscarried, we simply pick another child of the same parents to inhabit, or, we choose another couple to be our parents. We do not choose a human to inhabit based on his/her physical appearance, talents, career, lifestyle, or wealth. Those things do not matter to us as spiritual beings.

Do we as Light Beings ask permission to incarnate into a human's body?

Human Perspective. Unawakened souls believe they are human beings who are separate entities from our Creator. This erroneous belief sets up a conflict between humans and Source as we souls struggle under the burden of the belief that life happens to us without our permission. Naturally, a human who believes himself or herself to be a victim of fate will chafe at the thought that no one asked him/her whether he/she agreed to be born.

Light Being Perspective. We do not ask or receive permission to enter into a manifested human body. We feel no need to do so, as we do not consider manifestations to be real. To us Light Beings, asking permission to enter a manifestation would be equivalent to a human asking permission to watch a dream from the perspective of one of his or her own dream characters.

Source's Perspective. Human manifestations are thoughts that exist solely for the purpose of Source using them as vehicles for experiencing the physical world. Source does not need its own thoughts' permission to incarnate into them any more than you need your dream character's permission to watch the dream through its eyes.

How and with whom does pre-birth planning take place?

Reincarnation planning takes place while we are in the stage of eternal life that our religions call heaven or paradise. This is the state of awareness that NDErs usually visit. However, I was past the incarnation phase of eternal life before this incarnation into Nanci. So my NDE did not automatically take me to the state of awareness in which we decide whether and how to incarnate. I do, however, remember a few Knowings on this topic. We preview the lives of several human couples and choose one to be our parents. We do not base reincarnation decisions on the attributes of a particular child they produce. We base the decision on whether a potential child's life will produce experiences consistent with the theme of human life we are studying, or the goal we wish to reach, rather than any particular feature of his or her body or success by human standards.

This reincarnation selection process I remembered in the afterlife took place entirely in my own mind. There were no guides or Light Being helpers, as books I have read suggest.

Do we reproduce physical attributes from an earlier lifetime's body in our current body?

I do not have specific memories about this particular aspect of reincarnation. My impression is that if a Light Being soul remembers a particular attribute of a body it has inhabited, such as a birthmark or injury, it is theoretically possible to manifest that attribute into the body of a current incarnation. But it would have to be a very small change in the body. I remember when I was a very small child I would look into a mirror and say to myself, "This looks wrong." So I secretly taped my eyes into an upward slant and tried to color my skin yellow with crayons. I was Asian in the last human incarnation I had before this one, and apparently I remembered that appearance.

I have spent an entire lifetime trying to tan my skin into the color I remember having in that other lifetime. No matter how hard I have tried to manifest my former Asian looks onto this body, though, I have been unsuccessful. So, I would have to say that, in general, we do not manifest former hosts' attributes into a current incarnation.

Do we plan the events of a human life we select?

Human Perspective. Humans have been told by psychics and spiritual authors that we souls engage in pre-birth planning that may include selecting a particular career or event to experience. This belief comforts us to the extent that it helps explain why certain things happen in our human lives. It gives the body a sense of control over its own destiny. But this message is inaccurate based on what I learned in the afterlife.

Light Being Perspective. According to the Knowings I received, we do not plan our human life. We manifest it, moment by moment based upon our then current beliefs about life and Source. During the one incarnation planning event I remembered while in the afterlife, I noted that I did not plan specific talents, events, jobs, characteristics of a mate, wealth, or lifestyle choices for that physical life. Those things do not matter at all if we incarnate solely to perform one task, or to be there to support a loved one through incarnation. And if we incarnate in order to study a feature of human life, these things do not matter unless they relate to our theme of study. Only humans care about these aspects of life.

We are in Light Being form when we choose reincarnation, and, as spiritual beings, we do not care what type of house we will live in, what our job will be, how much money we will have, or who our friends and loved ones will be in the way humans do. Those things are important only to humans because humans base judgments on them in order to create status hierarchies. All we souls care about is whether the life we select will produce the opportunities for us to experience more of the theme of physical life we have chosen to study. Remember, human life is not real to us as Light Beings. It is like a virtual reality game in which the only thing that matters is whether we are able to allow our true nature, and unconditional love, to show through the avatar we select. Incarnation is a mental and emotional challenge. The physical matter details are not important to us if they do not relate to our chosen goal or theme of life.

Why is wealth immaterial to the selection process when we obviously have a need for money in human life?

Wealth is immaterial because we Light Being souls manifest our human lives as we go along. We cannot tell much about a particular human's future financial status before it is born and we start manifesting its life. Every life is always subject to change. This is why I encourage conscious manifesting so much in my books and workshops. We can change our lives by manifesting differently.

The quest for wealth can sometimes impede our spiritual goals. My own experience is a good example. Before I died I was hardwired to succeed at all costs. I pursued the almighty buck as though my life depended on it. Then I found out my life exists whether or not I'm in a human body, whether or not I'm a success by human standards, and whether or not I have money. I was embarrassed in the afterlife by how much my blended human/soul personality had been formed by ego, fear, and the quest for financial security at the cost of developing loving relationships. I felt like a dog that had chased its tail its entire life.

What determines our next birth and things associated with our next birth?

Our own choices, based on our reasons for deciding to participate in the incarnation phase of afterlife, determine our next birth and all of its aspects. From what I could see in the afterlife, no one else is involved.

If we inhabit a rock, how do we leave it since a rock does not die? It can be around for billions of years.

We Light Being souls can decide to terminate our incarnation into any type of physical matter at any time. Normally, we do so when we have experienced what we sought and the physical matter's life cycle is complete. But, we don't have to stay inside a rock until it is demolished. We just leave it.

Do we have to incarnate on Earth or can we go to another planet and experience life there?

We Light Beings can, and do, incarnate into any type of physical matter anywhere in the universe.

Is Earth the only planet where we have physicality/duality?

We are Light Beings with no physicality at all. The only way we experience physicality is by inhabiting some type of physical matter, whether solid, liquid, or gaseous, and sharing its physical life. We can choose to inhabit physical matter anywhere in the universe. We are not limited to Earth. Wherever we incarnate, we create a duality of physical matter outside with Light Being soul inside.

Is it true that some other planets are like vacation planets and Earth is the most challenging planet to be on?

That's how I remember it. But I would say that Earth is one of the more challenging habitats because its physical stability is ever-changing and its inhabitants are so primitive.

Is it true that the other planets don't have a money system and we don't eat, have sex, or have bodies there?

No, that is not correct. Each place is different. Some societies in other parts of the universe have monetary systems. Some types of physical matter we inhabit are not alive, in the way humans use that word, and therefore do not eat. Yet many species are alive and must sustain themselves by taking in nutrients, like plants and animals do. Some species have sex, some don't. We have human bodies only while on Earth.

What percentage of our Light Being Energy do we invest into physical matter when we incarnate?

I don't remember the answer to this question. My impression is that it varies depending upon the incarnation skill level and goals of the particular Light Being.

Would it be possible for us to be invested in different physical entities simultaneously?

I received no Knowings that would suggest we Light Beings incarnate into two bodies simultaneously, but, theoretically, we have the power to do so.

If the reason we incarnate into physical lives is mostly for the experience, why would the soul carry emotional scars from life to life?

For the same reasons that humans carry emotional scars. Physical life is hard emotionally. Because the soul lives forever, those scars can be carried for longer than one physical lifetime if not resolved.

Isn't that like judging what we did in the previous life to be wrong and that's why we're scarred by it?

A human might take this viewpoint. But right or wrong has nothing to do with emotional scarring in many instances. For example, giving birth, having surgery, and growing independent from our parents can emotionally scar us, but none of these things would be adjudged by humans to be "wrong."

Do families travel together and so reincarnate together?

My understanding regarding family is that these ties appear in both physical life and the afterlife in some form.

Human Perspective. On the animal level, humans have ties that are biological and emotional. Animals have blood lines and shared DNA that create an instinctive bonding, including maternal and paternal instinct.

Light Being Perspective. On the Light Being level, we have something like a family as well, but it is composed of different individuals than our human family. The five Light Beings I met during my NDE—whom I call my "Light Guys"—are my closest, most beloved eternal friends. They are my family at the afterlife level of existence although none of them are in my present human family. I vaguely recall that we Light Beings all have groups like that and that the members incorporate into physical matter together. Based on the Knowings I received, "families" of Light Being friends tend to travel together and reincarnate together. The difference between human families and Light Being friends, however, is that our spiritual group does not always reincarnate into the same human family. Many times some of these Light Being souls will be part of our human family, but some will be friends, co-workers, or others in a position to affect our incarnated lives.

Can our human goals and desires be in conflict, or even competition, with our Light Being goals?

Most of the time they are, I learned. Among the first huge downloads of Knowings I received in the afterlife was one about human nature and how it differs from our true spiritual nature. Humans have one goal—to survive—and all of their desires relate to that solitary goal. We Light Beings have no survival worries, so we are free to focus on quality of life rather than sheer existence. Humans are designed and have evolved to be self-absorbed, controlling, competitive, fearful, irresponsible, judgmental, resistant to change, emotionally immature, ego-centered, and suspicious. Our true nature as parts of Source, however, is to be other-oriented, accepting, egalitarian, compassionate, responsible, non-judgmental, always growing, emotionally stable, motivated by what is best for all, and honest. I think you can see how these diametrically opposed personality traits could generate conflicting goals, desires, and emotions about many human experiences. But that is precisely why we choose human life. It is a challenge we Light Beings take on to see how we handle these conflicts.

Is the focus of selecting human lives based on hardships and difficult situations?

No. Only humans focus on hardships and difficult situations to the exclusion of all of the joyous and peaceful events of their lives. It is part of Source-designed human nature to remember far more of the hurts, pains, disappointments, struggles, and victimization we suffer than the good things about life. The hardships would seem far less significant if we were able to put them into context with all the wonderful sensations, successes, accomplishments, surprises, and joys we also experience in human life but tend to take for granted.

When we Light Beings choose a human life to share, we do not do it with the idea that we will experience a lot of heartache. We do not focus on hardships and difficult situations. Instead, we focus on opportunities to have the experiences we seek. Some of the themes of human life we can choose do include hardships and difficult situations, and some do not.

Don't some souls come back as enlightened beings because of their past work and effort?

Human Perspective. Our religions have espoused the belief that we are actually human beings and that we can enter an earth-like afterlife as humans. Those that also believe in reincarnation explain the phenomenon as repeated opportunities for a human to earn the afterlife through good deeds and service to our Creator. And, because this whole theory is based on and reflects human experience, it includes the concept that hard work in life gains us spiritual enlightenment.

Light Being Perspective. Enlightenment comes from remembering Universal Knowledge, not from anything we do in human life. Reading a million spiritual books, doing good deeds, and complying with religious precepts has no impact on enlightenment unless those acts cause us to remember Universal Knowledge.

We souls each have our own degree of spiritual enlightenment while in human bodies. The degree of enlightenment depends on how effective the veil of amnesia is, and how much Universal Knowledge we remember, not what our host body in another lifetime did or didn't do. These soul degrees of enlightenment are not comparable, or related in any way, to our levels of enlightenment in the afterlife. We are all "enlightened beings" while in the afterlife, but very little of that knowledge transfers through the veil of amnesia into our lives as humans' souls.

Do we as Light Beings benefit from having reincarnated dur-

ing this lifetime or only after we leave the human body at death?

I don't know what type of "benefit" is implied in this question. We Light Beings do not actually benefit from incarnation, other than it fulfills our purpose. I guess it is possible that a Light Being soul could benefit from previous experiences during subsequent incarnations if it can remember having a particular talent or skill in another life. For example, I know one person who learns languages extremely easily. He says he simply remembers them from prior human lifetimes once he hears them again.

Since there is access to the past, present, and future when we are Light Beings, can we choose to enter into a human body from the past or the future as opposed to the present?

The concepts of past, present, and future are artificial human constructs. Time does not exist once we leave the human body so there is no past, present, or future earth history. The only time that exists outside the human experience is the everlasting now. In effect, we always enter into human life in the present day from Light Being perspective because the present moment is the only time convention we have.

Why do some NDErs believe in DNA cellular memory versus reincarnation?

I have no idea whether or why some NDErs believe in cellular memory but not reincarnation. I have never read an NDE account that mentions this. Perhaps these NDErs had such a brief experience that they did not receive any Knowings on reincarnation and have used human logic and education to come to the conclusion that cellular memory exists rather than reincarnation. Scientifically, cellular memory as an explanation for reincarnation does not work because: (a) the cells that make up a present host body are completely unrelated to the cells that made up any previous host body and have different DNA, and (b) cells can only reproduce DNA and other cellular material, not a Light Being soul's memories.

Life Preview

Do we get to preview the life of the human we will incarnate into?

We have a limited preview of some of the moments of a physical life before we enter it, whether human or otherwise, before making the incarnation decision. The events we witness are *potential* life experiences. They are not set in stone because manifesting is continuous.

While receiving reincarnation Knowings, I remembered one of my own reincarnation selection events. I remembered seeing several scenes in the lives of Nanci's parents and older sister. In one of them, I felt I was standing on the front bench seat of a car right beside my older sister, even though I hadn't yet been born into Nanci. My perspective on the scene was very adult, as I was concerned that my parents had left their little girl alone in the car. I learned in recent years that the event actually happened, and that my father left my sister alone for only a few minutes while he ran into a hospital emergency room to sign papers so that my mother could be admitted.

What if the preview of a human life we consider looks bad and we reject it. Whose life did we preview? Someone who never existed? How can someone who never existed have a life to preview?

Regardless of whether we choose to inhabit a human whose life we previewed, the human still exists in the manifested world. While in the afterlife, I was given Knowings to the effect that Light Being souls do not animate humans. Nor does one Light Being individually create a human to inhabit. Humans are not outward reflections of the soul inside. Humans are manifested creatures who are born, live, and die regardless of whether they are inhabited by Light Beings.

Doesn't the life preview mean there's no free choice? We can't change things? We can't make our lives "happen" because we saw the whole thing before we were born?

First, we do not preview the whole lives of the potential offspring of the parents we are considering. We sample events and get the overall gist of each one's personality and potential for manifested life.

Second, I have tried to emphasize that we *do* have freedom of choice and *can* change our human experiences. Human lives are manifestations and, therefore, by definition are subject to change. Most of us simply allow our human hosts to live their lives without us exerting much control over events. But it does not have to be that way. One of the major reasons I returned to Nanci's life from the afterlife is to spread the Knowings I received. We can change things. We can take more control over the humans we inhabit. We are *not* chained to humans' emotions, motivations, instincts, and drives. We do not have to "go along for the ride," but can consciously choose to use our powers of accessing Universal Knowledge, manifesting, Light Being perspective, unconditional love, multiple levels of awareness, and other spiritual abilities to improve our body's life and the lives of others. But we must wake up to, and accept, our true nature as part of Source in order to know we have this option. This is the eternal truth that so many messengers from Source have come into human life at this time in history to spread. We need to wake up to our true spiritual nature in order to improve earth life.

Purpose of Reincarnation

The purpose of reincarnation is simply to give us the broadest possible understanding of the physical experiences that can potentially arise related to the theme we have chosen for our incarnations. For example, if our theme is retaliation, we will incarnate into every species in the universe that is capable of retaliation and live many physical lives of each, in order to get a 360-degree perspective on what retaliation is all about and how it feels in different bodies. We Light Beings pick a theme that represents an emotion or trait foreign to Source's innate nature so that Source can experience how it feels to have that emotion or trait.

We also have the option of incarnating to perform a specific task or to be another soul's support person. If so, the part of our human's life unrelated to the task or support role will have no purpose whatsoever. This fact probably offends some readers who believe human life is important. And it is—to humans. We Light Being souls, on the other hand, know that human life is not real and do not chafe at spending an entire human lifetime incarnated in physical matter in order to do something for those souls we love.

Is reincarnation punishment for failing our life's mission?

No. Reincarnation is always a personal choice. We can choose to incarnate once, many times, or not at all. Source would never punish us for serving the purpose for which we were created, even if we failed to perform a particular task we intended to perform.

Are some Light Being souls here to perform a particular exercise for Source as part of a mission, and if they fail, would they have to come back and repeat that life?

Yes, some Light Being souls have a mission and, no, they do not have to repeat a human life if they fail in their mission. For example, I came back from the afterlife on March 14, 1994, to spread the information I gained through Knowings. In 2001, I was called back into the afterlife to meet with the council of Light Beings that monitors my mission. They informed me that Nanci's body was dying and I had a choice to make. I could return to Nanci's body, which would recover, and complete my mission, but I would have to suffer through the remainder of her life full of life-threatening diseases, handicaps, and loss of loved ones. Or, I could return home to the afterlife even though I had not completed my mission (my first book was not published until 2007) and my failure would not be held against me. I chose to stay with Nanci and called 911 immediately upon returning to my body. I was in the hospital three days but did make a full recovery. I started writing in earnest during the year off work it took me to recover.

The idea that we are here because we have a mission or task to perform to Source's expectations, usually in order to get into heaven, arises from fear of death. Humans instinctively know they will die. Unawakened souls, gathering their information only from humans, have the hope that if they know exactly what to do, and how to do it, then they could earn their way into heaven. Because they are unawakened, these souls do not remember that going back to the heaven level of awareness is automatic for us Light Beings. We do not have to earn it.

The concept of punishment for failure is likewise human. Humans fear retribution from Source because they experience it from one another in the animalistic competitive cultures they have created. Unawakened souls project human nature onto Source in the honest belief it creates an accurate picture of the Creator. But it does not. Source does not judge or engage in retribution.

The assumption that reincarnation is punishment for failure to achieve a spiritual goal is grounded in human physical and emotional pain. When we reincarnate, it is because we have chosen to do so in order to garner yet another perspective on our chosen topic or fulfill an agreement with another Light Being. We are not sent by Source as punishment for failure, or anything else. We enter into physical life knowing full well what it will be like.

The idea of returning to human life can seem like punishment to someone who has lived with pain. But we Light Beings do not consider reincarnation to be punishment. Living what seems to be a life separate from Source is the very purpose for which we were imagined.

How does Source keep tabs on which Light Being has been successful in its mission and which has not?

It doesn't. Source showed me that our only mission while in physical matter is to experience that type of life, whatever comes our way. There is no possibility that we can fail at it. Most of us perform no specific mission for Source. Therefore Source has no need either to keep tabs on us or judge whether we have been successful. Simply having experiences is success!

The few Light Being souls who have chosen to have a specific mission are monitored by panels or councils of Light Beings in the afterlife who help guide us and keep us on track. I had personal experience during an NDE and visit to my council of Light Beings that if we fail at the mission we choose, we are given a choice to either stay here and try again or go home with no stigma of failure. This NDE is detailed in chapter 10 of *BACKWARDS Guidebook*. Another excellent description of an NDEr's meeting with her council of Light Beings appears in *Application of Impossible Things: My Near-Death Experience in Iraq* by Natalie Sudman.

What Happens When We Finish Incarnating

Incarnation is only the second segment of life, with the first stage being existence in Source's mind. Between incarnations, we Light Beings continue to live in a non-physical state of mind that religions call heaven or paradise. I learned while living in the afterlife that what religions call heaven, the place NDErs visit, is merely a way station where we can rest, heal, recharge our batteries (so to speak), and digest all that we have experienced and integrate it into our eternal personalities before the next incarnation.

After we complete our desired incarnation phase, or if we skip it, we leave the state of awareness we call the afterlife and continue to experience eternal life by merging into other Light Beings, one at a time or as a group. We experience their physical lives vicariously, either as them or as ourselves. We literally live the events of another Light Being's physical lives as though we were actually there. It feels completely real, even though we are aware that we are not actually living those lives in the physical world. This process gives us the benefit of perspective without the need for a linear sequence of events. At this level of awareness, we no longer think of ourselves as beings. We are simply minds. The illusion of having any type of form disappears, and we exist as free-floating consciousness. In the next segment of eternal life, we merge our Energy into the Energy of several other free-floating consciousnesses at the same time and exist as a multi-personality entity. I describe how both of these phases felt to me in *BACKWARDS*.

The final experience is awakening to the realization that we are in fact Source itself and are simply imagining that we are separate beings out gallivanting around the universe and afterlife. I describe this process, and how it felt to me, in detail in *BACKWARDS Beliefs*.

Is it possible for a Light Being to remain a part of Source and stop reincarnating on Earth?

Yes, and some Light Beings never incarnate. We remain part of Source at all times, whether we incarnate or not. Separation is only an illusion. We incarnate into all kinds of things and creatures throughout the universe, not just on Earth. Someone who no longer wishes to come to Earth may choose to enter into some other object or creature on another planet or in another part of the universe. We usually do not stop incarnating, however, until we have reached a point where we are ready to move on to the segment of eternal life in which we live vicariously by merging into other Light Beings and experiencing their memories of physical lives lived.

Suppose an evil person dies, and his soul wishes not to be part of the birth and death cycle. Is this possible?

There are no evil souls or humans—only behaviors that society labels evil. Yes, the Light Being described can choose not to reincarnate, but it will not be because of any allegedly evil acts its former host performed. Incarnation is always voluntary.

Karma

Ancient scriptures, including the Bhagavad Gita, speak of an end to karma as requiring both good deeds and spirituality in the physical world and a desire to be free from the birth/death cycle forever. Is all this necessary to get out of the reincarnation phase of life?

No. Nothing I learned in the afterlife supports this belief. In fact, Source does not expect us to perform good deeds or become more spiritual while in physical life. Knowings informed me that incarnation is always a matter of our own free choice and has nothing whatsoever to do with any deeds or misdeeds we may have participated in while in physical form. We can *choose* to stop incarnating at any time. And we automatically stop incarnating when we are ready for the next segment of eternal life, which involves vicarious living through merger into other Light Beings.

Are we going to have to pay back in karma for causing others pain, hurt, anger, etc?

There is no law of karma except as a concept of human creation based on fear. I discuss this in the *BACKWARDS Guidebook* and on my CD titled *The Purpose of Life*.

Some might interpret the life review as a payback for causing another pain, though that is not its purpose.

The way I understand it, from when I was awakening within Source, is that our choice of human for reincarnation has nothing to do with how we acted in a previous life. It will be a life where we can experience the theme or other goal we selected. For example, if we selected the theme of human murder, we might commit murder in this life. Then, in our next life, we may be the murder victim. That's not karma operating because we aren't subjected to being murdered as a *consequence* of the first life. We have merely *chosen* to experience the direct opposite of the first life. We could just as easily have chosen a life where we are the parent or spouse or employer of the murder victim and experience murder from that angle. Then, several lives down the line, we could be the murder victim again. Because everything exists in the present moment in the afterlife, we Light Beings do not see correlations between lives that human linear sequencing creates.

What's the most important thing a soul can do in this lifetime to ensure a great future after this lifetime is completed?

Not a thing. You don't have to do anything to ensure a great afterlife or eternal life because it is automatic. But I realize saying that isn't very helpful. So I suggest that we show more love. Find something to love about everything, every experience, and every person. My five Light Guys told me over and over as I returned to my body: "Love is all that matters."

Amnesia of Other Lives Lived

Do you remember ever experiencing déjà vu, and if so, how

do you explain it?

Yes, I have. Several times. Déjà vu is the sensation of a soul physically living through a memory it has from previewing a human life before choosing to enter into it. The event seems familiar because it is remembered by the Light Being soul, though not by the human host. This is one of many events that allows us to recognize that we souls are separate identities from the bodies we inhabit.

Isn't it unfair and illogical that, although we may have lived many past lives as humans, not only can we not remember any of those lives but we also cannot remember the eons of time we supposedly spent in the heaven realm before incarnating into a human now?

Amnesia of who we really are may seem unfair and illogical from the human perspective, but it is not from the spiritual or Source's perspective.

The amnesia we suffer about our eternal life, and what we call past lives, is the combined result of several processes. First, when we incarnate, we alone decide how much of our awareness to invest into physical form. This may be what accounts for the fact that some of us remember more of our other physical lives and eternal truths than others. Thus the part of us experiencing human life, by design, does not have full awareness, much less full memory.

Second, the density of physical matter dumbs us down. We cannot remember our eternal lives because humans are too physically dense to hold much intelligence or memory. I felt this to excruciating effect when I returned to my body after my NDE. I fought going back into Nanci because I did not want to lose the information I had gained in the afterlife. I could feel knowledge figuratively slipping through my fingers as I was stuffed back into this flesh. I actually felt constriction or denseness as Nanci's flesh stole my memories. So, before I fully recombined with Nanci's body, I memorized as much as I could before the Knowings evaporated.

Third, Source designed us, its mental characters, to have amnesia of our true nature in order to make its experiences of physical life more real. Source's goal is to have genuine emotions, spontaneous reactions, and believable experiences of all types. If we remembered who we really are, how we got here, and the other physical lives we have lived, human life might not seem as real as it does. (But, I can tell you from personal experience that knowing this life is not real does not prevent it from feeling real for me.)

20

Hell

I LEARNED, AS I MERGED INTO SOURCE, THAT THERE
is no place, or level of existence, where Source sends souls for all eternity to suffer for their physical hosts' behavior.

How did you come to the conclusion that Hell doesn't exist?

I *didn't* come to this conclusion. The information was planted
directly into my mind in the middle of my NDE, and then again as
I relived Creation of the universe. I saw while inside Source that no
place we would call Hell existed before, during, or after this universe
was created. Source did not create a free standing, open to all, hellish environment in its mind for itself/us to experience. Source does,
however, allow us Light Beings to temporarily manifest our own personal hells.

**Several NDErs describe their descent into an actual hell. How
can that be if there is no hell, according to you?**

Based upon my reading of their accounts, and the fact that I went
further into the afterlife than those NDErs, my explanation for these
accounts of visions of hell is the spiritual power of manifesting.

There is a wonderful book that puts hellish NDEs into context,
titled *Blessing in Disguise: The Other Side of the Near-Death Experience*,
by Barbara Rommer, MD. Dr. Rommer collected negative NDE ac-

counts from her patients and others, categorized them according to their common elements, and explained how they happened. I recommend Dr. Rommer's book because it includes the NDErs' own explanations for why they experienced a hellish environment.

I naturally view other NDE accounts in comparison to my own. My understanding is that when I died, it was my time to leave human life permanently. I never reached a barrier beyond which I could not pass. I was never told I had to go back to human life. And, no one resuscitated me before I returned to Nanci's body voluntarily. Consequently, it is my understanding that what I went through is the full-blown process we all follow after death to transition back to our natural spiritual state, and ultimately to awaken as Source. I experienced steps that are much deeper in the transition process than maybe 99 percent of near-death and afterlife experiencers. That gives me a perspective from which I can place others' accounts into a rough transition process timeline. And, because of the depth of my NDE, I know that impressions and insights garnered early in an NDE change as you get deeper into the afterlife. That's what happened to me. Universal Knowledge informed me that the crossing over and transition to Light Being life processes apply to everyone.

Although I was given no Knowings specifically about hellish NDEs, I can extrapolate from other afterlife Knowings and personal experience to explain them. Based upon the hellish NDE accounts I have read or heard, my understanding is that the experiencer unknowingly, and unwittingly, manifested the hellish physical environment he feared. I personally give credibility to hellish NDE accounts. I believe these NDErs truly experienced what they report. But I also believe these NDErs did not see and enter the Light, panicked, and in fear manifested the hellish experiences they suffered.

Universal Knowledge informed me that we Light Beings have the ability to manifest what humans perceive to be physical matter. We are each capable of creating our own personal hell at any stage of our existence, including during near-death experiences. Our thoughts can create the same physical matter we see on earth. And, though our manifestations may take time to materialize when we are in a body, we manifest physical reality instantly once we leave the body. All it takes is momentary expectation that we will see certain things for us to manifest into our physical reality what we truly, deeply believe. These manifestations are as real to the NDErs as anything on earth.

There are several stages in the after-death transition process when we might manifest what we expect to see in the afterlife based on our beliefs. The hellish NDE accounts I have read occur before the NDEr sees the Light and enters it. This is manifesting prime time after death. If we know we are dying, or are about to die, it is human nature to turn our thoughts to what we expect to happen after death. Someone who has been steeped in a religious tradition that teaches the existence of hell, and who deeply believes in and fears hell, can easily manifest that belief into his/her own hellish physical reality when he/she leaves the body. This manifested hell is created before the person enters the Light and feels Source's incredible love.

Rev. Howard Storm's hellish experience is a perfect example of what I mean. He was in a French hospital in excruciating pain that was not being treated, had an out-of-body experience, and manifested his own feared version of hell. I learned in the afterlife that we Light Being souls try to communicate with our host bodies via nightmares to alert our sleeping bodies to danger. We will generate whatever scary or hellish nightmare is necessary to get the body to wake and remove the danger. In Rev. Storm's case, I believe he was having nightmares warning him that his body was being torn apart by pain that could kill him.

Rev. Storm claims in his book [*My Descent Into Death: A Second Chance at Life*] that, at the time of his out-of-body experience, he did not believe in heaven, hell, or God. But, his childhood Christian beliefs rose to the surface in response to the nightmares and his fear of dying. He saw the Light, and a Being of Light, when he started singing the children's hymn, "Jesus loves me./ This I know ..." Rev. Storm believes Jesus, whom he interpreted the Light Being to be, saved him from hell. However, I believe switching his attention and intention from anguish to the Light broke the hellish manifestation. His experience after seeing the Light Being progressed as the typical positive NDE.

Mellen-Thomas Benedict's NDE started in "hell" as well. When he became aware that he was trapped in his own negative thoughts and fears, he shifted his attention and saw the Light. He admits in his CDs that he knew he was manifesting the hellish experience out of fear.

Our understanding of what is happening to us during an NDE or afterlife experience depends upon how far into the transition process we get; our personal frame of reference, such as religious beliefs, education level, personality, etc.; and our emotions at the time of death.

For example, someone who just sees the Light, and then returns to the body, may very reasonably assume the Light is God, Jesus, or an angel, if his or her religion includes these celestial figures. Those of us who enter the Light realize it is none of these. Someone who enters into the Light but goes no further may believe he or she has merged into God. Those of us who actually merged into Source later in the process know going into the Light is not a merger into God. Someone who gets back into body right after experiencing a hellish manifestation will be absolutely convinced that hell is real. Those NDErs, like Mr. Benedict, who move past the manifesting phase know it is not. Each soul's understanding of what happened to it is limited by how far it went in the after-death process.

Universal Knowledge explained to me that during the early stages of a near-death or afterlife experience, we still perceive everything the same way we did in the body. It takes quite a bit of processing for that perspective to be shorn and replaced with what I call Light Being perspective. Thus, if NDErs did not get far enough in the transition process to gain the Light Being perspective, they return absolutely convinced of their human-based interpretation of what they went through. Physical environments are believed to be real, until the soul's awareness is raised high enough to understand they are manifested. Spiritual beings appear with human-like bodies, until later in the transition when Knowings allow the soul to understand that bodies do not exist in a spiritual level of awareness.

Sometimes a person who reports a hellish or frightening NDE experienced the same phenomena as those who report wonderful experiences. The difference is in the attitude and interpretation of the experiencer. One soul's dark, hellish "nothingness" is another soul's dark, comforting, supportive void. One soul's tunnel of horrors sucking him out of life is another soul's glorious trip through the universe. Looking outward produces more comforting impressions than focusing on oneself and what has been left behind.

Finally, a few of the frightening accounts I have read were penned by people, like Rev. Storm, who do not claim to have died. According to their accounts, the experiences happened when they were in excruciating pain, feverish, blacked out, or overdosed on drugs. I am not qualified to comment on what goes on in those altered states of consciousness but they are not NDEs unless the soul leaves the body.

There Is No Eternal Punishment

If it doesn't matter whether I'm loving and kind—or mean and hateful—why am I sending you a birthday card?

One of my friends sent me a birthday card with this joke in it, and it echoes a sentiment I hear over and over from readers. It is very hard to accept that Source does not punish us for misbehavior—or sin, as some call it—when our organized religions have for millennia told us the opposite. On May 13, 2014, in a teleconference call with some of my spiritual writer colleagues, Neale Donald Walsch give the best response to this concern that I have heard. He explained that after he had written about a third of his best selling *Conversations with God: An Uncommon Dialogue, Book 1*, he got this message from God: There is no such thing as the Ten Commandments. We are One. Who would I command? Who would I punish? Myself?

Source has no more interest in punishing its different personalities (you and me) than we have in punishing our dream characters. The key to accepting that there is no punishment in the afterlife is accepting that you are literally a facet of Source's personality and consciousness, just as our dream characters are facets of our own personality and consciousness.

The fact that we are not punished in the afterlife for our human behaviors does not, however, mean that our actions here do not matter. They matter a great deal to those around us. Every action has a consequence, not only for those directly impacted by it, but for ourselves and everyone else. We see those consequences quite clearly in our human lives. We feel them exquisitely in our life reviews in the afterlife. We have the power to hurt or heal with our words, our touch, and our actions.

Our actions in physical life also matter a great deal to us as eternal beings. We do not stop being who we are after these bodies die. We still believe we are separate beings from Source. We still have emotions. We still have the same personalities. And we remember every single detail of every moment of our physical lives. We remember all too clearly how many of our human behaviors contradicted our true nature as unconditionally loving parts of Source. Those memories are very powerful and influence how we see ourselves. How do you want to remember human life? As a wonderful adventure? Or as a place where you acted like an animal?

You seem to be saying God doesn't care. If this information were to get into the wrong hands ... do you realize how chaotic this planet would be? Killing someone because you feel like it and God doesn't care. There's no hell, so who cares? This woman [Nanci Danison] is very dangerous.

This reader's opinion appeared in an Amazon.com review of my first book. People worry that if God does not punish us, humans will run amok. Threatening punishment is the traditional way to control humans. But it only works with those willing and able to exercise self-control. As a defense attorney, I have observed that even immediate punishment at the hands of our government, including prison terms, loss of all possessions, and complete humiliation before one's peers, does not deter some people from bad behavior. The threat of punishment in an afterlife, which no one has proven beyond a reasonable doubt to exist, has no impact at all on criminals. In addition, those who act on impulse are not controlled by the risk of punishment, here or in the afterlife.

I propose appealing to a higher power—the power of the Light Being soul within the human body. Innately, we souls take responsibility for our own behavior and respect others' rights. We can and do take control of the bodies we inhabit to prevent acting out their most violent or antisocial tendencies. Most humans behave nonviolently because we souls inside restrain them. We control our hosts to prevent harm to others. We are peaceful. We souls exercise our spiritual power to prevent the chaos my reader fears, whether or not there is punishment in the afterlife.

I believe the solution to human violence lies in enlightenment. Awakening *all* of us to our true nature as parts of a loving Source would be a more effective way of preventing chaos than playing on fear of punishment. We souls have a lot more power than our bodies. And we have a stronger incentive—love.

Wouldn't we be less likely to end up in Hell had we remained ignorant of all this and done our best anyway? Doesn't having this knowledge multiply the consequences of any sins we commit?

No. More knowledge does bring more responsibility, but the truth does not change. There is no hell and we Light Beings are not punished in the afterlife for what our human hosts do during their manifested lives.

What part does the Devil play in this life?

None. It does not exist except as a mythical literary figure.

The Bible clearly states that the Devil can transform himself into an Angel of Light. Isn't this true?

While watching Creation, I witnessed no angels existing after the universe was manifested. Nor did any exist before Source manifested the universe. I received no Knowings suggesting angels as described in the Bible ever existed. What people call angels are Light Beings like you and me in the afterlife who appear in spiritual form to humans or NDErs.

It was made very clear to me in the afterlife that there is no devil. Source created no devil and none existed before Creation. Satan is a human myth first documented in Jewish religious literature after that faith evolved from believing in many gods to monotheism. Satan is used to explain the inconsistency between a loving Yahweh and the evil we observe on Earth.[9]

If there is no hell, why have there been people who have been demonically possessed and have been delivered?

According to information I was given in the afterlife, there's no such thing as demonic possession because there are no demons. I have no idea what actually goes on with people who claim to have been possessed.

21

My Near-Death Experiences

MY MOST PROFOUND NEAR-DEATH EXPERIENCE OC-
curred in 1994 during a needle localization procedure performed just
before a lumpectomy for suspected breast cancer. A detailed account
of how I died, a chronological description of the events of my afterlife
journey, and the story of my return to human life are documented in
full in my previous three books. I also describe two additional brief
NDEs during which I met with my council of Light Beings.

My 1994 Near-Death Experience Events

**My study group wants to know if you experienced a life re-
view when you crossed over.**

Yes, I had a life review in the afterlife. But I didn't pay much attention to it because I was simultaneously remembering hundreds or
thousands of other physical lives I had led. The few details I remember of the life review are recorded in chapter 21 of *BACKWARDS*. I
had another life review three years later, during what started out as a
meditation session and ended up being a trip back into the afterlife.
That one is described in chapter 15 of *BACKWARDS Guidebook*.

**When you received the memories of your past lives, did you
feel you would retain that knowledge perfectly and forever?**

Yes. We Light Beings perfectly preserve forever all our memories of every single moment of every physical life we have ever lived, as well as all the memories of our eternal non-physical lives. However, we can access those memories on demand only while we are in spiritual form. I can't remember much at all about my other physical lives since I've returned to this body. Scientists erroneously believe memory resides inside the human brain. It does not. Only the chemical reaction portion of memories, such as what we experience with trauma, illness or injury, are stored in the body. The Light Being soul records all experiences it shared with the human body. *All* memories are stored in Source's knowledge base, what I call Universal Knowledge.

You said that the human being dies. Then you said that after you died you asked all the questions to which you wanted answers. Wasn't it the human side of you that was asking the questions? How can this be if the human is dead?

I'm sorry I didn't make that clearer. It was not a "human side of me" seeking answers because I am not a human, and, therefore, have no human side. These were the spiritual questions that I had as an unawakened Light Being soul living within Nanci's body. We do not instantly awaken as an enlightened being just by entering the Light. There is a transition process we go through that gradually acclimates us to spiritual life and deprograms our human mindset.

When you had your NDE you went beyond what other NDErs describe as heaven and merged into Source. Do you know why you could do this and other NDErs couldn't?

Most NDErs are resuscitated or return voluntarily to the body before they experience all that I did. From my perspective of having gone through the whole transformation process and return to Source, I estimate that most NDErs whose accounts I have heard or read barely glimpsed the afterlife. I assume this is because it simply wasn't their time to die and/or they were resuscitated before they got very far. I believe I had a deeper experience because it *was* my time to die and no one resuscitated me. Knowings informed me that we all go through some variation of what I did when our bodies die permanently.

Some NDErs have an experience that is more judgmental, learning. Some, like yours, are more removed from the attachments of this world, with less learning and more observation. Why do you think that is?

NDE researchers identify at least two types of near-death experiences based on content: ones that are personal to the person having the NDE, and ones that are transcendental in nature. Mine was transcendental. I believe those NDErs who receive information (learning) pertinent to their human lives died before their time. They were given guidance during their NDEs that could help them after they returned to human life. I further believe those NDErs who have transcendental experiences died when it *was* their time to die. There was no need for guidance useful back in human life because the NDEr was not anticipated to return to human life.

I disagree that my NDE had less learning than others. Ninety percent of my experience consisted of learning the precepts of Universal Knowledge contained in my books.

Does the fact that you didn't see the part of heaven where souls reincarnate mean you had evolved to a point where a physical body was no longer needed?

Shortly after I met my five dearest Light Being friends, they began telepathically conversing with me. From what they said, my understanding is that I had already finished the incarnation stage of life, and had been fully reintegrated into Source, before choosing to incarnate into Nanci. Therefore, when Nanci died I did not return to the incarnation phase of the afterlife, which is the stage of eternal life most NDErs visit.

PS. Physical bodies are never "needed," and inhabiting them does not evolve Light Beings. (See chapter 18, titled "Evolution.")

You just said you were finished with incarnations, but when you died you obviously weren't Mother Theresa. You don't appear

to have been the kind of person who most would think was so spiritually evolved they wouldn't need to reincarnate anymore because they learned how to love unconditionally. Isn't the purpose of reincarnation to learn the lesson of unconditional love?

I agree with my reader's assessment of my human life. My conduct is not up to Mother Theresa standards. But no one's has to be in order to choose to stop incarnating. One of the many things NDE accounts teach us about the afterlife is that we do not have to be Mother Theresa to get into heaven. NDEr Dannion Brinkley (*Saved By The Light*) was a bully and mean prankster when he died. NDEr Ned Dougherty (*Fast Lane To Heaven*) was a night club owner who enjoyed the wilder things in life before he died.

The purpose of reincarnation is not to learn unconditional love. (See chapter 8, titled "Purpose of Life.") Unconditional love is an innate characteristic of our true identities as parts of Source. However, when we incarnate into humans we forget who we really are, think we are human, and accept and act from human nature, which is far, far from being unconditionally loving.

If you remember nothing else from this book, please try to remember this: You cannot look at someone's human actions and get an accurate idea of the degree of spiritual awareness he/she has in the afterlife. Judging people, their actions, their level of evolution, etc., is a human character trait that may give accurate information for survival purposes, but it is totally inaccurate when it comes to spiritual matters.

Reading your NDE account on NDERF's[10] (Near-Death Experience Research Foundation) website confused me. You said: "I delved deeper into life after death than I had thought possible in an NDE," and "Nah, I can't be dead. I didn't go through a tunnel into the Light." These statements seem to indicate you had some knowledge of NDEs before your experience. But when the interviewer asked you if you were familiar with NDEs prior to your experience, you said no. Can you explain the contradiction?

At the time of my NDE I had never heard the term "near-death experience," had no idea that it is a known medical phenomenon, and had not read the few existing NDE books. So I did not know that others had experienced a small part of what I had. Years after my 1994 NDE, I read a lot of NDE books and accounts. My statement that I had "delved deeper into life after death than I had thought possible in an NDE," was made years after my NDE, and after comparing my NDE with other NDE accounts and research. It was not something I thought during the NDE.

As for my other statement, when I first got out of body, I did say to myself: "I know what this is. I'm supposed to go into the Light." I recognized what was happening, as it was happening, from vague memories of previous human deaths, not from knowledge about NDEs. But I didn't remember enough at the time to predict what would happen next; each step clicked with me after the fact. My understanding through the entire experience was that I was completely finished with human life and would not be returning to it. I was told during the NDE that I had come directly out of Source, having completed all my stages of physical and spiritual life before taking up residence in the body of Nanci. I was once again reintegrating into Source when I made the decision to return to Nanci's body. As this was happening, I was surprised that it was possible to return to an existing human body from that far along in the reintegration process. Knowings informed me that it was not the usual situation.

In all of the past lives that you were able to remember in the afterlife, did you ever inhabit an inanimate object?

Yes. I remembered those lives while in the afterlife, but cannot retrieve the memories now.

When you were trying to make your decision about whether or not to come back, if you had said to Source, "Thy will be done, not mine," would Source have wanted you to return?

I learned in the afterlife that my will *is* Source's will. I was reared in a religion that preached subservience to God. This question arises from that same thinking. We are *not* subservient to Source. We are literally parts of Source. I cannot imagine the Source I know ever wanting or expecting such a thing as it's "will [to] be done" if it differed from the will of a Light Being part of Source. Source's core personality never imposes its will upon any of its mental characters. Inasmuch as we are simply thoughts in Source's repertoire of imagined characters, everything we decide is Source's will.

You have said you didn't learn any Knowings about forgiveness in the afterlife. Was that because you were well beyond the need for any forgiveness at that point? Don't we need to learn forgiveness in order to get into the afterlife?

No. One of the issues my readers have with my message is that I say there is no need for forgiveness in the afterlife because Source does not judge us. There is nothing to forgive when no behavior is judged to be a sin once we leave the sting of human judgment. I did not learn a single thing about forgiveness in the afterlife because the concept simply does not exist there. Unconditional love and the absence of judgment make it irrelevant. No one needs to learn forgiveness in order to enter the afterlife. I see learning forgiveness as very important to human life because the human personality does not forgive easily. Life on earth would be a lot more pleasant if there were more forgiveness.

How is it that you are able to retain so much of your experience? This happened to you back in 1994, a one time occurrence. How specifically have you been able to remember it?

Many NDErs receive gifts as part of the experience—such as psychic ability, being healed from the condition that caused death, or other gifts you may have read about in NDE accounts. My gift, apparently, was the ability to remember more of the experience than is typical. NDE events are far more real than anything in human life, and therefore, make a greater memory impression. Even then, what I remember is a tiny fraction of the information I perused while in the afterlife. I also worked very hard to remember as many Knowings as I could while I was getting back into Nanci's body.

Can you explain how you were able to memorize the knowl-

edge you gained in the afterlife while you reentered your body?

Intelligence, consciousness, and memory all reside in the Light Being soul living within the human body. All the human brain does is run the biological functions. But we souls are restricted in what we can remember while inside humans due to the amnesia of incarnation.

My whole purpose in returning to human life was to tell people what I learned in the afterlife. So I worked very hard to memorize Knowings I'd received in the afterlife as I was pulled backwards in a whirlwind from the afterlife back into my body. It was like cramming for the hardest test I would ever have to take. There was *so much* and I wanted to remember it all. Nevertheless, I lost a lot of memory as I reentered and reintegrated with Nanci's body. That is why I can give full answers to some questions and no answer to others.

Which concepts in your books originated in your afterlife experience?

All of them. All the concepts and information in my books came to me as Knowings while I was in the afterlife, except for the chapters about what happened to me immediately before and after the NDE, and, some of the examples I use. But none of the information I received in the afterlife was in words. As I wrote my books, I had to fish for the best words to explain what I understood from wordless Knowings.

One of my readers kidded me: "You got all this information from your NDE? It figures that this assignment would have to be given to an attorney." Yep, I got all of the information in my books (and tons more) during my NDE—except for those instances when I say something happened at a different time.

In *BACKWARDS*, you say that the Second Epoch, according to your best recollection, will terminate around 2013-2015. But then you say a little bit later that, "my sense is that the current Epoch ends during my remaining human lifetime, which I estimate to end around 2033." Which is it? How will we know when the Second Epoch ends? Will it be something so subtle it won't be

obvious?

The change in epochs is an ongoing transition that no one can pin down to precise dates. What I said is that my best memory of when the *most obvious* transition events will occur is sometime around the 2013-2015 time frame "when a more pronounced transition to the Third Epoch will begin."[11] That's when I thought the financial system would collapse, based on what I remember watching Earth's future unfurl in the afterlife. The world's financial structure is wobbling now, so I was pretty close on dates. When I said: "My sense is that the current epoch ends during my remaining human lifetime, which I estimate to end around 2033," I meant that my current human life appears to end around 2033. The years 2013-2015 are within my current human lifespan, so the statements do not conflict. Please keep in mind that I made no attempt to remember what I saw of Earth's future because I had no idea I would be returning as I watched human history in the afterlife. My estimates are just that, not memories of Universal Knowledge.

The transition probably will not be obvious to anyone but those of us who have seen the future. Later, looking back on the transition years with the benefit of hindsight, everyone will recognize the life-changing events. The transition will take decades. It could even take centuries. Every NDEr who has seen the future has gotten the time frames wrong. I have read NDE books from the 1980s in which the experiencers consistently agreed the world would end in 1988.

Anyway, because there is no time construct when we are out of human bodies, there's really no way to tell with any accuracy when future events will occur. In other words, don't quit your day job.

What is your definition of meditation and what is the goal/end result that meditations are trying to create?

To me, meditation is any technique that quiets the words that flow incessantly through our minds. Quieting the mind is necessary to listen to Universal Knowledge, get guidance from the part of us still in the afterlife, and to focus our attention and intention to manifest consciously.

MY NEAR-DEATH EXPERIENCES

Aftereffects of 1994 Near-Death Experience

You have said that when you were in the afterlife you couldn't believe human life was ever real. Is the reverse true? Now that you're back, do you say, "I can't believe I ever thought human life wasn't real!"

No. I know for a fact that human life is not real, even though it still feels as real to me now as it did before I died. That's how powerful the amnesia is that Source designed to keep its mental characters from questioning the reality of their physical experiences. But spiritual truth is more powerful, to me.

Do you ever find that, although you never forget the truths you learned in the afterlife, you get so involved in day-to-day life that you put them on the back burner?

Yes, of course. I still get caught up in daily human life, and believe it matters though I know most of it doesn't.

Do you see life as a Light Being does, as Source does, or both?

Many times I have no more awareness than any other soul. Much, or most, of the time I think and perceive as a Light Being soul, which is a blend of Light Being and human personality traits. Only occasionally do I see things as Source does. Even when I see life from Source's perspective, however, it doesn't necessarily mean I can act accordingly.

Why did you abandon your Catholic faith in favor of your NDE?

To me, it's the difference between blind faith and actual knowledge. All my spiritual questions were answered while I was in the afterlife. Religions are all based on faith and beliefs, rather than fact. I feel like I have been given the facts. Therefore, I no longer need a faith-based religion.

In one of your videos on YouTube you mentioned that since your NDE you can now speak to your dead parents. How?

I don't speak to them in conversations, or the way a medium claims to do it. But I can feel their love ,and they do help me by giving me healing Energy. Also, my mother talks to me from time to time in dreams. Unfortunately, I can't usually remember what she said when I awaken.

How do you deal with the so-called "Bible thumpers?"

I appreciate their perspective because I used to share it. When I am asked a loaded question I just answer it directly and truthfully based on what I learned in the afterlife. I don't feel my job is to convince people of what I learned. I'm just here to deliver the message.

Why didn't Source bestow perfect health on your physical body for your remaining years?

I wish. Humans get damaged by what they eat, what they do, exposure to the environment, aging, etc. That's just the way biology works, and Source does not intervene to change its laws of nature. I knew before my NDE that my body was at high risk for breast cancer. I held it off for seventeen years before it laid me low. And I have other medical conditions from a lawyer's high stress life. I was also told when I died in 2001 that if I came back to this body I would suffer for the rest of her life. Once again, I chose to come back to complete my mission.

It would be nice if Source would let you go back and easily get more information whenever you wanted to, without having another near-death experience. Why can't you do that?

Like many of us, I do get Universal Knowledge from time to time. I don't disseminate it to others because I know it has been filtered through my human perspective. I want to give people only the purest information I have, which is from my time in the afterlife.

My Later NDEs

You state *(in BACKWARDS Guidebook)* that in 2001 you met with your council [of Light Beings guiding your life], which in-

cluded your parents, who appeared as themselves momentarily and then suddenly removed their human faces and appeared as Light Beings. That startled me no end! Did that freak you out too? Can Light Beings make themselves appear in whatever way they want?

Yes, it did freak me out. I remember thinking at the time, "Gee, I would have shown them [my parents] a whole lot more respect if I'd known they were on my council." We Light Beings have no physical appearance. But in the afterlife we can manifest any physical appearance we want. We can take it on and off, like my parents did; or change it, such as to look younger than our former bodies looked at death; or forgo any sort of physical appearance. We obviously can't do this while inside bodies or I'd look a lot better. Ha, ha.

Comments on My Books

Why did you wait so long to publish?

The timing just worked out that way. I didn't write the bulk of my complete manuscript until 2001, during a time I was too sick to work for a year. I didn't create my first book, *BACKWARDS: Returning to Our Source for Answers*, until 2005. A foreign publisher conditionally accepted it for publication but couldn't find a satisfactory U.S. distributor for its catalog of titles. That left me stranded until I met my current publisher in 2007.

If you chose to come back to share what you learned in the afterlife, shouldn't you give it away for free?

I do give a lot of it away for free. I answer e-mails, post comments on YouTube, post videos on YouTube, and write an extensive monthly newsletter answering readers' questions (you can subscribe on my website) for free.

With books, a publisher has to make a choice among printed books, electronic books, and posting a manuscript on the Internet.

No publisher would accept a book for publication if it was available for free on the Internet because there would be no way to assure enough sales to recover expenses. There are huge expenses associated with editing, proofreading, designing, marketing, and selling an E-book. Additional expenses for printing, warehousing, insurance, and order fulfillment apply to paper books. Book wholesalers pay distributors 50% or less of the book's list price. Distributors take their cut from that less than 50% figure to cover charges for warehousing, insurance, order fulfillment, shipping and sometimes time charges. All told, publishers get paid a fraction of a book's list price and have to pay all their business expenses out of those small dollar amounts. Only when a book sells in the tens of thousands does it start to make a profit for a publisher. Only a few thousand of my books have sold. So there has been no profit yet.

Producing a professional quality book for download from the Internet is not free anyway. Professional editors, book layout designers, and cover designers all have to be paid. In addition, I had to pay thousands of dollars to various publishers and photographers to purchase licenses to use quotes and images for which they hold the copyrights. I have put roughly $35,000-$40,000 of my own money into getting my books published and marketed.

More important to me is the fact that posting a book on the Internet does not reach my entire potential audience. Publishing industry data from 2014 discloses that only around 15% of books are purchased in digital format, including all of the Nook, Kindle, and free books on the Internet. Given a choice between reaching only 15% of my potential readers by posting to the Internet, or reaching 100% by selling paper books, I chose to reach the widest audience I could.

If the purpose of human experience is just that—to have a human experience—why do we need someone to come back and tell us that?

Because we have forgotten, and so have adopted all kinds of scary and burdensome theories about the purpose of life. We all know this truth while in the afterlife, but the veil of amnesia that stifles our memory when we incarnate prevents us from remembering the purpose of life while here. In addition, I wanted to remind Light Being souls about who they really are. I believed before returning to this life that sharing the truths I learned in the afterlife would ease suffering back on earth. I felt at the time I chose to return that my life as Nanci would have been far less traumatic had I known some of what I learned in the afterlife. I don't think I would have put so much pressure on myself.

You said Light Beings do not judge things as evil or not evil. Yet in your book you clearly encourage readers to adopt a more spiritual life style. Don't you think that is value judging?

I don't think I actually advocate a more spiritual life. I report what I was told in the afterlife would make human life a little easier. The more harmony we can establish between ourselves as Light Being souls and our host bodies, the happier we can be. I state outright in *BACKWARDS Guidebook*, and in my interview with Ted Henry of ABC News on my YouTube channel, that there's no downside to not becoming more spiritual because we are here to experience life as a human does. We get plenty of experience as spiritual beings while in the afterlife.

Why do you have to sound so preachy in your books? Simply state what you experienced and let readers draw their own conclusions. They know it will likely apply to everyone.

I do not intend to sound preachy, and have experimented with various ways of trying to get around leaving that impression. This reader admonishes that I should state only what I experienced. That's what I did. I stated only what I experienced. Most of my NDE consisted of receiving the Knowings that fill my books, which were delivered to me along with the message that they apply to everyone. They are Universal Knowledge. The Knowings are not interpretations that came to me afterward. Nor are they my own sermons on how people should behave. They are the thoughts I received while I was in the Light. The Knowings came in the form of "we this" and "we that" in a way I understood to mean that what I was being given was true for everyone. So that's how I stated it. The example the reader gives of an NDE account describes what happened to the NDEr, not the Knowings he or she was given about life, death, and the afterlife, during the NDE. When I describe in my books what happened to me in the afterlife, I do it the same way. But I have yet to identify a method of doing essentially the same thing for the Knowings.

My first draft of the manuscript was written all in the first person, as all "I." You can imagine how well that would have gone over! I am trying to walk a tightrope between sounding as if I think I'm the Second Coming—which clearly I am not—and sharing my story as I actually experienced it.

How do you explain the fact that there's a whole other "reporting," for lack of a better word, on the afterlife from certain NDE circles?

I know. So far as I can determine from other NDErs' accounts, those folks did not get very far into the afterlife. I say this because I went through what they did, but then went way past it. My guess is they are completely unaware of some of the things I experienced simply because they didn't get as far into the afterlife as I did.

There seems to be a huge gap, if not a discrepancy, between your version of what happens after death versus what Christianity teaches. Why is that?

I recognized that discrepancy immediately upon entering the Light. Before my NDE, I totally believed in Christianity. I was very distraught about the conflict between my Catholic religion and the Knowings I received. I think this is why I was given a full review of religious history during my NDE. My book *BACKWARDS Beliefs* details everything I remember from my NDE of the history of religion's role in human development. When I was writing the book, I combined what I saw in the afterlife with scholarly research published since my NDE that confirmed what I saw.

I believe that what Christianity teaches about death was constructed gradually over decades to keep the religion alive. The Kingdom of God movement (the precursor to Christianity) was originally founded as a heretic branch of Judaism that preached that a Jewish Messiah would create a new Israelite Kingdom of God on earth to overthrow the Roman Empire's occupation of Palestine. This new kingdom would be egalitarian and based on brotherhood. When that didn't happen, and Palestine lost the 60-70 A.D. war with Rome, there appeared to be no hope for the Kingdom of God on earth. So, church fathers moved the Kingdom of God from an earthly setting to a heavenly one, claiming that must have been what Jesus meant, although he never said it. Human bodies had to be resurrected from the grave in order to get them into this new Kingdom of God. But this new dogma kept the Christian Church from dying out after having been proved wrong. Prior to this shift in location, Christianity had no dogma relating to an afterlife because Judaism had no formal concept of an afterlife.

I don't know the mind of God/Source. No one does. A human mind can only interpret with human understanding what Source/God is and/or what Source/God may think and feel. Do you agree?

I do agree that a human mind cannot know the mind of Source and can only interpret religious precepts from human experience. That is precisely why I do not believe psychics, mediums, channels, religious leaders, or spiritual writers in general are accurate sources of spiritual information. They give us human perspective because they did not get their information in the afterlife.

I do not believe the Knowings I was given while in the afterlife are affected by the limitations of human understanding. I had made the transition out of human ways of thinking and into Light Being awareness before I received most of the Universal Knowledge. In addition, while I was awakening as Source I shared Source's essence, thoughts, and feelings. That is how I can tell you what Source is and how it thinks.

All Light Beings can know the mind of Source because we *are* Source.

My whole purpose in being here is to awaken the Light Beings inside humans and get them to rise above human understanding and remember who and what they are, so they, too, can see things as an awakened soul does.

NOTES

[1]   Raymond A. Moody, MD, *Life After Life* (New York: Bantam 1975).

[2]   Although this message is delivered lovingly and delicately, I know at least two NDErs who took it as rejection by God. They spent their entire human lives trying to understand why.

[3]   The interview with Colton Burpo is included in the "Special Movie Edition" of *Heaven Is For Real* by Todd Burpo and Lynn Vincent (Nashville: W Publishing Group 2010), p. 171.

[4]   As a result of lack of oxygen to the brain during my NDE, I lost almost all memory of both foreign languages, as well as my ability to read music and play the piano. I also lost a tremendous amount of memory of my life as Nanci before the NDE.

[5]   Nanci L. Danison, *BACKWARDS: Returning to Our Source For Answers* (Columbus, OH: A.P. Lee & Co., Ltd. 2007), 67.

[6]   Nanci L. Danison, *BACKWARDS Guidebook* (Columbus, OH: A.P. Lee & Co., Ltd. 2009), 43-44.

[7]   Bart D. Ehrman, *Misquoting Jesus: The Story Behind Who Changed the Bible and Why* (New York: HarperCollins, 2005).

[8]   Nanci L. Danison, *BACKWARDS: Returning to Our Source For Answers* (Columbus, OH: A.P. Lee & Co., Ltd. 2007), 42.

9   T.J. Wray and Gregory Mobley, *The Birth of Satan: Tracing the Devil's Biblical Roots* (New York: Palgrave Macmillan, 2005).

10   The link is http://www.nderf.org/NDERF/NDE_Experiences/nanci_d_possible_nde.htm.

11   Nanci L. Danison, *BACKWARDS: Returning to Our Source for Answers* (Columbus, OH: A.P. Lee & Co., Ltd. 2007), 251.

About the Author

Nanci L. Danison holds a B.S. degree Magna Cum Laude with double majors in biology and chemistry, a B.A. degree Magna Cum Laude in Psychology, and a Doctorate in Jurisprudence. Until 1994, she was living the life of a successful trial lawyer in a large midwestern law firm. She often lectured on a national level and wrote on health law topics for other lawyers and the health care industry. Nanci at one time appeared on the Noon News for local TV stations in public service spots for the Bar Association, one of the activities that earned her a Jaycees' "Ten Outstanding Citizens Award" for community service. Then she had a near-death experience (NDE).

After returning from beyond, Nanci left the security of her big firm and started a successful solo practice in health law. Her activities post-NDE include being named in the *1998 Who's Who in American Law*, earning a pilot's license in 2000, and being listed in the *2006-2016 Bar Registry of Preeminent Lawyers*. Nanci has retired from the practice of law and writes books on what she remembers from her life in the Light.